M000207208

Inside the Muslim Brotherhood

RELIGION AND GLOBAL POLITICS

SERIES EDITOR
John L. Esposito
University Professor and Director
Prince Alwaleed Bin Talal Center for Muslim-Christian Understanding
Georgetown University

ISLAMIC LEVIATHAN
*Islam and the Making
of State Power*
Seyyed Vali Reza Nasr

RACHID GHANNOUCHI
A Democrat Within Islamism
Azzam S. Tamimi

BALKAN IDOLS
*Religion and Nationalism in
Yugoslav States*
Vjekoslav Perica

ISLAMIC POLITICAL IDENTITY
IN TURKEY
M. Hakan Yavuz

RELIGION AND POLITICS IN
POST-COMMUNIST ROMANIA
Lavinia Stan and Lucian Turcescu

PIETY AND POLITICS
Islamism in Contemporary Malaysia
Joseph Chinyong Liow

TERROR IN THE LAND OF THE
HOLY SPIRIT
*Guatemala under General Efrain Rios
Montt, 1982–1983*
Virginia Garrard-Burnett

IN THE HOUSE OF WAR
Dutch Islam Observed
Sam Cherribi

BEING YOUNG AND MUSLIM
*New Cultural Politics in the Global
South and North*
Asef Bayat and Linda Herrera

CHURCH, STATE,
AND DEMOCRACY IN
EXPANDING EUROPE
Lavinia Stan and Lucian Turcescu

THE HEADSCARF CONTROVERSY
Secularism and Freedom of Religion
Hilal Elver

THE HOUSE OF SERVICE
*The Gülen Movement and Islam's
Third Way*
David Tittensor

MAPPING THE LEGAL
BOUNDARIES OF BELONGING
*Religion and Multiculturalism from
Israel to Canada*
Edited by René Provost

RELIGIOUS SECULARITY
*A Theological Challenge to the
Islamic State*
Naser Ghobadzadeh

THE MIDDLE PATH OF
MODERATION IN ISLAM
The Qur'ānic Principle of Wasaṭiyyah
Mohammad Hashim Kamali

CONTAINING BALKAN
NATIONALISM
*Imperial Russia and Ottoman
Christians (1856–1914)*
Denis Vovchenko

INSIDE THE MUSLIM
BROTHERHOOD
Religion, Identity, and Politics
Khalil al-Anani

Inside the Muslim Brotherhood

Religion, Identity, and Politics

KHALIL AL-ANANI

OXFORD
UNIVERSITY PRESS

OXFORD
UNIVERSITY PRESS

Oxford University Press is a department of the University of Oxford. It furthers the University's objective of excellence in research, scholarship, and education by publishing worldwide. Oxford is a registered trade mark of Oxford University Press in the UK and certain other countries.

Published in the United States of America by Oxford University Press 198 Madison Avenue, New York, NY 10016, United States of America.

© Oxford University Press 2016

Library of Congress Cataloging-in-Publication Data
Names: al-Anani, Khalil, author.
Title: Inside the Muslim Brotherhood : religion, identity, and politics / Khalil al-Anani.
Description: New York, NY : Oxford University Press, [2016] | Includes index.
Identifiers: LCCN 2016006858| ISBN 9780190279738 (cloth : alk. paper) | ISBN 9780190279745 (updf)
Subjects: LCSH: Jam'īyat al-Ikhwān al-Muslimīn (Egypt) | Egypt—Politics and government—1981– | Islam and politics—Egypt.
Classification: LCC BP10.J383 A635 2016 | DDC 322.4/20962—dc23
LC record available at http://lccn.loc.gov/2016006858

3 5 7 9 8 6 4
Printed by Sheridan Books, Inc., United States of America

To Howaida, Mohamed, and Aly,
my sources of love, success, and joy

Contents

List of Illustrations ix

Acknowledgments xi

Note on Transliteration xv

1. Introduction: Unpacking the Brotherhood 1

2. Debating Islamism and Theorizing the Brotherhood 14

3. Constructing Islamic Collective Identity 34

4. The Power of the *Jama'a*: The Enduring Legacy
   of Hasan al-Banna 50

5. The Brotherhood's Art of Recruitment 67

6. *Tarbiyya* and Consolidating the Brotherhood's Identity 82

7. The Brotherhood's Organization, Structure, and Ideology 99

8. *Ikhwanism:* The Brotherhood's Code of Identity 118

9. Enforced Coherence: The Brotherhood under
   Regime Repression 135

10. Conclusion 155

Notes 162

Index 191

List of Illustrations

Figures

3.1 Components of the Identity Construction Process 48
4.1 Al-Banna's Framework of Islamic Identity 56
4.2 The *Jama'a* Paradigm 59
5.1 Stages of the Brotherhood's Recruitment Strategy 72
6.1 Venues of Socialization (*Tarbiyya*)
in the Brotherhood 87
6.2 The Brotherhood's Multitiered System
of Membership 93
7.1 The Vertical Structure of the Brotherhood 104
7.2 The Horizontal Structure of the Brotherhood 105

Table

5.1 Mashhur's Blueprint of the Individual Call 78

Acknowledgments

THIS BOOK WOULD not have been possible without the support of many people. It originated with a doctoral thesis I researched, wrote, and successfully defended at the School of Government and International Affairs at Durham University. As a result I am indebted to Professor James Piscatori, who supervised my thesis and provided me with invaluable guidance and advice. Throughout my doctoral study Jim was more than a supervisor; he was a mentor and a friend who encouraged me to pursue my research and career objectives. I am grateful to Mehmet Asutay, professor of Middle Eastern and Islamic studies at Durham University, a source of inspiration and invaluable support. His course on methodology was intellectually stimulating and enlightening. I would also like to thank Dr. Frederic Volpi for his insightful comments.

I owe a deep debt of gratitude to the El-Masry Foundation for Community Service in Egypt, which sponsored and supported my postgraduate studies at Durham University. In particular I am thankful to Nashwa Bayoum, Tamer Attya, Heba Isaac, and other staff for their support and understanding. I am also grateful to my friend Mahmoud Mohieldin, professor of economics at Cairo University, who encouraged me throughout this project. I owe special recognition and gratitude to Chris Kato, my research assistant, who helped me diligently throughout this project. Chris spent hours revising and editing the manuscript and provided invaluable comments and feedback.

I am thankful to several leaders, members, and ex-members of the Muslim Brotherhood in Egypt who agreed to be interviewed for this project and provided vital thoughts and ideas that deepened my understanding of the organization: Esam Al-'Aryan, Abdul Khaliq Al-Sherif, Khaled Hamza, Mohamed Hamza, Abdurrahman Ayyash, Sherif Ayman, Ammar El-Beltagy, Mohamed Mustafa, Kamal El-Helbawy, Abdurrahman

Mansour, Eslam Ahmed, Mohamed Yussif, Ibrahim Saleh, Mohamed Soliman, Salah Abdul Halim, Mohamed Ayoub, Ayman Ashraf, Mohamed al-Naggar, and Mohamed Sarhan. For their time and attention I would also like to thank the interviewees who requested their names not be mentioned.

I thank friends, colleagues, and scholars who influenced my research either through their writings and scholarship or by engagement and discussion: Colin Turner, John Esposito, Nathan Brown, Olivier Roy, Asef Bayat, Carrie Rosfesky Wickham, Alberto Melucci, Salwa Ismail, Jillian Schewedler, Abdelwahab El-Affendi, Marc Lynch, Jason Brownlee, Emad El-Din Shahin, Peter Mandaville, M. Hakan Yavuz, Tarek Masoud, Mona El-Ghobashy, Maszlee Malik, Samer Shehata, Mohamed Abu Rumman, Alaa El-Nadi, Mu'taz Al-Khatib, Omar Ashour, Ahmad Atif Ahmad, Ziad Munson, Saif El-Din Abdelfattah, Heba Ezzat Raouf, Osama El-Ghazaly Harb, Radwan El-Said, Shadi Hamid, Tamara Wittes, Michele Dunne, Jeroen Gunning, Roel Meijer, Ibrahim El-Bayoumi Ghanim, Mohamed El-Menshawy, the late Husam Tammam, Nabil Abdel Fattah, Tareq Al-Beshry, and the late Mohamed El-Sayyid Said. My apologies if I missed someone who deserves to be acknowledged. Any errors, omissions, and misunderstandings in this book are solely my own.

I am grateful to Oxford University Press and its staff and partners, particularly Executive Editor Cynthia Read, who was so patient and understanding throughout the journey of putting together this book. I also thank the editorial team at OUP particularly Glenn Ramirez, David Joseph, copy editor Judith Hoover who made this book possible. Special thanks go to the anonymous reviewers for their invaluable comments on the initial manuscript.

I am grateful to Abdou Mousa Bermawy and Ahmad Helmy for designing the cover art of the book and to the Design Team at OUP who worked on it.

This project would not have been finished without my family's prayers and constant support. I am indebted to my father, the late Mohamed Khalil al-Anani, who passed away before the book was finished. His diligent spirit was always a source of inspiration. My mother, Fatima Mohamed Salem, has been a key supporter throughout my life journey. Her unwavering encouragement, faith, and wisdom helped me endure many difficulties.

I would like to thank Howaida Soliman who is not simply my beloved spouse but is also my friend and companion. Without her endless love, faith, and encouragement, I would not have been able to finish this book. No words can express my gratitude to her. Finally I would like to thank my two boys, Mohamed and Aly. I am grateful for their patience and for enduring days when I could not play with them. May I provide you both as much joy as you have given me.

To all my family I dedicate this book.

Note on Transliteration

THROUGHOUT THIS BOOK I have adopted a simplified transliteration scheme that roughly follows the logic of the Library of Congress system, except principally for the diacritics. I have generally designated the 'ayn (e.g., *shari'a, da'wa, jama'a*) and medial *hamza* (Qur'an, not Quran), but not the terminal *hamza* (*'ulama*, e.g., not *'ulama'*). The spellings of individual and place names that are commonly used in English, particularly as used in reference to Egypt, are adopted here—for example, Badie (not Badi'), Ismailia (not Isma'iliyya). "Mohamed" is thus used for all individuals except the Prophet Muhammad.

Inside the Muslim Brotherhood

I

Introduction

UNPACKING THE BROTHERHOOD

THIS BOOK UNPACKS the Muslim Brotherhood in Egypt. Unlike other works that tend to focus on the Brotherhood's *external* behavior and activism, or what can be called the "outer" layer, this book concentrates on the *internal* dynamics, processes, and interactions that shape its identity and politics. In this respect I uncover how the Brotherhood as a sociopolitical movement came to be. I unravel the tangled processes of recruitment, socialization, indoctrination, and identification that forge the Brotherhood's identity and explore how this identity is constructed in everyday life. Put differently, this book is a journey that explores the *inside* world of the Brotherhood through the eyes of its members. By demystifying the multifaceted character of the Brotherhood, I explain how the Brotherhood constructs its identity, how one becomes an *ikhwani* (a Brotherhood member), and how this affiliation manifests itself in one's everyday life. I explain the intricate and disciplined structure of the movement, how it has survived repression, and the relationship between its identity and its durability. As an ethnographic and analytical study, this book contributes to the growing literature on the Muslim Brotherhood and sheds light on some of its understudied aspects.

This book is the culmination of my studies and observations of the Muslim Brotherhood for more than a decade. I started researching the Brotherhood in 2004, when Mohamed Mahdi Akef was chosen to become the new general guide (*al-murshid al-'am*). It was incredibly difficult to conduct field research during that time due to security repression and surveillance of the movement, and it took me months to build trustful relationships with the Brotherhood's leaders and members.

I published my first book on the Brotherhood in 2007 in Arabic, *The Muslim Brotherhood in Egypt: Gerontocracy Fighting against Time*, in which I explained the startling rise of the Brotherhood in the 2005 parliamentary elections and its impact on the movement's politics and ideology. A few years later I realized that I had only scratched the surface and had little knowledge of the Brotherhood's intricate structure and dynamics. Therefore this book delves into more detail regarding the movement's internal politics and paints a clear picture of the dynamics and processes that shape its ideology, behavior, and activism. Informed by dozens of interviews, discussions, meetings, and informal conversations with leaders and members representing different generations and geographical areas across Egypt, this book provides a detailed account of the interplay of religion, identity, and politics within the movement. It also contributes to the theoretical debate on how to study Islamists and whether or not they should be considered "social movements." By doing so this book challenges some of the conventional and dominant narratives about Islamists and Islamism as a whole.

The Brotherhood's Identity

To understand the Brotherhood's activism, one needs to deconstruct the underlying factors that shape and motivate it. It is my contention that identity is one of the key drivers of the Brotherhood's activism. I define *identity* in this book as the code of norms and values that guides and inspires individuals in everyday life. This code stems from multiple factors and is subject to intense socialization and indoctrination processes. As Craig Calhoun points out, identity is produced by acts of individual will.[1] Along these lines in chapter 3 I explain that identity cannot be measured; however, it can be imagined and manifested.

I argue that the Brotherhood's collective identity is the outcome of multiple processes and factors. Building on Alberto Melucci's seminal work on collective identity I trace how the Brotherhood constructs its identity through ideational as well as institutional factors. For Melucci collective identity is not a datum or an essence, a "thing" with a "real" existence, but the outcome of negotiations, bargains, exchanges, decisions, and conflicts among actors.[2] He aptly defines *collective identity* as "a process in which actors produce the common cognitive frameworks that enable them to assess their environment and to calculate the costs and benefits of their action."[3] It is also a reflection of the mutually reinforcing processes and interactions that occur within social movements and are shaped by the opportunities and constraints in the external environment.[4] Throughout this book I employ Melucci's interactive and analytical concept of collective identity to uncover the processes that shape the Brotherhood's identity and explain how it came to be.

Over the past two decades collective identity has been a subject of extensive scholarly work to better understand the rationale of collective action. Scholars have studied the relationship between culture and collective action, identity and modes of mobilization, interests and the incentives of participation in collective action, and grievances and collective identity.[5] Despite the literature's useful contributions, it is mainly concerned with investigating the impact of identity on collective action, but not the other way around, that is, how a movement reshapes its individuals' identity in everyday life. This book seeks to fill this gap in the literature by examining the impact of collective action on individuals' identity, in other words, how a social movement transforms its members' mindset, worldviews, and perceptions—their identity. By deconstructing the process of identity construction, I explain how the Brotherhood recruits members, indoctrinates them, and reshapes their worldview.

The Brotherhood's identity formation is intertwined with other processes of recruitment, indoctrination, and identification. As I explain in the following chapters, these processes occur simultaneously and serve as a concrete foundation for the Brotherhood's identity and structure. They also correspond with the Brotherhood's objectives and ideology. In fact it is these very rules that distinguish the Brotherhood from other Islamist social movements. By deftly weaving a web of internal relations, culture, norms, and values, the Brotherhood produced a distinctive code of identity that enabled its survival against all odds.

As I show in chapter 5, the Brotherhood has an intricate, multitiered system of membership, with sympathizers at the bottom and the most active and committed members at the top. This system not only facilitates the alignment of members' behavior with the Brotherhood's objectives and ideology but it also ensures their loyalty and commitment to the leadership. The membership structure also plays a pivotal role in protecting the movement from state infiltration. It is with this system that the Brotherhood selects, trains, indoctrinates, and scrutinizes prospective members' attitudes and behavior before granting them full membership.

I contend that the relationship between the Brotherhood's membership and its identity is robust, although it has been overlooked in the literature. As I will clarify, the recruitment and promotion system was designed to correspond with the identification process. In order to rise within the movement's ranks, members must meet certain requirements and carry out certain activities. These reflect members' degree of loyalty and willingness to submit to the Brotherhood's ideology and leadership.

Ikhwanism *as a Form of "Distinctive" Identity*

The key question this book explores is how one becomes an *ikhwani* and how this affiliation manifests itself in everyday life. Answering this question reveals many facets of the Brotherhood's identity. As discussed earlier, the Brotherhood's identity is not merely a product of the religious or theological convictions of members; rather it is a socially constructed product of the movement's organizational dynamics, symbolic production, and ideational framework set by its leaders and ideologues. Accordingly this identity is contested in everyday life by similar or rival identities and, more important, within the movement itself. As a social entity every organization encounters different views and conflicting interests of its members, leaders, and stakeholders. Without a strong sense of identity, these organizations may be more vulnerable to fracturing and splitting.

As a social movement the Brotherhood has built a distinctive form of identity that differentiates it and its members from other groups and allows it to maintain its activism. I call this identity *ikhwanism*, referring to the cognitive code of norms, values, and regulations that guides and directs members in their everyday lives. When individuals join the movement, they abide by its rules and regulations; after a while, they start to act not as individuals but as brothers (*ikhwan*). This sense of *ikhwanism*, or togetherness, helps the Brotherhood generate collective action, deepen the commitment of its members, and enhance the resilience of the movement as a whole. As I explain in chapter 8, *ikhwanism* is not a rigid set of sacred or spiritual values but rather a constellation of social and organizational norms that are created and utilized in everyday life. Moreover *ikhwanism* does not negate other facets of members' personal identities. To be and to behave as an *ikhwani* does not conflict with a member's social identity as a father or brother or professional identity as a lawyer, doctor, or teacher. In fact the uniqueness of the Brotherhood's identity is that its members have multiple layers of identity that facilitate the dissemination of its ideology in society.

As the Brotherhood's code of identity *ikhwanism* consists of five key norms and values: allegiance (*bay'a*), obedience (*ta'ah*), trust (*thiqa*), commitment (*iltizam*), and loyalty (*intima*). These reflect the Brotherhood's distinct identity and define its role in the lives of its members. They play a key role in *ikhwanizing* the private and social sphere of the Brotherhood and strengthening the loyalty of its members.

The Jama'a *Paradigm*

Ikhwanism does not operate in a vacuum; it needs an organizational structure that can activate and sustain it in everyday life. There is a crucial link between the Brotherhood's identity and its structure. This is tailored to intensify and enhance the indoctrination process. The Brotherhood's regulations and norms require members to behave in a manner that complies firmly with its objectives and ideology. According to Melucci, norms refer to the "point at which operational needs (the allocation of resources) come together with the needs of integration and control (power)."[6] These norms help the Brotherhood institutionalize its ideology. The regularity of the movement's activities (e.g., seminars, battalion training, camps) helps members interact, communicate, and, most important, acclimate themselves to its norms and regulations. The incessant processes of indoctrination, ritualization, and habituation reshape individuals' identities and foster a strong sense of self-identification.

The Brotherhood's organizational structure was created by its founder, Hasan al-Banna, and is maintained by his successors. As I explain in chapter 3, al-Banna created a unique organizational structure that blends the movement's mission, ideology, objectives, and strategy. I call this the *jama'a* (groupness) paradigm: an organizational framework that connects the movement's religious, social, and organizational aspects and galvanizes them in everyday life. This framework also responds to the spiritual, material, and social needs of the Brotherhood's members by enhancing their solidarity and strengthening their social bonds. Furthermore this organizational structure has generated a unique system of values and norms that defines the Brotherhood's disciplined and cohesive character.

Interestingly, despite the complexity of the organizational structure, it is far from rigid or static. In fact, as I explain in the following chapters, it is elastic, inclusive, and adaptable. It helps the Brotherhood recruit, accommodate, and assimilate members from diverse social, cultural, educational, professional, and geographic backgrounds, integrating them all under the umbrella of the *jama'a*.

The *jama'a* paradigm is the outcome of complex processes of social networking and indoctrination. As a social movement the Brotherhood allocates resources, mobilizes individuals, and sets ideological frameworks that bind members together and foster their commitment. It consistently capitalizes on social networks, familial relationships, and religious bonds in order to expand its constituency. The *jama'a* paradigm is the lynchpin of the Brotherhood's collective identity and serves as the foundation for its activism and unity. Al-Banna and his successors always stressed the importance of being part of a group or a movement, a *jama'a*; in fact the Brotherhood's organizational structure is based on the very idea of collectiveness, or being a *jama'a*.

The Brotherhood's Durability

Over the past century the Brotherhood has demonstrated a remarkable degree of resilience. Founded in 1928 as a religious and charitable organization, it played a key role in shaping Egypt's politics and society. During the 1930s it was mainly involved in charitable and social activities, with little interest in politics. Entry into politics came in the early 1940s, when al-Banna decided to run in the parliamentary election of 1942, though he eventually withdrew in light of pressure from the government.[7] At the end of the 1940s the Brotherhood's military wing (the Special Apparatus) engaged in violence against British authorities and Egyptian officials, leading to the assassination of al-Banna on February 12, 1949, and the dissolution of the movement. Under the Nasser regime the Brotherhood was subject to harsh repression and even eradication attempts during the 1950s and 1960s. This repression peaked after the movement was outlawed in 1954; hundreds of its members were arrested, prosecuted in military courts, and tortured. However, the Brotherhood experienced a resurgence in the early 1970s after President Anwar Sadat took power. His more accommodating stance led to the release of many members and their return to political life. Building from this point, the Brotherhood returned to prominence and became an influential actor in Egyptian society. It plunged into formal politics, expanded its social network, and reached out to liberal and secular forces during the 1980s. However, this growth caused the Brotherhood to be perceived as a threat to the Mubarak regime in the 1990s, and once again it became a target of regime repression. The relationship between President Hosni Mubarak and the Brotherhood reached an impasse after the fraudulent 2010 elections, when the Brotherhood won no seats and boycotted the second round of voting.

It was not until the popular uprising of January 25, 2011, and the ouster of Mubarak that the Brotherhood reemerged as a key political force. In June 2012 Mohamed Morsi, chairman of the Brotherhood's Freedom and Justice Party (FJP), became Egypt's first democratically elected president. However, after only one year in power Morsi was ousted by the military on July 3, 2013, following mass protests. Since then the Brotherhood has witnessed one of the greatest crises in its history: hundreds of its members and supporters have been killed,[8] thousands are in prison or in exile,[9] and several key leaders, including the movement's most senior leader, General Guide Mohamed Badie, have been sentenced to death.[10] In addition the movement's financial assets have been frozen, and its charity and educational centers have been seized by the government.[11]

Yet despite this unprecedented repression, the Brotherhood survives and maintains its activism, particularly in rural and suburban areas. This extraordinary ability to endure and accommodate repression constitutes one of the Brotherhood's most defining features. Not only has it survived multiple waves of regime oppression and exclusion, but it has also sustained its structure and preserved its identity. It is due to this resilient identity that the Brotherhood has been able to survive and maintain its activism.

The durability of the Brotherhood has puzzled scholars and observers; however, it has not received much attention in scholarly work. This book provides an explanation for this dilemma. The Brotherhood is not a mere political force that seeks power; it is an identity-maker that aims to reshape societal norms and individualities as Islamic. It is thus heavily involved in meaning construction and symbolic production that shape its members' worldviews and perceptions. These processes, as I shall explain, help the movement accommodate repression by connecting members and enhancing their solidarity, particularly during difficult times.

Repression sometimes plays into the hands of the Brotherhood and enables it to achieve three key goals: garnering public support, reinforcing internal coherence, and avoiding internal change. As I explain in chapter 9, the Mubarak regime's attempts to destroy the movement actually helped it survive and expand. I also explain why the Brotherhood did not experience major internal splits or schisms over the past three decades, despite a number of disputes between the old and the new guard and between the conservatives and the so-called reformists.

Rethinking the Brotherhood

This book is not simply a synopsis of findings on Islamism, and it looks beyond the stereotypes and clichés about Islamists as rigid and immutable actors. It therefore does not treat Islamists as monolithic or homogeneous but as sociopolitical agents involved in the production of meanings and symbols in everyday life. In other words, this book is concerned with the nature of Islamists as social actors who have material and ideational interests in altering societal norms to match their ideology and objectives.

The chief question I seek to answer is this: How does the Brotherhood create its identity in everyday life? I have divided my response into a group of subquestions: What are the key processes of identity construction in the Brotherhood? What is the code of norms and values that guides the Brotherhood's members? What is the role of the Brotherhood's structure in fostering and consolidating members' identity? What is the impact of repression on the Brotherhood's coherence and unity? How may identity preserve and maintain the Brotherhood's activism?

These questions are answered by the book's chief contention: the Brotherhood's identity is the culmination of intricate and intensive processes of recruitment, identification, socialization, and indoctrination. These processes are significantly affected by the external environment, particularly whether it is inclusive or exclusive, authoritarian or democratic, oppressive or friendly. I follow constructivism as a theoretical framework for this study. Building on the seminal work of Peter Berger and Thomas Luckmann, I argue that identity per se is a "social construct" and is therefore subject to multiple factors and variables. Social constructivism challenges the idea that identity is an immutable phenomenon. In fact as a socially created reality, identity reflects the interaction between individuals and society whereby both constitute each other. It is the outcome of these processes of interactions between the self and society, individuals and groups, structures and meanings that take place in everyday life. Berger and Luckmann demonstrate that identity is formed by social processes and is maintained, modified, and reshaped by social relations.[12]

The strength of constructivism as an interpretive framework lies in its ability to uncover the ways individuals and groups participate in the creation of their perceived social realities. According to Hakan Yavuz, constructivism stresses human agency as the prime mover of history and assumes that society is a human construction, so it is subject to multiple interpretations and influences.[13] As Vivien Burr points out, constructivism is "an artifact of a social group."[14] As members in that group, individuals tend to surround themselves with constructed meanings and symbolic relationships that foster their activism and give purpose to their actions.

Beyond Social Movement Theory

Over the past decade an influential body of scholarship has sought to integrate the study of Islamist activism into the field of social movements. Despite the significant contribution of this new trend in enhancing the understanding of Islamism as a multifaceted phenomenon, further efforts are still needed. And despite the importance of social movement theory (notions of mobilization, allocating resources, grievances, culture, framing, etc.), it is not sufficient to capture the essence of Islamism or to draw an accurate picture of its intricate nature; it is necessary to integrate other scholarly disciplines and approaches. Therefore, besides social movement theory, I incorporate social psychology, sociology of religion, and comparative politics.

I use social psychology to understand the changes and shifts in individuals' identities and perceptions within the Brotherhood. I build on the work of Bert Klandermans and Dirk Oegema, Hank Johnston, and John Drury and Steve Reicher to analyze individuals' motivations to join social movements and to be involved in different forms of collective action.[15] I extend the insights from these scholars into the realm of Islamist movements, specifically the Muslim Brotherhood, in order to explain the indoctrination and self-identification processes that occur. Social psychology enables us to uncover the interactive relationships between the movement and its members, the impact of collective action on their identity, and the underlying drivers of their activism and political participation.[16]

I use sociology of religion to examine the role of religion in constructing identity. Islamist social movements use religion both as a frame of reference and as an organizational mechanism. This instrumentalization of religion is crucial for Islamists to conduct recruitment, indoctrination, and solidarity building among the rank and file. The Brotherhood reaches out to new members using an integrated and well-crafted strategy. It adopts different tactics and tools in order to disseminate its discourse and ideology; the most important of these is preaching (*da'wa*). The *du'ah* (preachers) operate as active recruiters who seek to expand and widen the Brotherhood's social networks. This can be achieved with a wide range of tools, including educational, social, cultural, and recreational activities. I call this recruiting strategy "chasing the prey" to describe how the *du'ah* (the recruiters) tend to target religious-leaning individuals. Once detected these individuals become subject to a gradual yet intensive process of indoctrination that reshapes their mindset and worldview. A second recruitment tool is the Brotherhood's religious rituals and weekly gatherings. Several members I interviewed emphasized the role of these meetings in fostering a sense of belonging and commitment to the Brotherhood's ideology and leadership.

Since the Brotherhood is operating in a highly authoritarian and hostile environment, it is vital to understand the impact of this environment on the movement's behavior and activism and, more important, on its internal politics and dynamics. I tackle this issue with a comparative politics approach, by analyzing the relationship between authoritarianism and organizational cohesion, and find that regime repression has played a significant role in shaping the Brotherhood's internal dynamics and organization. Repression is not always a curse but can sometimes favor the victim. The Brotherhood not only accommodated Mubarak's repression; it employed that repression to gain public support and to maintain cohesiveness and solidarity among its members. The Brotherhood capitalized on regime repression by creating what I call the *mehna* (adversity or affliction) narrative. This narrative enabled the movement to create sympathy for them as victims of the regime. At the same time, this framing of regime repression deepens members' loyalty to and support of the leadership. However, this is not to say that repression comes without cost or that the movement seeks it. Rather my point is that its response to repression can help explain the dialectical relationship between repression and the Brotherhood's internal cohesion.

Moreover I argue that repression, among other factors, has played a key role in shaping the Brotherhood's internal balance of power. Since the mid-1990s repression has enabled the conservative faction within the movement to control the organization at the expense of the so-called reformists. While the reformists had a key role in the movement during the 1970s and 1980s, they were excluded and marginalized in the following decades.

Research Methodology

This study is primarily based on qualitative discursive analysis. As Corbin and Strauss explain, qualitative research produces findings not arrived at by means of statistical procedures or other means of quantification.[17] This research can be about persons, lives, stories, or behavior, or about organizational functioning, social movements, or interactional relationships. In order to obtain an in-depth understanding of the Brotherhood's identity and internal dynamics, my research incorporates both primary and secondary data. The primary data are from observations and interviews; the secondary data consist of information and documents such as official statements, textbooks, leaflets, and writings of the movement's founder and ideologues.

In terms of research methods, this study relies mainly on semistructured interviews conducted with Brotherhood members, leaders, and experts. They were conducted in a way that reflects the Brotherhood's diversity and complexity. Therefore some of the interviews took place in cities and urban areas such as Cairo and Alexandria, while others were conducted in more rural areas such as Al-Sharqia, Al-Dakahlia, and Al-Minya. I also visited some of the FJP's regional branches and held meetings with several low-level members and middle-ranking leaders. Most of the interviews were conducted between 2009 and 2013, and while most were conducted face-to-face, some were done through Skype or phone conversations. Some interviewees allowed their names to be mentioned, while other preferred to remain anonymous or provide pseudonyms to avoid regime retaliation.

Mapping the Book

This book is divided into eight chapters. In chapter 2 I provide a survey of the literature and scholarly contributions to the study of Islamist movements, with a special focus on the Muslim Brotherhood. Using critical analysis I examine theoretical and analytical approaches that have been applied to the study of Islamism since the 1980s. In particular I probe the "essentialist" and "contextualist" narratives that have dominated the study of Islamist movements over the past three decades. This reveals the problems of dealing with Islamism as a monolithic phenomenon, as essentialists argue, and as a reaction to the modernization and urbanization crises plaguing the Middle East since the second half of the twentieth century, as the contextualists contend. The chapter also provides a critical examination of emerging social movement trends that have been used to analyze Islamist movements over the past decade. Nevertheless, despite my critique of social movement theory, I view it as a useful tool if combined with other theoretical disciplines. To this end my study interweaves social movement theory with social constructivism in order to analyze the Brotherhood's politics and identity.

Chapter 3 articulates the study's theoretical framework. The departure point of this study is social constructivism combined with social movement theory in order to provide a better understanding of the Brotherhood's identity. In chapter 4 I trace the role of Hasan al-Banna, the founder and chief ideologue of the Brotherhood, in articulating the movement's identity framework. By investigating al-Banna's ideological and intellectual upbringing, I reveal how his legacy has affected the Brotherhood and shaped its identity. I investigate the *"jama'a* paradigm," which distinguishes the Brotherhood and allows it to maintain its identity and activism during difficult times.

In chapter 5 I delve deeply into the internal elements of the Muslim Brotherhood to shed light on its recruitment and mobilization strategy. In particular I explain how the Brotherhood leverages what I call "chasing the prey" in order to recruit and attract new members. This chapter also explains the different phases of the Brotherhood's recruitment strategy and how they correspond with the socialization and indoctrination process.

Chapter 6 continues the examination of how the Brotherhood consolidates its identity through an internalization of its ideology, norms, and objectives. It provides an original and detailed account of the socialization and indoctrination process that takes places within the Brotherhood. By integrating the ideational and institutional factors, I propose a new model to explain how the Brotherhood reshapes and consolidates its members' identities. This framework is called the "incubation model," an intensive socialization process that transforms an individual's perceptions and views to align with the movement's ideology, norms, and objectives. The model incorporates two primary components: the Brotherhood's unique socialization process, known as *tarbiyya*, and its multitiered system of membership. I show how the Brotherhood blends its socialization process with an organized membership structure to consolidate and reinforce its members' identities.

Chapter 7 builds upon the incubation model to examine the interplay between the Brotherhood's organizational structure and ideology. I begin by revealing how the movement's structure has enabled it to endure regime repression and expand its activism over the decades. I provide a fresh look into the Brotherhood's structure by exploring the relationship between its different organizational levels (*usra, shu'ba, mantiqa*, etc.) and discussing the impact of amendments to the bylaws and charter. The chapter also illustrates the Brotherhood's organizational problems and how they hinder its image and performance.

In chapter 8 I analyze the notion of *ikhwanism* and argue that it serves as the code of identity that works to preserve the movement's activism and survival. I explore the Brotherhood's norms and regulations that encompass members in everyday life, highlighting five key norms: *bay'a* (allegiance), *ta'ah* (obedience), *thiqa* (trust), *iltizam* (commitment), and *intima* (loyalty). The chapter shows how the Brotherhood's structure and its members internalize these norms.

In chapter 9 I demonstrate the vital role that repression plays in shaping the internal dynamics of the movement. The Brotherhood utilizes repression to maintain coherence and solidarity within its ranks. I also reveal the shifts in the balance of power within the Brotherhood by examining the relationship between different factions and generations. In this respect an important caveat is worth mentioning. This book covers the Brotherhood primarily during the Mubarak era (1981–2011). However, I touch upon developments and dynamics in the post-2011 period insofar as they relate to the book's major themes and topics.

2

Debating Islamism and Theorizing the Brotherhood

HOW SHOULD WE study Islamism? This perennial question has overshadowed the realm of Islamist politics in recent decades. Despite the burgeoning literature on Islamist movements, agreement among scholars over terminology, classification, and analytical framework has proven elusive.[1] In fact it appears that as more literature is produced, less agreement among scholars is reached. This irony is due to many factors; among them is the multifaceted character of Islamism, which requires a significant amount of effort to accurately understand it and an interdisciplinary approach to explain its changing behavior and tactics. Such an approach should combine disciplines such as sociology, social psychology, and the study of social movements in order to comprehensively and compellingly capture changes in Islamists' ideology, discourse, behavior, and strategy over time.

Further, the state of the field is subject to political developments and contestation in the Muslim world, which impact the way scholars and analysts perceive Islamism.[2] Media coverage of these developments tends to essentialize and decontextualize them, and analysts often juxtapose them in order to advance certain views and objectives. For example, the rise of the self-proclaimed Islamic State of Iraq and al-Sham (ISIS) has shaped public discussions and even academic debates on Islam, Muslims, and Islamism. I described this as the "ISIS-ification" of Islamist politics, whereby Islamism is viewed through the lens of ISIS.[3] It is true that scholars should not overlook or disregard serious phenomena like ISIS, but a problem arises when it is treated as the norm and not the exception.

Similarly the events of 9/11 had an enormous impact on Islamist politics. Since then Islamism has transformed into a broader label encompassing different and sometimes contradictory groups of Islamists that have no commonalities except the usage of religion in their discourse. Terminology such as *fundamentalism, revivalism, radicalism, reformism, Salafism, and conservatism* are used indiscriminately as synonyms.[4] In addition movements as diverse as the Egyptian Muslim Brotherhood, the Turkish Justice and Development Party, the Palestinian Hamas, and the Moroccan Justice and Development Party are sometimes studied as though they were identical. It is true that some of these groups share similar ideas or religious references; however, they vary greatly in their strategy, discourse, and tactics. This is not to say that Islamism as a field of inquiry is difficult to grasp or is intrinsically different from other research fields but rather to highlight the need to move beyond the existing analytical formulas that dominate our thinking and analysis and seek more nuanced and explanatory frameworks.

In this chapter I survey the academic literature and scholarly contributions to the study of Islamism, shedding light on how scholars have studied and interpreted Islamists' ideology, discourse, and activism. I also examine different theoretical and analytical approaches that have dominated the realm of Islamism over the past few decades. Most important I critically investigate the literature on the Brotherhood. Until recently the Brotherhood was one of the most academically understudied movements in light of its history, importance, and influence; the number of academic works on the group, in both English and Arabic, was not abundant until the 2000s due to several theoretical and practical factors. With regard to the former, as mentioned, the study of Islamism has been a subject of debate and disagreement among scholars, impacting the status of the field and creating divisions on how to study it. Scholarship has been dominated by essentialist and Orientalist views that treat it as an immutable phenomenon; thus the academic literature on Islamists, at least until 9/11, was highly reductionist and shallow. As a religiopolitical phenomenon, Islamism is a victim of the "modernity paradigm," which focuses on structural and cultural interpretations of the religious element and treats it as irrelevant.[5] Consequently the analytical and interpretative frameworks applied to Islamism can be both flawed and superficial.

On a practical level the Brotherhood's secretive and disciplined character has kept scholars from engaging with its members and receiving access to its records and archives. Meeting with cadres requires significant time and effort in order to gain their trust and confidence. While meeting with leaders is relatively easy because they tend to be more public and accessible, interviewing the low- and middle-ranking members can be daunting because they are more reticent to be identified. Security surveillance and the fear of regime repression are pervasive, so the threat of retribution imposes a serious impediment for both the interviewed and the interviewer. This was until the uprising of 2011 when the Brotherhood was legalized and its members became free to speak and to open up. However, the coup of 2013 reversed the situation and it became tremendously difficult to get hold of the Brotherhood's members who are either in prison or exile.

Studying Islam: An Enduring Debate

The academic theorization of religion has proven to be problematic. Not only has the study of religion undergone several changes over the past few decades, but scholarship on religion and religious movements has become significantly intertwined with other disciplines in order to reach consensus on how to study religion. Social scientists, for example, tend to tackle religion as a social phenomenon with different manifestations in everyday life, whereas theologians are interested in its sacred and metaphysical character. Nevertheless controversy over the study of religion has not precluded sociologists, anthropologists, psychologists, and political scientists from developing theoretical frameworks to expound the intricacy of religious phenomena. A growing body of cross-discipline studies has enhanced our understanding of religious movements and activism by tackling different aspects of this phenomenon.

Max Weber's and Emile Durkheim's contributions in the sociology of religion demonstrate how complex it is to construe religious behavior. Weber draws our attention to the role of individuals, such as prophets, priests, saints, and religious leaders, in shaping religious beliefs, worldviews, and values systems;[6] Durkheim gives society the final word in defining these outcomes.[7] Thus many Weberians and Durkheimians *study religion differently, if not contradictorily.*[8]

Studying Islam and Muslims is not an exception. The vast majority of scholarly work on Islamist politics raises more questions than answers. While some scholars are preoccupied by Islam as a faith and a system of beliefs, others focus on its cultural, social, and political components and manifestations. Notwithstanding the considerable literature on Islam, the Muslim world, and Islamist movements, social scientists, historians, and theologians who study Islam are faced with significant difficulties in scrutinizing its real essence. According to Richard Martin, those who study Islam "have come under increasing attack in recent years for their academic provincialism and for the distorted images of Islamic peoples and cultures many say they have created."[9] The real problem in studying Islam, however, is not the lack of knowledge about it as a system of beliefs but the tendency to confuse and conflate Muslim cultures, societies, and movements. For example, a substantial number of studies have persistently conflated the terms *Muslims* and *Islamists*, and *Islamists, fundamentalists, Salafis,* and *jihadists* have been used interchangeably and sometimes synonymously.[10] The ascendance of violent and radical movements, such as ISIS and Al-Qaeda, particularly in the wake of 9/11, has also created difficulties in categorizing Islamist movements. For instance, scholars have failed to distinguish between radical and moderate movements, religious and political groups, and fundamental and reformist parties. Put differently, the diversity of Islamist actors leads to a deep misunderstanding of Islam and Muslim politics. To avoid generalizations about Islam and Muslims, James Piscatori explains, scholars must ask two important questions, "Whose Islam and when?,"[11] to which I add "and where?" John Esposito elucidates this dilemma by revealing the multiplicity of Islamic interpretations: "While we commonly speak of 'Islam,' many Islams or interpretations of Islam exist. The images and realities of Islam and of Muslims are multiple and diverse: religiously, culturally, economically, and politically. Muslims are the majority in some fifty-seven countries, and they represent many nationalities, languages, ethnic and tribal groups, and customs."[12]

The crucial question remains: How should Islam be studied? This question entails various ontological and epistemological dilemmas embedded in the confusion between Islam as a faith system and a political ideology. Indeed studying Islam is usually accompanied by questions about its political ethos. While some scholars impugn the proposition that Islam is a "political religion,"[13] others believe it is inherently political.[14] Despite the belated recognition that studying Islam is a thorny and polemical phenomenon, reductionist approaches can still be found. Further, the ascendancy of a monolithic image of Islam and Muslims hinders many scholars from discerning the vast differences among Muslim societies. A number of scholars, including Samuel Huntington,[15] Bernard Lewis,[16]

Bassam Tibi,[17] and Daniel Pipes,[18] tend to view Muslim communities as homogeneous, stagnant, and static. Edward Said underscores this problem as part of Orientalism's legacy, which obscures appropriate understanding of Islam:

There are numerous methodological and intellectual problems that still need settling: Is there such a thing as Islamic behaviour? What connects Islam at the level of everyday life to Islam at the level of doctrine in the various Islamic societies? How really useful is "Islam" as a concept for understanding Morocco and Saudi Arabia and Syria and Indonesia? If we come to realize that, as many scholars have recently noted, Islamic doctrine can be seen as justifying capitalism as well as socialism, militancy as well as fatalism, ecumenism as well as exclusivism, we begin to sense the tremendous lag between academic descriptions of Islam (that are inevitably caricatured in the media) and the particular realities to be found within the Islamic world.[19]

This Orientalist tendency was reinforced by the 9/11 attacks, which added more prejudices to the study of Islam. Since then two arguments have persisted. The first assumes Islam has an authentic problem with politics. Embedded in an essentialist view, this thesis amalgamates culture and politics, norms and practices, and text and context.[20] The second contends that Islam as a faith system is incompatible with modernity.[21] These two arguments dominated the scholarly perspective toward Islam and Muslims during the 1980s and 1990s and led some to believe that Islam is characterized by an inherent political and religious exceptionalism.[22]

However, several scholars have refuted these arguments. Nazih Ayubi, for instance, claims that original sources of Islam (the Qur'an and Sunna) have very little to say about politics, that Islam does not determine a specific form for the state or government, and that political Islam is a new "invention" that does not represent a "going back" to any situation that existed in the past. According to Ayubi, *ulama* (Muslim scholars) politicized Islam by incorporating Islamic jurisprudence and *shari'a* into state law and functions.[23] The flaw in the argument that Islam and politics are inseparable lies in its tendency to disregard the cultural and political nature of Muslim societies.

Many scholars find the argument that Islam is incompatible with modernity or democracy unconvincing. Asef Bayat points out that viewing

Muslims as "exceptional" or as having a peculiar position on democracy overlooks the internal dynamics, changes, and diversity that exist within these communities.[24] In fact the tendency to decontextualize Islam and Muslims and treat them as abstract or given is responsible for this prevalent misconception among scholars and policymakers alike.

Theoretical Approaches to Studying Islamism

The literature on Islamist movements presents a considerably diverse array of theoretical approaches and frameworks. However, before demonstrating this diversity, three important observations need to be highlighted. The first is the profound impact of the 1979 Iranian Revolution on this literature, which encouraged many scholars to study Islam and Islamism and to revisit secularization theory and reconsider its self-fulfilling prophecy about religion and its role in public life. Foucault described the Iranian Revolution as the "first post-modern revolution of our time," while Anthony Giddens saw it as a sign of "the crisis of modernity."[25] The second is the rise of militant Islamists in Egypt, Algeria, Saudi Arabia, Lebanon, and Afghanistan during the 1980s and 1990s, which reinforced negative perspectives regarding Islamism in general. Third is the outrage that followed 9/11, which led many scholars to reconsider their theories on how to study Islamism and unpack its multifaceted activism.

In this respect the literature on the resurgence of Islamist movements can be divided into three key trends: the crisis approach, the cultural (also known as essentialist) approach, and the social movements approach.

The Crisis Approach

This trend emphasizes the significance of the political and socioeconomic context in explaining the rise of Islamist movements. According to its proponents, the rise of Islamist movements is merely a reaction to the political and economic crises that afflicted Arab countries during the second half of the twentieth century. The economic and social failures of the Arab state fueled the ascendance of Islamists and legitimized their cause. While some scholars focused on the crisis of legitimacy that confronted Arab regimes after the War of 1967, others concentrated on the rampant urbanization, poverty, and unemployment that plagued Arab societies. On the former, Michael Hudson puts forward the idea that most Arab regimes faced a serious crisis of legitimacy that affected their image and power: "The shortage of this indispensable political resource [legitimacy] largely accounts for the volatile nature of Arab politics and the autocratic, unstable character of all the present Arab governments."[26] On the latter, Ali E. Dessouki contends that the revival of Islamic movements is the "product of a crisis situation characterized by economic difficulties, moral and ideological confusion, and political instability."[27]

Some advocates of this trend also focus on the role of the Arab defeat in the War of 1967 in fueling Islamism. The defeat diminished the appeal of Arab nationalism as a secular ideology and encouraged Islamism to replace it.[28] Some however, do not share this view. François Burgat observes that many Arab intellectuals shifted their position from nationalism to Islamism by the end of the 1970s. Among others he refers to figures such as Rachid el-Ghanouchi, the leader of the Tunisian Ennahda movement, and Tariq Al-Bishri, the renowned Egyptian judge and intellectual, who changed their ideas and discourse after the demise of Arab nationalism.[29] Yvonne Haddad asserts that the 1967 defeat is not the sole reason for the growth of Islamist movements. Although she recognizes the war's role in reviving religious sentiment (Islamic, Christian, and Jewish alike), she also highlights the domestic and international contexts that led to the defeat and its consequences.[30]

Lisa Anderson argues that the appeal of Islamist movements is not confined to the crisis of Arab nationalism but is the result of structural and institutional problems of Arab states. She explains that the persistence of absolute monarchies and authoritarian regimes in the region created political and social grievances that were then seized on by Islamist movements.[31] Gudrun Krämer expands on Anderson's idea by exploring the consequences of restricted political liberalization policies on Islamist activism. She argues that Islamist movements became a key oppositional force as a result of the unavoidable political opening that occurred in the Arab world during the 1980s and 1990s. According to Krämer, restricted political pluralism coupled with economic deprivation and social turmoil paved the way for the emergence of Islamists.[32]

In addition the urbanization of many Arab societies from the 1970s onward created significant socioeconomic problems. The marginalization and subsequent alienation of large portions of the lower and middle classes provided ideal conditions for Islamist recruitment. Over the past three decades the bulk of Islamist movements have come from urban and suburban areas. Ayubi asserts that the appeal of Islamists is an upshot of the urbanization and modernization crises in many Arab states. Policies promoting rapid urbanization in countries such as Egypt and Syria left many of the poor frustrated and alienated. This alienation benefited Islamists, who offered a new path of engagement, particularly for youth.[33] Mark Tessler writes that support for Islamist movements stems primarily from economic and political circumstances rather than religious or cultural traditions. He found that young Arabs have been particularly impacted by the failure of economic and developmental policies led by Arab governments, an outcome that fuels disenchantment and dissatisfaction.[34]

According to advocates of this approach, countries with greater income inequality such as Egypt, Tunisia, Yemen, Jordan, and Morocco encountered economic hardship as a result of privatization and structural adjustment policies. The socioeconomic consequences of these policies created an ideal environment for Islamists to exploit; in particular the vacuum created by the state's withdrawal encouraged Islamists to fill the void by expanding their social service and economic welfare networks. Islamist movements penetrated civil and public spheres and rooted themselves in universities, professional associations, unions, and schools, creating a strong network of supporters and beneficiaries. They launched what Saad Eddin Ibrahim calls "Islamic business," which served as a vessel to recruit members and spread their ideology more effectively among the population.[35] In Egypt, for instance, the Muslim Brotherhood encouraged its members and supporters to establish Islamic institutions, banking centers, schools, health clinics, and other enterprises. It succeeded in extending its service coverage to the poor and middle classes around the country. Similarly in Algeria economic liberalization played a crucial role in feeding the growth of Islamists. According to Dirk Vandewalle, the structural economic reforms had an immediate impact on the poor and generated support for the Islamic Salvation Front.[36] The pioneering role of Islamist networks in building religious and public institutions, such as mosques, clinics, and day care centers, proved advantageous to Islamists in the political arena. Tessler claims that Islamist movements, unlike secular parties, have the benefit of criticizing Arab regimes and delivering services at the same time.[37]

Despite the importance of the crisis approach in explaining the emergence of Islamist movements, many scholars have highlighted its shortcomings. Salwa Ismail, for instance, raises two main problems. First, it fails to capture the micro-level changes that shape the environment within which Islamist movements operate. Ismail finds "the focus on the macro level comes at the expense of the micro level where the everyday-life communities wrestle with the effects of the macro changes, initiate new forms of action, and struggle for and contribute to a reconfiguring of the political scene." Second is the inability to examine the impact of structural changes on cultural and symbolic aspects of everyday life. Although Ismail disagrees with the essentialist approach that gives primacy to culture over other factors, she considers the impact of political and economic transformations on shaping the public sphere where Islamists function.[38]

There are other problems with the crisis approach. It does not address why Islamist movements and not other ideological forces, such as leftists and liberals, are successful in seizing political and socioeconomic crises in order to gain support and attract the public. Similarly it does not provide a clear explanation for why people prefer to join Islamist organizations as opposed to other organizations. It fails to explain why most of these movements emerged before the creation of many Arab states. The Muslim Brotherhood, for example, was founded in 1928 and launched plenty of offshoots throughout the Arab world during the first half of the twentieth century. In fact this approach overlooks the role of religion in explaining the rise of Islamists. It is true that Islamist movements benefited from the failure of the Arab state; however, much of their support stems from their ideology and religious appeal. Moreover many Islamists are well educated and belong to the middle and upper-middle classes, an indication that the movements' appeal is not entirely based in lower classes that are more directly impacted by these crises.

The Essentialist Approach

The essentialist approach dominated the field of Islamic studies for decades. As mentioned earlier, the main premise of this approach is that the emergence of Islamist movements reflects the tension between Islam and modernity. Proponents of this trend argue that the rise of Islamist movements is merely a response to the inability of Muslim societies to reconcile modernity and democracy with their cultures and traditions. They claim Islam has a profound "cultural" and "ontological" problem with modernity.[39] They thus tend to identify Islamic culture as a rigid cluster of idioms and symbols that shapes the vision of Muslims toward the self and the other. As Hakan Yavuz explains, essentialists treat Islam as a set of fixed texts and doctrines.[40] Bassam Tibi, one of the most prominent essentialists, asserts that the problem of the Muslim world does not lie in the political ideology of Islamist movements but rather in the cultural crisis of Islam: "Ever since their encounter with the modern West in the course of the nineteenth century most Muslims have consistently been ill at ease with the cultural project of modernity, to which they were and still are exposed." Tibi describes modern Islam as characterized by a "defensive culture" that shapes Islamic political thought.[41] Despite his criticism of the philological and anthropological trends in the study of Islam, Tibi repeats the same mistake by suggesting that "historicizing" the Qur'an is a precondition for reforming Islam. In his own words, "If all kinds of essentialism are dismissed, and reference to the Qur'an itself is done in a historicizing manner, then it is possible to legitimate change in the direction of modernity."[42]

Daniel Pipes, another renowned essentialist, claims that Muslims have an unavoidable problem with modernity. According to Pipes, the "Muslim anomie" from modernity lies in the truth that Muslims are not able to adapt to Western civilization:

> Until 1800, Chinese, Indian and Islamicate civilizations enjoyed roughly the same social power as Europe and possessed full civilizations—with cities, classic traditions, written languages ... and formal institutions, which could compete with Europe's. Of these three people, the Muslims had much the hardest time coping with Europe's primacy.... Civilized peoples faced more difficulties than primitive peoples and Muslims faced more than the other civilized peoples. In short, Muslims experienced the greatest travails in coping with modernity; this was the special Muslim dilemma.[43]

However, Pipes's argument is built on a selective understanding of Islamic texts and on a Eurocentric narrative that is rooted in the hegemony of the Western modernity model over other cultures. For him Westernization is a prerequisite for modernization, and Muslims who live in the West cannot be both Muslims and Westerners at the same time. He advances the idea that Muslims should abandon *shari'a* and embrace secularism in order to modernize. Like Tibi, Pipes believes Muslims have to reconcile *shari'a* with the cultural dimension of modernity—in other words, to be Westernized: "Westernization being inimical to the observance of the *shari'a*, Muslim attitudes toward the west became embroiled in the question of fulfilling the sacred law [*shari'a*]. With Westernization becoming urgent, 'the crucial question is whether Islam should serve as a guide and inspiring ideal, or as a rule of life,' should Muslims abandon the Shari'a or keep it as always?"[44]

The essentialist perspective suffers many problems that are not limited to its Orientalist thrust but include theoretical and practical flaws. It fails to explain the diversity in Muslim societies and cultures; for example, all Muslims agree that the main Islamic divine texts are the Qur'an and Sunna but interpret them differently, and Muslims in Indonesia and Malaysia adopt different cultural and political styles from those who live in the Middle East. More important, this trend treats all Islamists as a homogeneous group with a regressive and backward understanding of religion. The Islamist spectrum covers many different kinds of Islamists, ranging from extremist radicals such as those in Al-Qaeda to progressive movements such as Ennahda in Tunisia and the Justice and Development Party in Turkey.

The most compelling critique of this approach is rooted in the field of poststructuralism. Recent scholarship reveals the inability of the essentialist narrative to explain religious phenomena, particularly in the Muslim world. Contemporary sociologists of religion, such as Peter Berger and Jose Casanova, stress the resurgent role of religion in the public sphere and acknowledge the failure of the secularism paradigm in explaining changes in religious phenomena. Berger explains, "The assumption that we live in a secularized world is false. . .. The proposition that modernity necessarily leads to a decline of religion is, in principle, 'value free.' "[45]

A critique of essentialism also emerged from the realm of postmodernity and multiculturalism. According to this trend, the main problem with essentialism is its reliance on modernity theory. James Piscatori and Dale Eickelman explore the limitations of the modernists' argument against the Muslim world by dismissing the causal relationship between modernization and Westernization. According to them, the main weakness of modernization theory "lies in the sharp contrast between two artificial constructs, 'modernity' and 'tradition.' "[46] They go further by emphasizing that Islamic "tradition" sometimes operated as a vehicle for revolutionary change. Fred Halliday expands on Eickelman and Piscatori's thoughts as he unpacks the ideological "defect" of the modernity narrative by criticizing the dichotomy of universalism vis-à-vis particularism. Halliday advances the idea that the particularism of the Middle East, like the universalism of the capitalist modernizer, is shaped by material and ideological interests. Unlike the essentialists, Halliday asserts the rise of Islamist movements is not a transhistorical phenomenon but rather a response to political and social conditions: "Where Islamist movements arise, or where particular groups identify themselves primarily as 'Muslim,' they are responding not to a timeless influence [as essentialists presume], but to the issues their societies and communities face today."[47]

Bobby Sayyid provides a robust critique of the modernist and Eurocentric narratives, arguing that modernity creates a hegemonic discourse similar to that which Islamists espouse. He finds that Islamists adopt a counterhegemonic movement based on Islamic particularism in order to protect their societies from the hegemony of the Western paradigm. He aptly observes, "An often made argument is that attempts to articulate Islamist positions on issues relating to human rights etc. are doomed to failure, since such positions are possible only through secularization; therefore, the only thing to do is to wait for Muslim societies to secularize."[48]

For some scholars the essentialist explanation of Muslims' position toward globalization and modernization is simplistic and inaccurate. Akbar Ahmed, for instance, reveals the superficiality of the essentialist argument by stressing what he claims is a global element of Islam: "Islamic history has had long periods in which we recognize elements from what we today call globalization: societies living within different ethnic, geographic and political boundaries, but speaking a language understood throughout, enjoying a common cultural sensibility and recognizing the same overarching ethos in the world-view."[49]

Another nuanced critique of essentialism comes from Olivier Roy, who rejects the rigid textual and cultural understanding of Islam and Islamism. According to Roy, Islamism is a modern phenomenon, not a traditional one. He compares Islamist groups with Marxist and revolutionary movements and rejects scholars who adopt a Weberian reading of Islam and treat it as a culture, a civilization, and a closed system. He explains, "The [Orientalist] presupposition consists, among Western specialists or essayists, in defining a timeless "Islamic Culture," a conceptual framework that structures both political life and urban architecture, the thoughts of the ulamas and of their detractors, and whose consequence would be the nonemergence of capitalism and the absence of an autonomous space for politics and institutions."[50]

Ultimately the essentialist trend fails to provide a compelling explanation of Islam and Islamism, leading to myriad critiques from scholars who sought to move beyond the essentialist narrative about Islam and Muslim societies as a whole.

Social Movement Theory

During the past decade several scholars have used social movement theory (SMT) to examine Islamist movements. They aim to overcome the shortcomings of other theoretical approaches that fail to explain the rise of Islamism. Instead of looking at texts, idioms, and ideologies, social movement scholars focus on everyday interactions and processes to understand how they shape Islamists' worldviews and identities. They investigate how Islamists allocate resources, recruit members, mobilize the public, build social networks, and frame their message to their followers. This trend treats Islamists as social agents seeking political and social change. Proponents view Islamism as an intricate and multifaceted phenomenon that cannot be understood without unpacking its *institutional* as well as *ideational* aspects (i.e., identity, framing, solidarity, emotions).[51]

This trend has three different but related strands: the first tackles Islamist movements in their political context and is called political process theory; the second focuses on political opportunity structures; the third addresses the cultural framing of Islamist movements. A brief discussion of these three strands demonstrates the pros and cons of applying them to the study of Islamism.

Political Process Theory

This strand investigates the impact of political context on Islamists and emphasizes the importance of political processes in shaping the behavior and strategy of Islamist movements. Proponents of this approach contend that the political environment determines resources, ideational frameworks, and institutional factors that shape Islamist movements. Repression impacts the movements and determines their ideological and political behavior. Mohammed Hafez finds the political process approach gives primacy to "process" over "structure" in creating collective action. According to Hafez, in order for Islamists to be engaged in collective action, they need to allocate resources that enable them to compete with their opponents.[52]

Despite its importance, this strand espouses a structural view that treats social movements as mechanical agents who react to the political environment without being able to change or alter it. Jeff Goodwin and James Jasper offer a lucid critique of the theory's structural bias. Although they acknowledge the contribution of political process theory to the study of social movements, they criticize the vagueness of its theoretical propositions. They state, "At best, [political process theory] in its current form provides a helpful, albeit limited, set of 'sensitizing concepts' for social movement research. It does not provide what it frequently and often implicitly promises: a causally adequate universal theory or 'model' of social movements."[53] Moreover this approach overlooks the dynamics and interactions occurring within social movements.

Political Opportunity Structures

This strand focuses on the political opportunities created by governments that enable social movements to mobilize people, allocate resources, and organize collective action. According to proponents, social movements seize political opportunities to press for more benefits.[54] These opportunities play a vital role in articulating the trajectory of social movements. Sidney Tarrow, for example, identifies four dimensions that provide incentives for participation in collective action: (1) access to participation; (2) shifts in ruling alignment; (3) building strong allies; and (4) splits within the ruling elite.[55] Building on Tarrow's insights, Quintan Wiktorowicz finds that political opportunities and constraints shape the calculations of Islamist movements and help them make rational decisions.[56] Hakan Yavuz goes further by emphasizing the role of opportunity space rather than opportunity structure in strengthening Islamist movements. According to him, opportunity spaces help Islamists articulate a new sociopolitical consciousness that can be utilized to achieve political change.[57]

Jeff Goodwin and James Jasper are among scholars who highlight the theoretical and analytical problems of this model. They question the tendency of its proponents to broaden or narrow their model in order to fit their analyses. As they put it, "the more broadly one defines political opportunities, the more trivial (and, ultimately, tautological) the political opportunity thesis becomes; conversely, the more narrowly one defines political opportunities, the more inadequate or implausible the political opportunity thesis becomes as an explanation for the rise of any particular social movement."[58] Furthermore this model fails to answer a crucial question: Why are Islamists able to capitalize on political opportunity structures to expand their gains while other groups cannot? In fact the political opportunities thesis conflates the emergence of social movements with their activism. The main assumption of this thesis is that people tend to join social movements whenever there is a political opportunity to do so. However, this does not explain whether movements create such an opportunity or simply exploit them. Despite stressing the importance of the political opportunity structure thesis, Ziad Munson criticizes its shortcomings when examining specific cases. Munson claims the political opportunity aspects mentioned by Tarrow fail to explain the rise of the Muslim Brotherhood in Egypt during the 1930s and 1940s. According to Munson, despite the repressive political environment in Egypt during that period, the Brotherhood succeeded in expanding its organizational and social structure to different urban areas.[59]

Cultural Framing Process

The third strand of SMT concentrates on cultural framing processes Islamists utilize to construct meaning.[60] Social movement theorists claim the process of creating or manufacturing meaning from traditional culture is complex and thus requires a certain level of framing alignment. David Snow and colleagues highlight four alignment processes social movements use to formulate their messages in relation to the existing culture: frame bridging, frame amplification, frame extension, and frame transformation.[61] Wiktorowicz contends that Islamist movements use framing mechanisms as interpretive devices that translate grievances and perceived opportunities into mobilization of resources and movement activism.[62]

Building on the framing process concept, Eickelman and Piscatori illustrate the importance of meaning manufacturing in the Muslim world. They argue that Muslim politics revolves around contesting both the interpretation of symbols and the control of the institutions that produce and sustain them, where Islam constitutes the language of politics and Islamic vocabulary contains words of political resonance.[63] Ismail takes their argument a step further by stressing the changing character of meanings and symbols when deployed in Islamist politics. Thus Ismail concludes that there are no inherited meanings to the texts.[64] The seminal work of Yavuz on Turkish political identity underscores Islamists' ability to interweave Islamic symbolism with the dynamics of everyday life.[65]

Despite the significant contributions of SMT in the study of collective action, it is still nascent in the field of Islamist movements, and more work needs to be done to gauge its ability to explain the behavior and tactics of Islamist groups. Moreover some sociologists believe SMT cannot be applied to religious movements. They assert these movements have an inherently backward nature that precludes them from being included in the study of social movements. Theorists such as Alain Touraine, Jürgen

Habermas, and Klaus Eder tend to exclude religious movements from the realm of new social movements, believing that religious movements do not present serious challenges to the prevailing social order.[66]

I argue that SMT provides valuable analytical tools to understand the dynamism and collective action of Islamist movements only if it can be incorporated into other analytical frameworks. Therefore, I combine SMT with the sociology of religion, social psychology, and comparative politics in order to better understand the Brotherhood's identity and activism.

Theorizing the Muslim Brotherhood

How can we study the Muslim Brotherhood? Is it a social agent or a religious movement? How can we explain its multifaceted character? And most important, how did the movement survive for decades despite regime repression? To put it simply, how can we theorize the Brotherhood?

These are a few questions that have preoccupied scholars studying the Brotherhood in recent years. Ironically, despite its long history and influence across the Muslim world, many aspects of the Brotherhood have yet to be uncovered.

Over the past few years several scholars from different academic and disciplinary backgrounds have produced a useful and influential body of literature on the Brotherhood. This literature can be divided into four main streams: the history of the Brotherhood, the social activism of the movement, the relationship between the Brotherhood and the Egyptian regime, and the ideological and organizational transformation of the movement.

Within the first stream is the seminal work of Richard Mitchell, which provides an insightful historical account of the movement in its early years.[67] Mitchell had extensive access to the Brotherhood's archives in the 1930s and 1940s, enabling him to uncover its ideology, organizational structure, and political history. However, since the publication of Mitchell's work, the Brotherhood has experienced significant changes and transformations that need to be further studied and investigated. Likewise Brynjar Lia's study provides a detailed account of the Brotherhood's internal dynamics and disputes between the 1930s and 1940s.[68] He extensively discusses the role al-Banna's charismatic leadership played in shaping the movement's ideology and organization. Although some parts of Lia's study repeat Mitchell's, Lia's analysis enhances our understanding of the formation of the Brotherhood as a mass social movement. Within the same stream is Barbara Zollner's study on Hasan al-Hudaybi, the second general guide of the Brotherhood. Zollner studies the relationship between the Brotherhood and the Nasser regime with special emphasis on how this relationship impacted the movement's ideology and leadership. She analyzes the role of al-Hudaybi in leading the Brotherhood during the crisis with Nasser's regime and reveals the impact of regime repression on the Brotherhood in the 1960s and how this inspired the radical ideas of Sayyid Qutb.[69]

The second stream discusses the Brotherhood's social formation and activism. Ziad Munson's pioneering study focuses on the Brotherhood's remarkable social capabilities during the 1930s and 1940s. More specifically he investigates the Brotherhood's ability to mobilize Egyptians across the country to such a successful degree that it became a mass social movement within only a few years. Based on original documents from the U.S. State Department between 1932 and 1954, Munson reveals the reasons behind the rapid development of the Brotherhood in urban and rural areas.[70] Abdullah Al-Arian's study provides a detailed account of the Brotherhood's activism in the 1970s. He highlights the "rebirth" of the Brotherhood in Egypt's universities after the years of repression under Nasser. According to Al-Arian, student activism enabled the Brotherhood to reemerge as an influential actor in Egyptian politics and society.[71]

The interplay between religion, activism, and politics is the theme of Carrie Wickham's influential study on the Brotherhood. Wickham details the Brotherhood's extraordinary mobilization capabilities and how they are shaped by the environment within which the movement operates. She maintains that the Brotherhood's activism during the 1980s and 1990s was due to "a deliberate process of mobilization initiated and sustained by Islamic counter-elites." She highlights the impact of political, social, and cultural environments on Islamic activism, which, she contends, contains both opportunities and constraints impacting Islamists' mobilization and activism.[72]

The third stream investigates the relationship between the Brotherhood and political regimes, particularly under Mubarak. While some scholars conclude that both parties benefited from this relationship (i.e., containing violent groups in exchange for the Brotherhood's political gains), others believe the relationship was more confrontational. Gilles Kepel, for example, asserts that Mubarak and the Brotherhood shared a common enemy in the form of violent Islamists who flourished in the 1980s. Accordingly the coexistence of the two parties was based on rational calculations.[73] However, Hesham Al-Awadi disagrees with Kepel's analysis and stresses that Mubarak attempted to eradicate the Brotherhood, particularly in the 1990s. Al-Awadi explains that the Brotherhood's gains in Parliament, professional syndicates, and universities threatened Mubarak's legitimacy and led him to launch an offensive campaign against the movement in the 1990s.[74] Wickham concurs with Al-Awadi and highlights the crackdown against the Brotherhood in the 1990s. She notes, "After more than a decade of toleration, the government launched a major counteroffensive against the Muslim Brotherhood, arresting many of its most dynamic leaders and hammering away at its reputation by condemning it as an 'illegal organization with ties to extremist groups.'"[75]

Clearly the popularity of the Brotherhood was a threat and source of discomfort to the Mubarak regime. How have scholars explained this popularity, especially when it manifests at the ballot box? Tarek Masoud provides a lucid and sophisticated analysis on this point. Unlike accounts that focus on ideology and religious appeal, Masoud attributes Islamists' electoral success to "structural factors that shape both citizens' choices and parties' strategies." He reveals the irony of Egyptian leftists' failure to use economic problems such as poverty and unemployment to win elections or enhance their popularity compared to Islamists.[76]

Another explanation for the success of Islamists in electoral politics is their adaptive tactics. Nathan Brown argues that regimes create a "red line" that binds Islamists from seeking a majority in elections. In authoritarian settings Islamists adeptly seize political opportunities to enhance their political gains, but they are also keen not to provoke the regime. Brown explains, "[Islamist movements] adapt their organization and bend their ideologies, but they are wary about the possibility that the political opening will fizzle or fail to deliver what they wish. The result is a cat-and-mouse game between dominant regimes and shrewd movements."[77]

The fourth stream deals with the ideological transformation and organizational changes within the Brotherhood. Unlike the Orientalist narrative, which treats Islamists as static and immutable actors, this stream underscores their dynamic nature. It argues that Islamists, like other social and political agents, are subject to ideological development and change. Mona El-Ghobashy provides compelling evidence for this argument. In her cogent study *The Metamorphosis of the Egyptian Muslim Brothers*, El-Ghobashy explains the shifts in the ideology and organization of the Brotherhood between the 1990s and 2000s. These changes arose from internal dynamics within the Brotherhood and from the movement's participation in party politics and adaptation to change in the political environment: "[The] ikhwan's energetic capitalization on Egypt's sliver of electoral competition for seats in Parliament, the professional unions, and municipal councils has had an especially profound effect on their political thought and organization."[78] Bruce Rutherford supports El-Ghobasy's insights on the Brotherhood's ideological evolution by highlighting the movement's ability to articulate what he calls "Islamic constitutionalism." According to Rutherford, this concept "advocates the adoption of laws that apply equally to ruler and ruled, the creation of institutions that regulate and constrain state power, and the protection of many civil and political rights. It also supports broad public participation in governance."[79]

On the organizational changes, El-Ghobashy refers to the generational shift within the Brotherhood after its repression during the 1960s. The 1970s witnessed the rise of a middle-aged generation who would go on to assume leadership positions in Parliament, universities, and professional syndicates in the 1980s and 1990s.[80] Brown also underlines the effect of this political opening on the Brotherhood's organizational structure. However, he places particular emphasis on the organizational cost of participation and its role in shaping the movement's calculations. He explains that the Brotherhood and other, similar groups actively weigh the risks of political participation with its impact on other activities. They tend to "leave a line of retreat, working to protect non-political activities and ensuring that the movement's goals are not forgotten by the entrance in the political process."[81]

These studies have enhanced our understanding of the Brotherhood's collective action and political activism beyond essentialist and Orientalist narratives. However, questions about the Brotherhood's identity, socialization and indoctrination processes, internal dynamics, and balance of power remain unanswered. This study attempts to provide plausible answers to these questions. Unlike studies that focus on the Brotherhood as a collective actor, I pay particular attention to the individual brothers (ikhwan), as they constitute the basic cell or unit of the movement's collective action.[82] Put differently, this study answers the crucial question of what it means for someone to be an ikhwani in everyday life.

Most studies on the Brotherhood tend to focus exclusively on one side or the other. By examining the processes of recruitment, social networking, and preaching, I explain how the Brotherhood adeptly turns its members into social entrepreneurs who play a crucial role in enabling the movement to expand its influence and constituency.

The starting point in most studies of the Muslim Brotherhood is the movement's external behavior, including its political activism, provision of social services, and electoral participation. These analyses fail to adequately emphasize how the internal workings of the Brotherhood impact these external processes. To fill this gap I investigate the interplay between the internal and the external. In particular I analyze how the internal world affects the Brotherhood's external behavior, and how this in turn shapes the movement's political and social activism. I also illustrate how the external environment impacts the Brotherhood's internal dynamics. Within this framework regime repression played a particularly important role in shifting the balance of power within the Brotherhood and shaping the movement's leadership over the past three decades.

3

Constructing Islamic Collective Identity

ISLAMISTS ARE NOT merely power seekers; they are also identity makers. They seek to make societal values and norms more Islamic. Their collective action aims to reshape individuals' identity and worldview. Therefore the question of how Islamists shape individuals' identity is crucial. Identity is not something *given*; rather it is a *constructed* concept that reflects individuals' sense of belonging to a certain family, group, tribe, or religion. Identity is therefore the byproduct of an intricate, dynamic process of constructing meanings in everyday life. In this chapter I explore how Islamist movements construct their collective identity. I uncover strategies, mechanisms, and tools that enable collective actors to produce meanings, symbols, norms, and values that shape their identity. My key objective is to propose an analytical framework that explains the process of identity construction within Islamist movements: How do social movements construct their identity? What are the components of collective identity? To what extent can collective identity sustain collective action? And what is the relationship, if any, between the political environment and identity formation processes?

The construction of Islamic collective identity is contingent upon the movement's aims and objectives, its internal structure, and the political environment within which it operates. I treat Islamic identity as a frame of reference that Islamists use to recruit members, generate collective action, and preserve their existence. I sketch the theoretical and scholarly debate on identity formation and explain how Islamist movements create their own collective identity. I explain how individual identity moves from the self to the social and then to the collective and how movements bridge the gap between these different levels of identity.

Echoes of the Self: What Is Identity?

The concept of identity is immensely problematic. Despite the plethora of literature on the subject, the concept itself remains somewhat of an enigma. Marilynn Brewer asserts that identity has no single or shared meaning, as "the problem with trying to extract any common definition is that the term is integrally embedded in separate theoretical structures and literatures with little or no cross-citation or mutual influence."[1] The multidimensional nature of identity perplexes scholars and has sparked fervent debate over its meaning and function. The sociologist Zygmunt Bauman, for example, considers identity a matter of grave concern because it contains vexing dilemmas for individuals and communities: "Identity-seekers invariably face the daunting task of 'squaring a circle': that generic phrase, as you know, implies tasks that can never be completed in a 'real time,' but are assumed to able to reach completion in the fullness of time—in infinity."[2]

In fact the difficulty of defining identity stems not only from its epistemological relativity but also from its multiple empirical usages. Identity is widely cited in psychology, sociology, anthropology, and, recently, political science; however, the roots of identity theory can be traced to the American sociologist George Herbert Mead's major work, *Mind, Self, and Society* (1934). Mead's classical framework of identity is based on the interaction between the self and society. He explores the genesis of the self as an organism that communicates with and responds to other social organisms. The interaction between the self and society he calls "the generalized other," which refers to individuals' tendency to behave as an "organized community," or social group. This process of interaction is contingent upon what he identifies as "self-consciousness." According to Mead, an individual organism enters the social environment through self-consciousness.[3]

Despite criticism of Mead's insights as simplistic and ambiguous, many theorists have built on his notion of "interactionism" in studying and interpreting social behavior.[4] Identity theory explains how social structures affect the self and how the self shapes social behaviors. The main assumption of identity theory is that the self is a multifaceted phenomenon that undertakes different social roles, "expectations attached to positions occupied in networks of relationships; identities are internalized role expectations."[5] Michael Hogg, Deborah Terry, and Katherine White, however, view the self as a reflection of society and argue that it should be regarded as an organized construct. According to them, identity theory "views the self not as an autonomous psychological entity but as a multifaceted social construct that emerges from people's roles in society; variation in self-concepts is due to the different roles that people occupy."[6]

Building on the notion of social roles, Sheldon Stryker and Peter Burke developed a subtheory of role identity that explains how social behavior becomes a role-choice behavior and why individuals choose one particular course of action.[7] This notion stems from Mead's concept of self-reflection, which he identifies as a prerequisite for social interaction. Peter Callero establishes the link between identity and social roles. He defines role-identity as "a particular social object that represents a dimension of the self." According to Callero, role-identity must be shared, socially recognized, and defined by action.[8]

The relationship between identity and social roles is paramount in Islamist movements. By creating a distinctive identity for their followers, Islamist groups can appeal to new constituents and expand their influence. In time members act as social entrepreneurs (du'ah) who embody the movement's values and ideology in everyday life. Furthermore this new identity gives Islamists a sense of differentiation and recognition in society, which is essential for recruiting new members and enhancing internal cohesiveness. Hogg and colleagues define role identities as "self-conceptions, self-referent cognitions, or self-definitions that people apply to themselves as a consequence of the structural role positions they occupy, and through a process of labeling or self-definition as a member of a particular social category."[9] In this sense identity is a crucial link between social structure and individual actions, which implies that identity should entail action in the first place.[10]

From the Self to the Social

Islamist movements are neither mechanical nor dogmatic agents; they are human and vibrant actors. As in any other group, members possess a wide range of personality traits, skills, and capabilities. However, for them to become productive and achieve the movement's objectives, they must move away from self-identity and take on the group's social identity.

Self-identity refers to personal traits that create a sense of self-reflection; social identity refers to traits in groups that create a sense of collectivity.[11] Charles Taylor believes the starting point of defining personal identity is to ask "Who am I, and where do I stand?" He explains, "My identity is defined by the commitments and identifications which provide a frame or horizon within which I can try to determine from case to case what is good, or valuable, or what ought to be done, or what I endorse or oppose."[12] The self cannot be revealed without being reflected by others. Mark Leary and June Tangney maintain that people view themselves as they believe others see them.[13] That is, the social aspect of personality comes to the fore when individuals conceive themselves as part of others' consciousness. This cognitive process of perceiving the self and "the other" has divided identity scholars into two camps. Some focus on self-identity, or what they call *identification* or *self-verification*; others tackle the social aspect of identity through *self-categorization*.[14] The former exemplifies identity theory as explained in the previous section, and the latter represents social identity theory, which explains group processes and intergroup relations. It ties identity to belonging to a social group, which is defined as "a set of individuals who hold a common social identification or views themselves as a part of social category." Jan Sets and Peter Burke contend that identity is the composition of two processes: identification and self-categorization. According to them, social identity is a "person's knowledge that he or she belongs to a social category or group."[15]

However, the division between the two levels of identity is not absolute. Proponents of both theories assert that identity cannot be defined without revealing its dualist character. Some tend to treat identity instrumentally depending on the context and the purpose of its use. In this context Stryker and Burke highlight three popular uses of identity: (1) to refer to the culture of a people, (2) to show identification with a collective or social category, and (3) to reflect parts of a self composed of different meanings and multiple roles.[16] Rogers Brubaker and Frederick Cooper stress the difference between using identity as a category of practice and as a category of analysis. Accordingly they highlight five different uses of identity: (1) to describe noninstrumental modes of social and political action, whether individual or collective; (2) to describe a common set of values among members of a group or category, which they call "sameness"; (3) to identify the integral aspects of "selfhood" of individuals and social groups; (4) to highlight the processual interactivity of collective understanding, solidarity, and groupness that enhance collective action; and (5) to reflect the unstable and fragmented nature of the contemporary self.[17]

An additional concept that links the self and social identity is identity salience, which refers to "the probability that an identity will be invoked across a variety of situations, or alternatively across persons in a given situation."[18] Identity salience denotes the multifaceted composition of self-identities and assumes identities are tied to roles and positions in organized social relations.[19] Further, a number of sociologists contend that salience facilitates the interplay between personal and social identity.[20] It helps individuals who undertake social roles to be involved in social groups and networks. Salience also enables social movements to recruit these individuals and generate collective action. Stryker and Burke find that the salience of religious identities predicts the time spent in religious activities, and the salience of religious identities is predicted by the commitment to role relationships based on religion.[21]

However, identity theorists have reached a consensus that identity is not a fixed and immutable concept, but rather an evolving process of "becoming" instead of "being."[22] I thus treat identity as both a fluid and a constructed concept. That is to say, despite the genesis of identity as a concept that can be manifested in different aspects of human behavior, its construction is determined by the agency of individual actors and the social context in which they operate. As Taylor aptly puts it, "answering the question of 'who I am' cannot be possible without defining where I [am] speaking from and to whom."[23]

Activating Identity: From the Social to the Collective

Islamists believe it is not enough to be a devout and pious Muslim; practicing and disseminating this piety in everyday life is paramount, and convincing others to follow Islamic teachings and adopt Islamic values is a religious duty. To this end social identity may not be sufficient to explain Islamists' activism. It is true that social identity is important in revealing individuals' tendency to interact and communicate with other social groups; however, it does not explain why certain individuals are keen to participate in collective action. Therefore, to understand the rationale of collective action, it is essential to distinguish between social identity and collective identity. The former refers to the physiological, structural relationships between the self and other social groups; the latter treats the self as an active agent in society. In other words, the social and physiological traits of individuals do not guarantee their involvement in collective action until these traits are activated by collective actors.[24] Collective identity therefore should not be perceived as an aggregation of social identities but as "constructed, activated, and sustained only through interaction in social movements' communities."[25] In short, collective identity exemplifies the locus of collective action.

For individuals to move from social to collective identity they must be involved in a collective action process that is organized, permanent, and meaningful. Social movements are the vehicle through which collective action and collective identity can be connected and sustained. William Gamson asserts that social movements tend to include relevant collective identities as part of their definition of the self.[26] According to Verta Taylor and Nancy Whittier, collective identities are rooted in the communities of social movements and "[derive] from members' common interests, experiences, and solidarity." In fact to some extent, a collective identity reflects the combination of cultural and ideational components of collective action. Taylor and Whittier stress the importance of culture in identity construction. They also contend that collective identity is more appropriate than ideology for understanding collective phenomena. For them, unpacking collective identity is fundamental to understand the complexity of collective action beyond structural views.[27]

Collective Identity and Social Movements

Collective identity is a key component of social movements' activism. The relationship between collective identity and collective action is reciprocal. Movements construct their identity through constant waves of collective action. In turn, collective action enables movements to sustain their identity and secure a sense of belonging for their members. Gamson highlights the key role of collective identity in preserving collective action. He contends that the durability of collective identity is contingent upon the ability of the collective actor to link solidarity, the movement, and its organizational layers in the participants' sense of self.[28] Similarly Alberto Melucci highlights three functions whereby collective identity ensures the persistence of social movements: (1) it regulates membership; (2) it sets the prerequisites for joining the movement; and (3) it draws on the criteria by which members recognize themselves and are in turn recognized by others.[29]

Scholarship on the importance of collective identity is rich and illuminating. Interest in studying the collective identity of social movements originated from changes across the world in the 1960s and 1970s brought about by the emergence of new social movements (NSMs) in Europe and the United States, which tackled issues such as feminism, environmentalism, and peace. More important, interest in collective identity reflects the mounting need to overcome the shortcomings of mobilization and political process models in studying social movements. Francesca Polletta and James Jasper believe social movement theorists focus on collective identity to fill the gap left by other models, to overcome the limitations of structural analyses of social movements, and to respond to the many new questions raised by social movements, such as Why do people take part in collective action? What are the catalysts of social movements' action? What is the role of social movements' identity in fueling collective action? They also assert that collective identity plays a crucial role in social movements' emergence, trajectories, and outcomes.[30] According to David Snow, Robert Benford, and Scott Hunt, the NSM perspective holds that the collective search for identity is a central aspect of movement formation: "Identity constructions, whether intended or not, are inherent in all social movements' framing activities."[31]

However, a number of sociologists believe the growing interest in studying identity instead reflects the crisis of the "modernity paradigm."[32] Alain Touraine, for example, addresses the need to study cultural aspects of social movements in postindustrial society. He describes social movements as "the combination of a principle of identity, a principle of opposition, and a principle of totality." The aim of NSMs, Touraine maintains, is not to change the state, as classical movements were doing, but to change society.[33] Melucci argues that postmodern society poses new challenges for individuals and movements and that social movements have therefore shifted their focus from structural issues (e.g., class, race) toward cultural and symbolic issues: "Collective identity is thus a process in which actors produce common cognitive frameworks that enable them to assess their environment and to calculate costs and benefits of their actions."[34]

More significant is Calhoun's contention that by focusing on identity, NSM theory deconstructs the essential and natural assumptions of social behavior. Although Calhoun criticizes the "newness" of social movements, he acknowledges that identity construction is the main activity for these "new" movements. Moreover he points out that despite the modern discourse on NSMs, modernity has imposed dilemmas that force these movements to respond by emphasizing their identity. He writes, "Recent approaches to issues of identity have stressed the incompleteness, fragmentation and contradictions of both collective and personal experience. They have shown how complex is the relationship among projects of identity, social demands and personal possibilities."[35]

Calhoun's insights on identity presume collective actors lack rationality and are merely reacting to identity dilemmas. Many social movement theorists, including Jean Cohen and Polletta and Jasper, have criticized this conclusion. Cohen insists that social movements are rational actors that create their own actions based on strategic calculations. She asserts most contemporary movements are involved in two main activities: identity creation and strategic or rational calculation.[36] Polletta and Jasper respond to Calhoun with compelling assumptions about the rationality of social movements. According to them, collective identity responds to the inadequacies of instrumental rationality as an explanation for strategic choice:

> Collective identity has been a way to get at the cultural effects of social movements. Dominant models of collective action have been better at measuring movement outcomes such as policy reform or expanded political representation than at gauging impacts outside the formal political sphere. But movements also transform cultural representations, social norms—how groups see themselves and are seen by others. Changes in collective identity captured movement impacts beyond institutional reform.[37]

By focusing on identity, NSM theory has fostered the cultural study of collective actors. Social movements are involved in articulating their own culture through meaning and symbolic codes. By creating a cognitive map for adherents, social movements can construct an identity distinctive from the dominant culture. According to Hank Johnston and Bert Klandermans, social movements invest in, add to, change, reconstruct, and reformulate a society's culture. They argue that by creating a distinctive culture, social movements can maintain activism and longevity.[38] Moreover, culture can be used as cognitive repertories to construct collective action and identity. According to Donatella Della Porta and Mario Diani, culture provides ideational elements such as beliefs, ceremonies, languages, and rituals that orient people and influence their identity.[39]

Social Constructivism and Identity

This debate reveals the interplay of concepts, models, and approaches on how to tackle collective identity. Building on these insights, I show that collective identity is a social construct that reflects the interactive relationship between structure and agency, meanings and actions, and values and interests. Collective actors are required to give meaning to what they are doing. Thus they are involved in the production of meanings, symbols, and values to ensure members' commitment and participation in collective action. The departure point of this study is Melucci's notion of collective identity. As noted earlier, Melucci's pioneering study, *Challenging Codes* (1996), helps us understand the complexity of identity construction in social movements by connecting their ideational and institutional aspects. For Melucci collective identity "is not a datum or an essence, a 'thing' with a 'real' existence."[40] Collective identity is a socially constructed phenomenon, a reflection of the multiple processes and interactions that occur inside social movements and that are shaped by the opportunities and constraints in the external environment.

To explain identity formulation within Islamist movements I have adopted social constructivism as a framework of analysis. Identity per se is a social construct. It is not something that can be measured; however, it can be imagined, sustained, and manifested in everyday life. Social constructivism enables an exploration, a deconstruction of the collective identity as it happens within social movements. Melucci claims that social constructivism reveals the collective agency of social actors by bridging the gap between objective conditions and subjective motives, behavior and meaning, and structure and agency.

Social constructivism challenges the idea that identity is an immutable phenomenon. Identity as a social reality reflects the interaction between individuals and society whereby each affects the other. As Karen Cerulo observes, every collective becomes a social artifact or entity molded, refabricated, and mobilized in accordance with reigning cultural scripts and centers of power.[41] Collective identity is the outcome of these processes of interactions between the self and society, individuals and groups, and structures and meanings, which take place in everyday life. According to Peter Berger and Thomas Luckmann, identity is part of everyday reality. It is "formed by social processes and is maintained, modified and reshaped by social relations."[42]

Hakan Yavuz asserts that stressing human agency as "the prime mover of history" is the main premise of constructivism.[43] It also allows for the examination of the complex relationship between individuals and society, agency and structure, symbols and action, and text and context. Most important, social constructivism illustrates how collective identity helps social movements generate collective action. Collective action, Melucci asserts, "must be understood in terms of the processes through which individuals communicate, negotiate, produce meanings and make decisions within a particular social field or environment."[44]

Furthermore social constructivism interprets how and why collective actors create a distinctive identity for their members. This identity helps movements to sustain their collective action and to counter other identity makers in society. Islamist movements, for example, tend to employ cultural and symbolic capital to construct their own collective identity as well as to respond to the challenges and pressures coming from other rivals, such as liberals, leftists, and especially the state. Put differently, social constructivism reveals the ways individuals and groups participate in creating their perceived social reality.

Islamic collective identity is an ongoing process of creating meanings, norms, images, and values for social agents. Such a process underlies individuals' worldview, perceptions, attitudes, and actions in response to the external world. By integrating cultural, institutional, and ideational frameworks, I uncover the process of identity formation as it occurs within Islamist movements. I use constructivism as an interpretive and interactive approach to examine multiple relationships between aims and interests, beliefs and practices, and the internal and external environment.

Constructing Islamic Collective Identity

The longevity of Islamist movements stems from their ability to grant their members a unique and distinctive identity. Islamist movements, more than other actors, are adept at generating a sense of differentiation and loyalty among members, which enables these movements to endure and gain support. It is this sense of distinctiveness that also helps Islamist movements recruit new members, reshape their worldview, and generate collective action. While religion underpins the movements' identity, they are keen to blend it with a political and social cause, such as political injustice, corruption, or unemployment, in order to appeal to a wider constituency. However, while it is true that Islamist movements are involved in political activities such as forming parties, contesting elections, and vying for public office, their ultimate goal remains determining society's norms, boundaries, and cognitive codes—its identity. Therefore they involve themselves in creating what Olivier Roy calls the "virtuous" society.[45] Yavuz finds that Islamists tend to reconstitute identities, institutional structures, ways of life, and the moral code of society by penetrating the cultural, economic, and educational spheres.[46] For most Islamist movements, producing an Islamic identity, regardless of what definition they attach to it, is critical for recruiting members, expanding their constituency, and especially continuing their activism.

By Islamic identity I mean the cognitive code of values, symbols, norms, rituals, idioms, and emotions that Islamist movements employ to forge individuals' worldview, behaviors, and attitudes—their identity. It also reflects the frame of reference for Islamist movements' collective action. This frame is used to mobilize adherents, nurture activism, and solidify their new identity. It helps individuals identify themselves as part of a robust and meaningful entity. Further, the process of Islamic identity formulation reflects an intertwined relationship between the movement's aims and objectives, internal system, and the environment within which it functions. The more deeply the movement can instill its aims, objectives, and norms into its members' individual identities, the stronger and more consolidated will be the collective identity.

This study integrates cultural and institutional aspects of Islamist movements in order to gain a better understanding of their identity construction process. As discussed earlier, this integration is crucial in overcoming the shortcomings of the political process and resource mobilization models in interpreting social movements' activism. The genesis of this integrative approach is Melucci's insight on collective identity as "an interactive process through which several individuals or groups define the meaning of their action and the field of opportunities and constraints of such an action" and as "the outcome of various axes of interaction between the collective actor, identification declared by the actor, and the identification given by others."[47]

Primarily, the leadership determines an Islamist movement's aims and objectives, which are divided into two categories: expressive, which refers to the ultimate goals that the movement seeks to pursue, and instrumental, which helps the movement to realize its aims. It is the leaders' task to align individuals' personal goals and objectives with those of the movement. For Islamists, establishing an Islamic state is an ultimate aim. They stress and propagate it in their statements, speeches, and leaflets. This aim can be realized through different instrumental goals, such as building a robust organization, having a wide and effective social network, and expanding their social base and constituency. Islamist leaders also play a key role in the framing process that occurs within their movement. It is through this process that Islamist movements can bind members together and guarantee their loyalty and allegiance. Erving Goffman defines framing as a "schemata of interpretation" that enables individuals "to locate, perceive, identify, and label" occurrences within their life space and the world at large."[48] According to Benford and Snow, framing is "an active, processual phenomenon that implies agency and contention at the level of reality construction."[49] This construction of reality is a key instrumental objective for Islamist movements. Islamist ideologues and figures have a significant impact on followers and the organizational bearings of the movement. Figures such as Hasan al-Banna, Sayyid Qutb, Abul A'la Maudidi, and Rachid el-Ghanouchi play a fundamental role in identifying their movements' aims, strategies, and tactics. In the case of the Muslim Brotherhood, al-Banna set a broad aim, namely to "dominate the world and [master] the humanity according to the teachings of Islam." He also provided the means for members to realize this aim by prescribing six instrumental objectives: building the Muslim individual, the Muslim family, an Islamic society, an Islamic government, an Islamic state, and an Islamic *umma* (*khilafa*). Many in the Brotherhood perceive these objectives as a blueprint for stages that should be followed in order to achieve the movement's ultimate goal. Al-Banna also articulated the Brotherhood's master framework and ideology, which remains influential and operative among its members to this day. To connect individuals to the movement's objectives, he stressed each member's responsibility in realizing them:

> The creation of nations, the education of people, the realization of hopes, and the defense of principles. The nation which tries to achieve this or the group which is calling for this will need at the very least a mighty spiritual strength which may be manifested in numerous ways: a strong will which no weakness can penetrate; a steady loyalty unassailable by fickleness or treachery; a noble spirit of self-sacrifice, unaffected by greed or avarice; a knowledge of the principles, having faith in them, evaluating them, and making sure they are immune to error. They must ensure that there is no

deviation, quibbling or betrayal about it (which are the characteristics of the soul). Upon this awesome spiritual strength and high principles will be erected, resurgent nations who will create educated and zealous people, [and] life will be renewed in those who have been deprived of it for many years.[50]

Nevertheless the distinction between expressive and instrumental objectives is not rigid. An instrumental objective can be treated at certain stages as expressive. For instance, during repression, survival of the movement becomes the ultimate goal. In fact the Brotherhood has successfully used this tactic to endure regime repression and to mitigate its consequences. When the movement was systematically repressed under Mubarak, it accommodated regime crackdown and maintained its organization. In other words, self-preservation can be the movement's ultimate goal at times.

In addition it is important to discuss whether the movement's ultimate target is the state, the society, or both. Islamist movements tend to target the state and society together. In this regard Yavuz suggested an operational and useful typology for Islamist movements based on their targets and strategies. Islamist movements can be divided into two main categories: society-oriented movements, which seek to change society from within, and state-oriented movements, which seek to change the political system and seize power as a tool to transform society. The latter is divided into subcategories: *revolutionary* movements, which reject the existing political system and use violence to change it, and *reformist* movements, which participate in political processes and are involved in building alliances with other parties in hopes of capturing the state or reshaping its policy.[51]

Despite the plausibility of Yavuz's typological framework, its terminology and classification are ambiguous and contradictory. For instance, it is not enough for an Islamist movement that abandons violence to be described as reformist. The Moroccan Al-Adl wal-Ihsan movement does not adopt violence, but it has a revolutionary agenda that targets state and society. Likewise one cannot put the Brotherhood in the same category as Al-Adl wal-Ihsan just because both abjure violence because there are significant differences between them. I contend that the Brotherhood is a movement that targets both the state and society; thus its ideology and strategy are formulated to change societal norms and values as well as to make the state more Islamic.

The second component of the identity construction process is the movement's internal structure, norms, and dynamics. According to Melucci, the internal system of the collective actor is designed to pursue the movement's objectives, adapt to the environment, and preserve unity.[52] It articulates the power dynamics and identifies organizational roles, membership and affiliation rules, and the structure of incentives. Together these components constitute the movement's character and identity. The internal system of Islamist movements has a significant impact on their identity and can be divided into inclusive and exclusive. The former is a flexible system of membership and affiliation based on a participatory style of management and interactions. The exclusive system is characterized by rigidity and homogeneity of membership and reflects an authoritarian style of management. For instance, movements that require intense ideological identification tend to impose an exclusive internal system that requires a high degree of commitment.[53] These exclusive organizations demand rigid discipline and intrude upon every aspect of their members' lives. Della Porta and Diani observe, "The greater the degree to which an organization is founded on symbolic incentives—either ideological or solidarisitc—the more exclusive it will be."[54] The importance of a movement's internal system stems from helping the members in allocating resources and building a solid network and enabling the movement to produce symbols, values, and rituals that form its collective identity. This identity also reflects conflict, negotiations, and bargaining relations within the movement, particularly between members and leadership.

The third component that shapes identity construction is the environment within which Islamist movements operate. Social movements do not operate in a vacuum. They naturally involve themselves in conflictual as well as cooperative relations with similar movements, potential competitors, and the state. This conflict defines the movement's strategies, objectives, and tactics. According to Melucci, the environment is made up of the wider society within which the movement is situated and draws its support base.[55] It contains the opportunities and constraints that enable the collective actor to formulate its collective identity. It also includes the "other" with or against whom the movement seeks to define itself. It both helps and hinders the movement's ability to delineate and sustain its character—its identity.

The impact of the environment on the identity construction process is therefore crucial. If the movement is operating within a hostile and repressive environment, its objectives, strategies, and behaviors can become radical.[56] The relationship between repression and radicalization of Islamist movements is evident.[57] A repressive environment heightens the necessity of affiliation. For instance, Islamist movements operating in a hostile and repressive environment tend to impose a high degree of commitment on members to ensure loyalty and maintain unity. During times of conflict the internal system of the movement reinforces and guarantees identity. In this context, Melucci states, "people feel a bond with others not because they share the same interests, but because they need that bond in order to make sense of what they are doing."[58]

As Figure 3.1 shows, the relationship between factors that shape Islamist movements' identity is reciprocal. They help the movement create its framework of identity that differentiates it from other movements and competitors. This framework enables Islamists to draw their objectives and targets, build their organization, and strategize their relationship with other adversaries. It also reflects how Islamist movements integrate religious, cultural, and institutional aspects of their organization in creating their identity.

Before applying this framework to the Brotherhood, three important points are worth mentioning. First is the interactive nature of this identity framework. I do not propose a linear relationship between the underpinning components of the movement's identity; instead I examine how these components are intertwined and affect each other. Second, this framework recognizes the importance of institutional as well as ideational factors

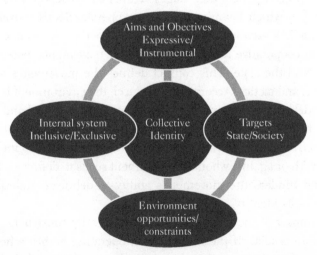

FIGURE 3.1 Components of the Identity Construction Process

in constructing the Brotherhood's identity. It thus considers structures such as mobilization, networking, and protesting, as well as the symbols, values, and norms of collective action. Third, and most important, this framework should be perceived as an analytical and operational approach that can help deconstruct the Brotherhood's identity formation process— "to dismantle the 'reified' appearance of those empirical dimensions of a social movement and to attain the constructive process behind them."[59]

4

The Power of the Jama'a

THE ENDURING LEGACY OF HASAN AL-BANNA

The current leadership of the Brotherhood doesn't understand al-Banna's teachings. They lack his charismatic skills and have diverted from the path he drew for the movement eight decades ago.

KAMA EL-HELBAWY IN INTERVIEW WITH THE AUTHOR,
December 3, 2009

HASAN AL-BANNA'S IMPACT on the Muslim Brotherhood is undeniable. His legacy extends beyond merely founding the movement; he branded its ideology, structure, and identity with his ideas and views. Al-Banna was not simply a religious scholar or preacher seeking spiritual salvation; he was also a social activist and political leader who sought to affect, and indeed change, the entire society. Despite his passing more than six decades ago, al-Banna remains the Brotherhood's chief ideologue and most influential leader. He set the movement's organizational and structural underpinnings, the ideology he crafted remains in effect today. In fact al-Banna's writings, statements, and epistles constitute an integral component of the Brotherhood's texts and socialization process. Nearly every Brotherhood member memorizes and glorifies al-Banna's epistles and strives to follow them in everyday life. Ironically, though, al-Banna's views remain the subject of debate within the Brotherhood because of differences among members in interpreting his statements and epistles and because some question the relevance and importance of his views in the modern day. The Brotherhood has revised some of these views, particularly those on political parties and the role of women in society. However, his views on organizational commitment, allegiance, obedience, and leadership remain influential and shape the Brotherhood's structure. Since al-Banna's death, the Brotherhood has not had a leader who comes close to matching his charisma and influence.

Scholarship on al-Banna tends to focus on his upbringing and personal journey, without much emphasis on his impact on the Brotherhood's identity.[1] Despite the contribution of this literature, many aspects of al-Banna's legacy have yet to be uncovered. This chapter provides a fresh account of al-Banna's role in shaping the Brotherhood's identity. I illustrate how al-Banna was able to articulate the foundational framework of the Brotherhood's identity. By setting its organizational structure, drawing its key objectives, and crafting its code of norms and values, al-Banna endowed the Brotherhood with a coherent and distinctive identity that has preserved the movement and nurtured its political and social activism.

Al-Banna's brilliance lay in his ability to interweave the collective identity of the Brotherhood through the Islamic notion of *jama'a*. In fact the very idea of the Brotherhood stems from this notion, which has significant religious, spiritual, and organizational connotations. It is rooted in Islamic traditions, specifically the Qur'an and Sunna, where Muslims are urged to act collectively in order to unite the entire *umma*.[2] As I explain in the following chapters, the norms of allegiance, obedience, and commitment are derived from the *jama'a* and its religious foundations. Moreover al-Banna transformed *jama'a* into an operative and functional structure that enables the Brotherhood to effectively recruit, manage, and direct its members, generate collective action, and maintain internal coherence.

Contextualizing al-Banna

In order to understand how al-Banna articulated the Brotherhood's collective identity, it is essential to contextualize his ideas and thoughts. Al-Banna was born on October 14, 1906, one year after the death of the renowned Islamic reformer Mohamed Abdu. He grew up in the small town of Mahmudiyya in the province of Buhayra, ninety miles northeast of Cairo, in a traditional Muslim family in which his father, Sheikh Ahmed Abdelrahman al-Banna, was an Islamic scholar and the local *imam* (prayer leader) of the mosque in Mahmudiyya. Al-Banna received his basic education and religious knowledge from his father and from the rural community in which he was raised.[3] From his early years he was an active member of his small, tight-knit community. As a young student he was profoundly influenced by the moral and spiritual atmosphere crafted by Sheikh Mohammed Zahran, the head of the primary school of Ar-rashad School. When the 1919 Revolution erupted al-Banna joined demonstrations against the British occupation, a decision that fostered his nationalist sentiment against foreign powers and would become a key component of the Brotherhood's ideology.[4] Despite his religious inclinations, he did not join Al-Azhar, the beacon of religious education in the Sunni Muslim world. Instead he chose to pursue his education in a modern school.[5] He joined Dar al-Mua'lmin (Primary Teaching School) in Damanhur, the capital city of Buhayara, where he was exposed to the Sufi Hassafiyya order.[6]

The most significant impact on al-Banna occurred when he moved to Cairo in 1923 to pursue his higher education at Dar-al-Ulum (House of Sciences). Al-Banna was stunned by the contrast between his life in rural Mahmudiyya and life in Cairo, where he was surrounded by all manifestations of modernity and exposed to the cultural and political debates taking place in the wake of the 1919 Revolution. For al-Banna, Cairo was not just a place for obtaining an educational degree; it was a symbolic battleground over values, morals, and, most important, identity.

Egypt's Identity Contested

At the turn of the twentieth century Egypt was confronted with an identity crisis. Some Egyptians wanted society to become more secular; others held on to the state's Islamic character, especially following the removal of the Ottoman caliphate in 1924. There was also a debate over how Egypt would achieve *nahdha* (renaissance).[7] This struggle involved two main intellectual camps: the so-called Western modernists (*tahdithyiun*) and the Islamic revivalists, or reformists (*islahyiun*).[8] The modernists said *nahdha* would not be possible without emulating the West and benefiting from its social, cultural, and political production. For them, modernization was the lynchpin of Egypt's push for independence. Therefore they believed national sentiment should be based on law and modern values instead of the long-standing system of Islamic conventions. In contrast, the Islamic revivalists believed *nahdha* and modernization should not come at the expense of Islamic values and morals. They maintained that Egyptians, as well as Muslims, could benefit from Western scientific and technological advancements without embracing Western values or lifestyles. For them, reinforcing Islamic sentiment was crucial to liberating Egypt and the Muslim world from imperialism and colonialism.[9]

The debate over Egypt's identity extended to religious circles. Islamic scholars feared that an Egyptian identity based on nationalism and modernism would be the beginning of the secularization of Egypt. They claimed liberal-secular intellectuals sought to emulate the Turkish model that separated Islam and politics and was led by the Turkish leader Mustafa Kemal Atatürk.[10] They also perceived secularists' celebration of the removal of the Ottoman caliphate in 1924 as a sign of betrayal and a threat to the Islamic character of Egypt.[11] Therefore it is no surprise that many Al-Azhar scholars sought to counter Atatürk's abolition of the caliphate by convening a conference in May 1926 to discuss its future. However, the delegates failed to reach a consensus on what should be done or who should be the new caliph.[12]

The debate following the demise of the Ottoman Empire was crucial in shaping al-Banna's views. In 1926 Sheikh Aly Abdel Raziq, an Azharite scholar and *shari'a* judge, published his controversial book, *Al-Islam wa' usul al-hukm* (Islam and the Foundations of Governance), in which he argues that Islam does not assign a specific type of government or political system, that the caliphate is not a religious duty that Muslims need to fulfill but a mundane choice. Abdel Raziq's views triggered contentious political and intellectual debate and widened the gap between secular and Islamic scholars. According to the Islamic camp, the removal of the caliphate was a sign of the demise of Muslims, who should exert effort to restore it.[13] However, liberals and modernists saw the end of the caliphate as a positive development, as it paved the way for dissolving the relationship between Egypt and the Ottoman Empire.[14] Al-Banna was struck by the celebration of the caliphate's abolition and argued that reviving it was an Islamic duty that Muslims should strive to fulfill.[15] In other words, the notion of pan-Islamism in al-Banna's ideology was born from the demise of the Islamic caliphate in Istanbul. Al-Banna considered the debate over Egypt's identity to be vital. He believed that the only way to preserve the Islamic character of Egypt was to embody Islamic teachings and values in everyday life. And the only way to achieve this goal was by establishing a movement capable of reshaping Muslims' perception and identity.

The Brotherhood as an Identity-Created Movement

The Brotherhood's creation was a response to the identity crisis that confronted Egypt during the first half of the twentieth century. For al-Banna it was essential to create an identity-based movement capable of embodying Islamic values and ideals in everyday life. He was not concerned with establishing an organization that would compete with other Islamic associations.[16] Instead he sought to establish a movement that could reshape societal norms, values, and practices to be more Islamic—to weave a new identity for Egyptian society. He wrote, "We call people to have a principle in their lives, to believe in it. . . . Our movement has a principle; our principle is calling for Islam. Islam in our understanding encompasses every aspect in our life. . . . Our call [*du'atuna*] stems from the Qur'an and Sunna."[17]

The quest for identity lies at the heart of al-Banna's ideology. He always believed reviving Islamic identity would not only insulate Muslims from Western subversion but would also provide them with an alternative system—socially, politically, economically, and culturally—that could challenge Western civilization. To legitimize the Brotherhood's cause and ideology, he addressed the rampant political and social problems facing Egypt during the 1920s and 1930s.[18] He strove to position himself and his movement as the savior, not only of Islam and Muslims but of the entire world. He succinctly stated, "Our call is a call of reviving and rescuing humanity."[19]

However, it should be noted that al-Banna was preoccupied with producing a model of identity that could attract a large number of Egyptians who felt alienated by the manifestation of Westernization in Egypt. Therefore he appealed to lower- and lower-middle-class Egyptians who were most significantly marginalized by the economic hardship and class divisions prevailing in Egypt during the 1930s and 1940s.[20]

In fact al-Banna was the first scholar to transform Islamic rhetoric over Egypt's identity from an elitist to a populist political and religious ideology. He was convinced that in order to revive and enhance Islamic identity one had to engage the public. In contrast to scholars such as Mohamed Abdu and Rashid Rida, who restricted their views on identity to elite and intellectual circles, al-Banna brought these conversations to the public. While Abdu and Rida focused on reforming religious institutions and discourse, al-Banna focused on reforming society as a whole. In this respect, Ghanim contends, al-Banna succeeded where other Islamic scholars failed. According to Ghanim, al-Banna was immensely affected by the plight of Islam and Muslims.[21] However, he leveraged this situation to galvanize Egyptians and generate Islamic collective action. As a result al-Banna's grassroots mobilization of Egyptian consciousness is one of the first manifestations of Islamic activism. Today, as Wilfred Smith notes, the Brotherhood seeks to "transform Islam into an operative force actively at work on modern problems."[22] Al-Banna criticized other Islamic organization for doing nothing to protect Muslims' identity. As one of his disciples puts it:

> The main concern of the existing Islamic groups was just to fill a part of the vacuum. Their aim was only to return people to Islam; however, it's the superficial Islam, the formal Islam, not the real one. However, al-Banna has sought to revive Islamic existence and provide Islam in a persuasive and new form. He sought to incite Islamic issues and defend Muslim nations through faith and thought, system and heritage, inside and outside.[23]Put differently, al-Banna sought to connect the past with the present, structure with agency, and text with context to forge the Brotherhood's identity.

Al-Banna's Comprehension of Islamic Identity

It was difficult for al-Banna to construct the Brotherhood's identity without first carving out the concept of "Islamic identity," which he called *al-fikra al-islamiyya*.[24] He envisioned Islamic identity as an inclusive, normative system of meanings, symbols, and practices that Muslims should abide by in everyday life. Indeed al-Banna was keen to distinguish himself from the prevailing Islamic discourse. Thus *al-fikra al-islamiyya* was perceived as innovative and attractive, granting al-Banna significant influence in the Islamic milieu. He also brought questions of identity to the fore in his tracts and statements, asking, "Who are you? What are the aims of your life? Do you truly understand Islam? Do you follow the Islamic teachings in everyday life?"[25]

Al-Banna crafted three primary dimensions of Islamic identity: comprehensiveness, adaptability and elasticity, and applicability (see Figure 4.1). However, it is vital to stress that al-Banna treated Islamic identity not as abstract and fixed but rather as dynamic and fluid, able to fit different political contexts.

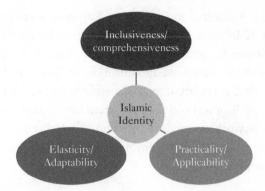

FIGURE 4.1 Al-Banna's Framework of Islamic Identity

Inclusiveness and Comprehensiveness

Al-Banna perceived Islamic identity to be an inclusive system of norms, values, and regulations capable of translating teachings and principles into the practices of everyday life. He believed Islam is a comprehensive creed that should encompass all aspects of human life. In one of his most stunning and enduring statements he emphasized, "We believe that Islam is an inclusive system; it is a faith and worship, a state, nationality and religion, a spirit and deed, a holy text and a sword. . . . The Glorious Qur'an considers these things to be the core of Islam."[26]

Al-Banna's notion of inclusiveness (*shumuliyyat al-islam*) is derived from his perception of Islam as a comprehensive way of life. Not surprisingly his solution for Egypt's political, economic, and social issues is the return to Islam as a comprehensive order for human existence.[27] This is an integral idea that shapes the worldview of the Brotherhood's members to this day. According to Abdullah Essam, a mid-ranking leader of the Brotherhood, Islam is an all-encompassing religion that fits in any society and survives any circumstance.[28]

Building on his concept of inclusiveness, al-Banna was able connect the mundane with the sacred, not with a dogmatic and theological approach but by articulating a practical and pragmatic platform for reform.[29] More important, he implanted the notion of inclusiveness in the minds and hearts of his followers by using expressive and emotional phrases. In one of his most influential statements, he describes himself this way:

I am a traveler seeking the truth, a human searching for the meaning of humanity and a citizen seeking dignity, freedom, stability and welfare under the shade of Islam. I am a free man who is aware of the purpose of his existence and who proclaims: "Truly, my prayer and my sacrifice, my living and my dying are all for Allah, the Lord of the worlds; no partner has He. This I am commanded and I am of the Muslims (who submit to Him)!" [Qur'an, 6, 162–163]. This is who I am. . . . Who are you?[30]

Al-Banna employed the notion of Islamic inclusiveness to delegitimize foreign ideologies such as communism and capitalism. He taught that Islam overrides socialism, capitalism, the East and the West, nationalism and universalism.[31] Ironically he used several Western concepts to outline his ideology, including freedom, elections, stability, and welfare. However, he was successful in framing and normalizing them to his audience as indigenous concepts.

Elasticity and Adaptability

The second key element of al-Banna's conception of Islamic identity is elasticity and adaptability. He argued that Islam transcends time and space and that it accommodates all other ideologies and philosophies. As the last revealed message, Islam is eternal and compatible with all ages and nations. In expounding on his argument, al-Banna emphasized that Islam is consistent with science, pointing to the fact that Islamic civilization contributed significantly to advancements in science and technology.[32]

Al-Banna's belief in the elasticity of Islamic identity is highlighted in his attempts to fit that identity into the existing Egyptian political system.[33] It is widely acknowledged that al-Banna did not seek to overthrow the political regime in Egypt during the 1930s and 1940s. In fact he praised constitutional government, which he believed was the most compatible with Islam due to its emphasis on accountability.[34] Despite bitter disputes between al-Banna and King Farouk's government, al-Banna never attempted to delegitimize the king. In fact he had a good relationship with the palace and acknowledged the legitimacy of Farouk despite the king's relationship with the British.[35] This flexibility is one of the key drivers of the Brotherhood's durability.

Applicability and Practicality

The third aspect of al-Banna's perception of Islamic identity concerns its broadly applicable nature. Unlike many of Islam's ideologues, al-Banna was highly pragmatic. It was useless, he insisted, to disseminate Islamic ideology without a practical platform that could attract and convince people. He titled one of his tracts "Are We Practical People?" ("Hal nahnu qawmun 'amaliyyun"), in which he stresses the importance of having a comprehensive and practical platform for reform. Al-Banna was keen to present himself not as a traditional theoretician but as a social activist. Drawing on the notion of inclusiveness, he stressed the comprehensiveness of Islamic methodology (*shumuliyyat al-manhj al-islami*), which implies Islamic identity cannot prevail without being applied as a detailed program for everyday life. He wrote, "If you study the Islamic teachings, you will find that Islam has set all proper rules and laws for human life; for men and women, for the family and nations."[36] Therefore al-Banna provided a detailed reform platform, ranging from political and social issues to health, science, and the ethics of everyday life.[37]

The Jama'a *Paradigm*

As the leader of a social movement, al-Banna articulated the overarching framework of the Brotherhood's identity by instilling a collective identity within its ideology, structure, and objectives. Whether or not he was aware of it, he integrated the ideational factors—Islamic symbols, rituals, and values—with the institutional aspects of the movement. He was keen to align the Brotherhood's members with the movement's aims and objectives. In other words, he constructed a sophisticated and coherent organization capable of both embodying his vision and ideology and becoming a mouthpiece for his ideas.

To integrate his vision of Islamic identity into the Brotherhood's ideology and structure, al-Banna created what I call the *jama'a* paradigm. The *jama'a* is the cognitive system that encompasses and guides Brotherhood members in everyday life, detailing its aims and objectives, duties and means, and phases and norms. It contains the Brotherhood's material, moral, and expressive aims, as well as its tools and strategies. Moreover

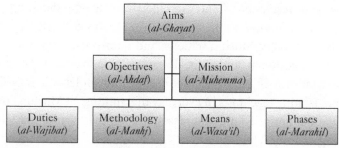

FIGURE 4.2 The *Jama'a* Paradigm

this paradigm creates a pattern of identity for the Brotherhood based on a sense of commitment and solidarity among members who act not as individuals but as a collective unit—as brothers.

The *jama'a* paradigm defines the movement's raison d'être, self-perception, and worldview. It constitutes the underpinnings of social agents' identity. Thus al-Banna constructed the framework of the Brotherhood's identity and sought to integrate it within the movement's structure and ideology. This cognitive map remains in effect to this day. However, it is not rigid or stale; on the contrary, it has worked for decades as a dynamic driver to transfer ideas into action, ideology into identity, and aims into reality.

As Figure 4.2 shows, the *jama'a* paradigm comprises seven integral and connected elements: aims (*al-ghay'at*), objectives (*al-ahdaf*), mission (*al-muhima*), duties (*al-wajibat*), methodology (*al-manhj*), means (*al-was'il*), and phases (*al-marahil*).[38]

Aims and Objectives

Al-Banna articulated three broad aims (*al-ghayat*) for the Brotherhood: (1) leading humanity toward greater well-being under the banner of Islam, (2) reinforcing Islamic identity among Muslims, and (3) creating a movement that embodies Islam in everyday life. He explained, "I devoted myself to one aim: to guide people to Islam by words and deeds and that is why I founded the Brotherhood to exemplify Islam in its aims and means."[39] By setting these aims al-Banna constructed a vibrant and enduring master frame for the Brotherhood. As Benford and Snow note, master frames link the beliefs and ideas of a protest group to political opportunity structures, which allow the social movement to spread its ideas and gain adherents.[40]

Al-Banna then introduced a cluster of instrumental objectives (*al-ahdaf*) in order to achieve these aims. These objectives can be divided into tentative and permanent. Tentative objectives include liberating Islamic countries from foreign occupation, resisting the materialistic and atheist wave that dominates Muslim nations, and reformulating political, social, economic, educational, and judicial systems to be based on Islamic principles. Permanent objectives include establishing an Islamic state that implements Islamic teachings in everyday life, uniting all Muslim countries under the banner of Islam, and disseminating the Islamic call (al-Da'wa al-Islamiyya) around the world.[41]

These aims and objectives are profoundly interconnected. They also play an integral role in aligning the movement's members with its ideology and leadership. Despite the broad ambiguity of the aims, they played a vital role in creating and legitimizing the Brotherhood's cause. Al-Banna, as well as his successors, employed these aims to recruit and attract individuals and, more important, to reshape their identity and connect them with the movement. As Melucci observes, the expressive function of a leader lies in his or her ability to offer symbolic objects for identification, around which the solidarity of the members and their individual identities coagulate.[42]

Al-Banna's aims are greatly broad and vague, which enables the Brotherhood to employ them flexibly to fit its mobilization and recruitment strategy. By setting general yet simple Islamic aims and objectives, the Brotherhood can successfully persuade large numbers of Egyptians to join the movement. These aims and objectives also enhance the Brotherhood's symbolic capital, as they resonate with the ordinary public who believe that Islam should not be separated from public life. They give the Brotherhood credibility and influence among other Islamic organizations. By linking Islam to reform and ideas to action, al-Banna ensured a powerful position for the Brotherhood in the religious market. These broad aims enable the Brotherhood to maintain unity and coherence. By aligning Brotherhood members with these aims, the possibility of division is more effectively contained. The Brotherhood tends to treat these aims as part of members' religious duties that must be fulfilled. Most important, these aims help the Brotherhood survive and gain support. That is, as long as these aims remain unaccomplished, the movement can continue to recruit members, allocate resources, and generate collective action.

Mission

Al-Banna also posited different meanings and connotations in relation to the Brotherhood's mission (al-muhema). He states, "Our mission [*muhimmatuna*] is to stand in the face of the prevalent wave of materialism." In a more detailed statement, he stresses that the Brotherhood's mission is to reform Egypt and enable it to lead the Muslim world. To this end he emphasizes that the realization of this mission includes the following indicators: (1) an efficient political system; (2) a new system of international relations; (3) a practical judiciary system; (4) an efficient economic system that ensures the independence of individuals, society, and the state; (5) a cultural and educational system that can overcome illiteracy and darkness; (6) a family system capable of rebuilding private and intimate relationships between Muslims; (7) a discipline system that can reform individuals' behaviors; and (8) a holistic spirit based on Islam that encompasses both the ruled and the rulers.[43]

The Brotherhood's mission is deeply intertwined with its aims and objectives. Interestingly al-Banna departed from the broad language associated with the aims and objectives by delineating the specific steps to be taken in order to achieve the movement's mission. He successfully infused a unique sense of responsibility and commitment to motivate members to change society. In addition he employed the mission to mobilize adherents and construct meaning for their action. The mission serves as the vehicle for linking the aims and duties (*al-wajibat*) that the *ikhwan* should undertake.

Duties

Al-Banna identified six key duties (*al-wajibat*) that the Brotherhood's members must practice in order to achieve the movement's objectives: (1) to be ready to make sacrifices for the sake of the mission; (2) to demarcate the real boundaries of Islam; (3) to help people follow and respect these boundaries; (4) to strive to achieve the Brotherhood's aims and objectives; (5) to adopt the Brotherhood's credo in everyday life; and (6) to believe these duties are derived from the teachings of Islam.[44] These duties are noticeably more individualized than the aims and mission of the movement as a whole. This individualization ensures that members remain committed and loyal to the Brotherhood's ideology and leadership. Al-Banna connected the fulfillment of these duties to organizational and personal promotion within the Brotherhood. As I explain in the next chapter, members who seek to move from one level to another within the Brotherhood must assume these duties and apply them in everyday life.

The more duties members strive to undertake, the higher the position they might attain.

Method

The Brotherhood's method (al-manhaj) is the disciplined approach with which the movement can achieve its ultimate goals. Al-Banna asserted that the movement's method should be based on three key principals: (1) faith in Islamic values and principles as the foundation for everyday life; (2) faith in incremental and comprehensive reform, which starts with individuals and then encompasses society; and (3) faith in practicality and connecting words with good deeds. Al-Banna advanced the idea that the Brotherhood should adopt a comprehensive manhaj in order to achieve its goals. In many of his epistles he stressed that Islamic methodology (shmūliya al-manhaj al-islami) should include all aspects of life: political, economic, social, and moral.[45] This holistic approach corresponds with the broadness of the Brotherhood's objectives. It is within this framework that the Brotherhood is capable of presenting itself as an all-encompassing movement seeking to reform and change societal norms and values to be more Islamic.

Means

Means (al-wasa'il) refer to the strategy and tools the Brotherhood utilizes to achieve its objectives: (1) deep faith, (2) precise organization, and (3) uninterrupted work. More specifically al-Banna established three tools for the Brotherhood to achieve its goals: propagating the Islamic call (da'wa) among the people through persuasion, expanding the movement's social network, and adopting a legitimate political and constitutional path to voice the Brotherhood's political views. Ironically, although al-Banna wanted to achieve fundamental change in Egypt, he stressed that this change should happen gradually. He consciously avoided revolutionary words and expressions in his epistles. He also reproved members who called for revolution as a means for change, writing, "The Brotherhood does not believe in revolution, and does not rely on it in achieving its goals and if it happened, we will not adopt it. . . .. Our task is to create a new generation of believers who can reformulate the Islamic umma in its all aspects of life." Al-Banna believed that without reshaping an individual's identity, any attempt to pursue change would be superficial and ineffective.[46]

Phases

To put all these elements into action, al-Banna established a firm order of phases (*al-marahil*) for the Brotherhood to follow. He underscored the importance of progressing in phases in order to ensure the movement achieved its objectives. He outlined three key stages: (1) disseminating the Brotherhood's ideology; (2) recruiting supporters, building the movement, and mobilizing its followers; and (3) implementing work and producing action.[47] These stages are not to be segregated but undertaken congruently in order to ensure the Brotherhood's endurance and dynamism.

Ultimately these stages reflect the Brotherhood's gradualist character. In fact al-Banna implanted this gradualism in the Brotherhood's structure and strategy, and the movement adopted a disciplined "bottom-up" policy to achieve its goals. This gradualism is based on the ripple effect of making *da'wa*, the task of reformulating individuals' identities to line up with Islamic values. This reformulation is set in motion by spreading the Brotherhood's ideas across the country through grassroots activities, such as education and social welfare, to recruit more members. Based on this gradualist and elastic approach, al-Banna was able to expand the network and base of the Brotherhood substantially.[48]

More significant, the gradualist approach operated as a link between the Brotherhood's expressive and instrumental goals. Thus al-Banna introduced a hierarchical structure of "mediating" steps to connect the tentative and ultimate objectives of the Brotherhood. This structure contains seven steps: (1) educating and forming the Muslim individual; (2) coalescing the Muslim individual into the Muslim family; (3) forming the Muslim family into the Muslim society; (4) forming the Muslim society into the Muslim government; (5) establishing an Islamic state through the Muslim government that governs according to Islamic precepts; (6) reunifying Muslim nations through the emergence of an Islamic state; and (7) retaining the supremacy of Islam through this new Muslim unity.[49]

Regardless of the viability of these phases, they entail significant symbolic power, enabling the Brotherhood's leadership to preserve the movement's coherence and dynamism. First, they underscore the bottom-up strategy of pursuing change by reformulating individuals' identities as a fundamental step in reshaping societal norms and values from below. Second, they serve as a roadmap for the Brotherhood's collective action. Members strive to meet this hierarchical order despite the long-term nature of the movement's objectives. Third, these incremental phases foster a sense of commitment and obligation among members, who remain keen to reach them. Fourth, they give the Brotherhood's leadership room for flexibility since the temporal link between the stages is blurred. As a result subordinates cannot accurately gauge the success of the leadership in achieving these phases. Fifth, the relationship between these phases is not clear-cut; the Brotherhood is operating at all phases and levels simultaneously.

Activating Identity in Everyday Life

The *jama'a* paradigm functions as the main framework of identity that binds the Brotherhood's members together and shapes their worldview. It is through this paradigm that the Brotherhood is able to connect the triangle of Islamic identity (inclusiveness, adaptability, and practicality) with the movement's organization and objectives. In fact the Brotherhood's members do not define themselves as individuals but as a community of brothers, or *ikhwan*. This collective identity is activated and stimulated in everyday life. The rank and file as well as the leaders act as a disciplined and committed organization. Many members believe following the rules and regulations of the movement is not only an organizational imperative but also a religious duty. Members strive to match their behaviors and practices with the Brotherhood's code of norms and standards. Nevertheless it is important to remember that the Brotherhood's norms and rules are not static or rigid but constitute a dynamic code of conduct reflecting social interactions within the organization. These norms and regulations help the Brotherhood to run its activities and to maintain internal coherence and unity. Given that the Brotherhood is composed of members from diverse social and educational backgrounds, organizational norms play a key role in fostering cohesiveness.

The Brotherhood's leaders and cadres adopted the *jama'a* paradigm following the death of al-Banna in 1949, enabling them to control the movement and maintain its activism. All general guides since al-Banna have stressed the need for members to act as a collective entity, or community of self-disciplined and pious Muslims. For instance, the emphasis on the comprehensiveness of Islam translated into the enduring character of the Brotherhood as a multifaceted movement. The result of this was the lasting and all-encompassing definition of the Brotherhood as "a Salafi call, a Sunni way, a Sufi truth, a political organization, an athletic group, an intellectual and scientific association, an economic company, and a social idea." This multifaceted definition reveals al-Banna's desire to portray the Brotherhood as an inclusive movement capable of achieving different goals through a "one-size-fits-all" approach. He described the Brotherhood as "a comprehensive movement contain[ing] all reform meanings."[50] This broad and inclusive definition instills the leaders with profound symbolic and religious power that enables them to generate collective action and expand the organization's network across different strata of society. It resonates with Egyptians who seek to join the Brotherhood for different reasons. And it differentiates the Brotherhood from other Islamic organizations that confine their ideology and activities to one dimension of everyday life.

The notion of inclusiveness has been repeatedly employed by al-Banna's successors. For instance, the current general guide, Mohamed Badie, asserts that the Brotherhood views Islam as a comprehensive system encompassing all aspects of life. In Badie's own words, "The Brotherhood does not differentiate between religion and politics. It views Islam as an inclusive system, it extends to all life's spheres, it encompasses politics, economics, society, culture, etc. We worship Allah by politics and *da'wa* together and do not separate between them."[51] This inclusiveness is embedded in the internal structure of the Brotherhood, which comprises distinct groups to supervise politics, social life, students, *da'wa*, and welfare.

Al-Banna's notion of adaptability has granted the Brotherhood a resilient and elastic identity, able to adapt to different political settings and to survive despite severe authoritarian conditions. Since its foundation in 1928 it has managed to sustain its structure and develop unique strategies in each era. This adaptability also enables the Brotherhood to expand its ideology and organizational network across different social strata, as well as in urban and rural areas. Moreover al-Banna articulated a pragmatic platform for change based on application of the movement's identity. This platform, which encompasses all aspects of social and political change, seeks to rebuild society and the state on the basis of Islam as perceived by the Brotherhood. Al-Banna asserted that the practicality of the *da'wa* is crucial to achieve the Brotherhood's goals. Accordingly the Brotherhood established many economic and charity organizations during the 1930s and 1940s.[52]

Opponents view the Brotherhood's pragmatism as opportunistic and deceptive, and they accuse the Brotherhood of using religion for political ends. However, the Brotherhood's pragmatism plays a vital role in attracting new members and sympathizers. Some members attribute their admiration of the Brotherhood to its practical nature. Salah Ghorab, a mid-ranking member, says, "I joined the Brotherhood because, in addition to its Islamic character, it provides me with essential guidelines that I need in my daily life politically, socially, and morally."[53]

In closing this chapter, four crucial points should be highlighted. First, the *jama'a* paradigm is a social construct that has been crafted over years of intricate development. Unsurprisingly it took al-Banna ten years to outline a set of clear aims, objectives, and phases for the movement. It was not until the Fifth Annual Conference of the Brotherhood in 1938 that he decided to unveil this paradigm and to become heavily involved in everyday politics.[54] Second, this paradigm is amenable and elastic rather than rigid. It is true that al-Banna sought to make the paradigm as vibrant as possible to enable organizational growth; however, he constructed it in a general and broad sense in order to fit different contexts. In fact it would have been quite difficult for the Brotherhood to survive regime repression without having such a coherent and solid sense of identity. Third, the concepts and terminology of the *jama'a* paradigm are broad and sometimes elusive, as al-Banna was inclined to use them interchangeably. For instance, he occasionally conflates aims with objectives, mission with duties, and method with means.

Al-Banna's influence on the Brotherhood is indisputable. As the Brotherhood's founder and chief ideologue, he determined its identity. By setting broad and strategic objectives he was able to connect subsequent generations to his legacy. To this day it is a common practice for the Brotherhood's leaders to invoke al-Banna's thoughts and statements to legitimize and enhance their positions within the movement. Through the *jama'a* paradigm al-Banna granted the Brotherhood a remarkably distinctive identity, enabling it to operate within different political environments. His epistles and statements constitute the main source of socialization and indoctrination within the Brotherhood. Each member must follow al-Banna's teachings and commands, and those who violate these rules are subject to criticism and censure. It is through this paradigm that the Brotherhood has been able to survive repression and remain an influential social and political force in Egypt ever since.

5

The Brotherhood's Art of Recruitment

*I didn't join the Brotherhood; I was selected. The
Brotherhood recruited me since I was eight years old
through its children's [bara'im] program in my village.*

ABDURRAHMAN AYYASH, former member of the
Brotherhood, interview with author, March 24, 2012

THE BROTHERHOOD IS a massive social movement that targets individuals from different social strata. To ensure cohesiveness it uses an intensive process of identification and socialization. Despite its populist character, becoming a member of the Brotherhood is not an easy task. Individuals must undergo an intricate and disciplined process of indoctrination before becoming full-fledged members. This process introduces new members to the norms and regulations of the movement as well as the precepts they should abide by in their everyday lives.

One of the key differences between the Brotherhood and other social movements is its membership system. Whereas membership in most social movements is open and accessible, membership in the Brotherhood and other Islamist movements is highly selective. Those who seek to join must possess certain traits and attitudes that allow them to advance the movement's objectives and abide by its rules and regulations. In fact individuals do not join the Brotherhood but are chosen by it. As one member puts it, "The movement selects its sons."[1] Also the Brotherhood scrutinizes members before officially extending an invitation to join. Functioning in a repressive environment in which it is frequently targeted by the ruling regime, the Brotherhood adheres to a policy of caution and vigilance in recruitment to avoid infiltration.

This chapter provides an extensive account of the Brotherhood's recruitment tactics and mobilization strategy, explaining how one becomes an *ikhwani* and revealing the impact of recruitment on that identity construction process. Affiliation and membership in the Brotherhood is a complex process that plays a crucial role in consolidating the Brotherhood's identity. As a social movement the Brotherhood requires that members internalize its ideology, norms, and code of values. This internalization process starts when individuals join the movement and continues until they become full-fledged members. The recruitment and promotion process enhances the Brotherhood's ability to engender solidarity and commitment among its members. It creates a sense of belonging and self-commitment (*iltizam*) among individuals keen to sacrifice their time, effort, money, and sometimes lives to achieve the group's objectives. Above all else it enables the movement to implant its set of norms and regulations within the mindset of the new members. By setting disciplined procedures for membership and promotion within the movement's structure, leaders can shape the worldview and identity of adherents. This identity-shaping process in turn helps the movement maintain coherence and unity.

Recruitment and Participation in Islamist Movements

Unlike most social movements, recruitment and participation in Islamist movements is an intricate, disciplined process. Since reshaping societal norms and values is a key objective, reformulating individuals' perceptions and worldview is of great importance to these movement's success. The selection and recruitment of members is a crucial component of the identity construction process that takes place in Islamist movements because it is through this process that the movement indoctrinates its followers, introduces them to the movement's norms and regulations, and internalizes its ideology.

Preaching (*da'wa*) is a vital tool for selecting and recruiting new members. Throughout the recruitment and mobilization process, the leaders align their practices and activities with Islamic norms and values. They strive to act as role models for their followers by linking their behavior to Islamic morals. Islamists also tend to link *da'wa* to their social and political activism. When they participate in elections, they do so not merely to win but also to recruit members and disseminate their ideology. Samer Shehata observes, "For the Muslim Brotherhood, electoral participation (and, later, membership in parliament) served as a mechanism to propagate its ideas and disseminate its ideology to wider segments of society."[2]

Individuals participate in Islamist movements for different reasons. While it is true that religion is a fundamental motivation for participation, it is not the only motivating force at work. Some join in order to receive social benefits and economic assistance, such as healthcare and free education, while others join to gain political privileges and influence. Salah Abdul Halim, a thirty-six-year-old member of the Muslim Brotherhood, claims that some individuals join for social purposes. He explains, "There are those who seek social promotion and others who need to improve their living conditions."[3] In fact in more undeveloped Muslim countries Islamist movements function as a vehicle for social mobility that provides members a clear-cut path to improve their social status. When they make *da'wa*, Islamists astutely blend religion with social and political grievances. As Wickham finds, "the Islamist *da'wa* tapped into [people's] grievances and portrayed Islam as the means to fundamentally transform the conditions in which they were rooted."[4]

Regardless of the underlying reasons for participation (e.g., interests, morals, emotions), the mode and process whereby recruits are selected and socialized is crucial in reshaping their identity. Therefore Islamist movements pay great attention to recruitment. Furthermore it is fundamentally important for Islamist movements to control the membership and recruitment process when they operate in authoritarian and repressive environments. To avoid regime penetration these movements closely monitor and scrutinize individuals before extending an invitation to join. As a result it can take months, even years before recruits become full members. Prospective members must also exhibit a high degree of commitment and loyalty to the movement's leadership and ideology. To this end they undergo an intensive process of identification and observation in order to enhance their commitment and prove their loyalty.

The influence of Islamist movements is especially pervasive among the lower and middle classes in Muslim countries. There the mobilization and recruitment strategy focuses mainly on the inhabitants of rural and impoverished suburban areas. Islamist movements therefore rely heavily on the social networks of friends, kinship, and neighbors to recruit new members. However, the ability to capitalize on these networks is contingent upon two factors: linking their recruitment tactics with *da'wa* activities and building and maintaining an intimate relationship with new members. Membership and affiliation in Islamist movements do not require individuals to break with previous social ties.[5] To the contrary, Islamist movements draw upon these linkages to attract new members, and the appeal of joining an Islamist movement often stems from the fact that they are an integral part of the existing social fabric. Islamist movements do not seek to disrupt this relationship but to imbue it with a more Islamic character. Ultimately the impact of Islamist movements is more visible in ethnically and socially divided societies because they can provide a network of safety and shared identity that transcends local loyalties.

The Brotherhood's Recruitment Strategy

The Brotherhood follows an astute and effective strategy of recruitment, which I call "chasing the prey." This strategy is based on a dynamic, interactive process between the recruiter (the hunter) and the potential member (the prey). During this process the former attempts to infiltrate the latter's private life and initiate a persistent but gradual psychological and ideological change that leads him to join the Brotherhood. The time invested varies across individuals, but the recruiter carefully surrounds the prey with Islamic idioms, symbols, and norms. He also capitalizes on the individual's religious and conservative values to facilitate the indoctrination process.

The Brotherhood utilizes many different tools to implement this strategy. The most effective tool is through social networks, such as kinship and friendship. The movement targets individuals in schools, workplaces, universities, and neighborhoods. In time the prey is subject to significant emotional, religious, and psychological influence, which facilitates his recruitment. However, at this stage recruiters and cadres take great pains to refrain from revealing their affiliation with the movement. At the inception of the recruitment process recruiters focus on propagating broad Islamic values and ethics among their networks. After a short period of time they gradually infuse their proselytizing message with the Brotherhood's ideology. Those who demonstrate religiosity and sympathy with the Brotherhood's cause become potential members. Once these potential members are identified, the recruiters chase them tirelessly until they officially join the movement; thereafter a new course of recruitment begins. At this stage the key message delivered to the prey is how to become a good Muslim in everyday life.

Preachers as Recruiters

The Brotherhood's recruitment strategy is embedded in its preaching activities. According to Shaykh Abdul Khaliq Al-Sherif, head of the Brotherhood's Da'wa Division, "The Brotherhood has been created for nothing but *da'wa*."[6] Al-Sherif notes that the Brotherhood has 140 preaching schools with at least 45,000 preachers from Al-Azhar and other educational institutions.[7] *Da'wa* is a fundamental tool for recruiting new members: individuals join the Brotherhood not only because of its social and political activism but also as a result of its preaching and outreach activities. Preachers (*du'ah*) act as recruiters who propagate and disseminate the Brotherhood's cause and ideology.[8] Due to the state's repression and security surveillance, *da'wa* is the Brotherhood's only way to communicate with its constituency. It is also through *du'ah* that the Brotherhood can maintain its influence among other Islamic organizations; therefore *du'ah* align their preaching activity with Islamic values and exhibit proper decorum. It should be noted that when reaching out to potential members through preaching, recruiters tend to frame their interactions with the banner of Islam and not the *ikhwan*. For the Brotherhood making *da'wa* is considered a religious duty that every member should fulfill. According to Al-Sherif, each member should act as a preacher (*da'iah*, singular of *du'ah*) in his family, among his friends, and with his colleagues at work.[9]

Stages of Recruitment: The Ripple Effect

The Brotherhood's recruitment strategy includes distinct but interlinked stages. These result in a "ripple effect," where each stage leads to the next in sequential order. This process originates from al-Banna's proselytization model, which highlights three main phases for recruiting members: (1) disseminating and proselytizing the Brotherhood's ideology; (2) spotting, selecting, and recruiting potential members; and (3) following and implementing the Brotherhood's ideology and commands in everyday life.[10] According to al-Banna, these phases must be applied strictly. The recruitment stages are the beginning of the long path toward full membership in the Brotherhood; they reflect the complexity and intensity of the recruitment process. However, these stages are not rigid or clear-cut in practice. Though recruiters may intend to follow the sequence according to al-Banna's model, actual recruitment varies based on an individual's response and readiness to adhere to the movement's ideology.

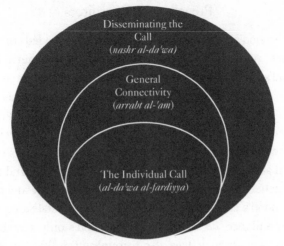

Disseminating the Call
(nashr al-da'wa)

General Connectivity
(arrabt al-'am)

The Individual Call
(al-da'wa al-fardiyya)

FIGURE 5.1 Stages of the Brotherhood's Recruitment Strategy

There are three stages: (1) disseminating the call (*nashr al-da'wa*), which aims to reach out to society broadly; (2) general connectivity (*arrabt al-'am*), which targets a narrow circle of individuals with whom each recruiter should operate; and (3) the individual call (*al-da'wa al-fardiyya*), which focuses on potential members. These stages are illustrated in Figure 5.1.

Disseminating the Call

This stage is the broadest in the sense that recruiters reach out to the entire public. The primary goal at this stage is to disseminate the Brotherhood's ideas and ideology among the general population. It follows al-Banna's command to spread the Brotherhood's ideology in both rural and urban areas.[11] The objectives of this stage are twofold: establishing the initial connection between recruiters and the public and refuting negative stereotypes perpetuated by the regime or the Brotherhood's political and religious adversaries. According to Eslam Ahmed, a twenty-eight-year-old member, "At this stage we seek to improve the image of the Brotherhood among people and not to ask them to join the movement. It is our very basic job."[12] This stage unleashes the first level of communication between the Brotherhood and the external world. It aims to reshape the image of the Brotherhood among people. According to Mustafa Mashhur (d. 2002), the fifth general guide (*al-murshid al-'am*), this stage familiarizes people with the Brotherhood's cause, and recruiters should take it with seriousness and devotion.[13] The forums used to achieve this stage's objectives include media campaigns, sermons in mosques, and public lectures. Throughout this stage recruiters tend to keep their affiliation with the movement a secret; they seek to be identified as good Muslims rather than as members of the Brotherhood. Therefore, when delivering talks and lectures as well as endorsing social activities, they stress that their purpose is for the sake of Islam alone.

General Connectivity

The second stage in the Brotherhood's recruitment strategy, general connectivity (*ar-rabt al-'am*), follows what al-Banna called *nashr al-fikra*, or spreading the Brotherhood's message among the public.[14] At this stage the scope for recruitment moves from broader society to target more specific networks and segments of society. This includes potential members who express sympathy for the Brotherhood's cause. Klandermans and Oegema define potential participants in a social movement as "those who take a positive stand towards a particular social movement."[15] Those who accept the Brotherhood's ideology and identify with its cause become the focus of recruiters. Once interested individuals are identified, a new course of action is followed to enhance their sympathy with and attachment to the movement. To this end recruiters infiltrate the private sphere of individuals' lives with simple messages on ideology and objectives. This connectivity is established through a variety of tactics, including organizing sports competitions and retreats, giving gifts, and distributing leaflets. According to Sherif Ayman, a twenty-six-year-old former member, these tactics create an intimate relationship between potential members and the Brotherhood's recruiters.[16]

The target audience at this stage is identified through social networks such as family, relatives, friends, neighbors, and work colleagues. These informal networks facilitate the Brotherhood's recruitment and mobilization process at a foundational level. Klandermans and Oegema write, "Networks condition whether people become targets of mobilization attempts. The more a movement's reach-out networks are woven into other organizations, the more people are reached by mobilization attempts."[17] The Brotherhood's recruiters strive to penetrate these networks and build friendly relationships with potential members. They also invest heavily in kinship and friendship in order to recruit new members. Eslam Ahmed explains, "At this stage recruiters focus on their relatives and families and attempt to persuade them to accept the Brotherhood's message."[18]

The Individual Call

The individual call (ad-da'wa al-fardiyya) is the most crucial stage in the recruitment process. After identifying potential members, recruiters begin to preach the Brotherhood's ideology and become more explicit about its objectives. This stage also constitutes the core of al-Banna's mobilization strategy. He wrote, "At this stage we should select sympathizers, prepare the soldiers, and mobilize supporters from those who have been identified and selected in previous stages."[19] At this point recruiters reveal their affiliation with the movement for the first time and focus on reshaping the perceptions and mindset of potential members. To achieve this they become heavily involved in constructing meaning and producing symbols to convince individuals to join the movement. This stage paves the way for active membership in the Brotherhood. The recruiters build strong relationships with potential members and introduce them to the Brotherhood's code of values and regulations. The process is completed when the prey demonstrates continued interest and falls into the hands of the hunter.

Islamist movements pay special attention to the individual call because of its crucial role in recruitment. For example, Abdul Halim al-Kinani, a middle-ranking leader in the Brotherhood and one of its recruiting theorists, defines the individual call as "a direct and personal communication between two individuals: the preacher who seeks to influence other people and a targeted person who should be transformed to become a devout Muslim."[20] Al-Kinani's definition details three key elements in the group's recruitment strategy. First, it draws a direct connection between the Brotherhood's recruiter and potential members. Second, it delineates that the aim of this connection is to alter potential members' perceptions and views. Third, this process takes place under the banner of Islam, which holds significant symbolic power.

In addition potential members who seek to be involved in the activities of the individual call should exhibit certain skills and characteristics. These activities are considered a religious duty. Alaa Muharram, one of the Brotherhood's recruitment leaders, believes recruiters should meet three conditions in order to participate in da'wa activity: desire, ability, and understanding.[21] Each of these elements is divided into two aspects. In terms of desire, the preacher (*da'iah*) should have the enthusiasm and motivation to disseminate the Islamic call; in terms of ability, he should have the knowledge and skills to do so; in terms of understanding, he should comprehend the internal and external environments that can impact his preaching activities. Al-Sherif says *du'ah* should be passionate, knowledgeable, truthful, patient, rational and wise, outspoken, and capable of reaching out to others.[22]

Stages of the Individual Call

The individual call is the threshold to joining the Brotherhood. Throughout this stage a potential member is subject to the recruiter's indoctrination and observation. Accordingly his behavior and attitude should be in line with the movement's commands and regulations. This transformation in the potential member's behavior does not happen all at once but gradually and by building an intimate relationship with the recruiter. Mashhur offers a clear and detailed blueprint for recruiters to follow while conducting the mission of the individual call. First is to detect the potential member. At this point the recruiter (*da'iah*) builds a personal relationship with the potential member using different means, such as gifts, home visits, and regular phone calls. It is the task of the *da'iah* to identify individuals who might be interested in embracing the Brotherhood's ideology. Once a potential member is detected, the recruiter permeates the individual's private sphere and surrounds him with Islamic symbols and idioms. According to Mashhur, this stage can take between three and four weeks.

The second stage is to encourage Islamic faith within potential members. The transition to this stage sees recruiters move from the personal to the religious level. Recruiters guide potential members to fulfill their religious duties, such as praying, reciting the Qur'an, and giving alms. The primary aim is to inspire the transformation process within a potential member's perceptions and behaviors. Sherif Ayman describes his own experience: "I felt as if I started a new life, or as if I was born again."[23] Recruiters use different tools to achieve this goal, such as videotapes, cassettes, and books. Mashhur suggests that this stage should last between four and six weeks.

The third stage of the individual call aims to instill the idea of Islamic comprehensiveness within a potential member. Here recruiters link ideas with practices. Hence they focus on how a potential member acts as a true Muslim in his everyday life. To accomplish this stage's goals, Mashhur suggests recruiters read Yusuf al-Qaradawi's *Shumuliyyat al-Islam* (The

Comprehensiveness of Islam) and Abul Hasan Ali Nadawi's *Madha Khasr al-'lam Binhitat al-Muslimin* (What Has the World Lost with the Degradation of Muslims?). This stage should last for one month; it ends when a potential member moves from internalizing Islamic values to practicing them in everyday life.

The fourth stage is "the duty to work for Islam" and focuses on activating the political identity of potential members. Mashhur explains that this occurs by increasing their knowledge about the plight of Muslims around the world. The main goal of recruiters at this stage is to invigorate pan-Islamic sentiment within potential members. Mashhur states, "The targeted person should become sympathetic with Muslims around the world, in Palestine, in Chechnya, in Kashmir, etc. and become eager to help and support them."[24] Media utilized to achieve this goal include newspapers, Islamic conferences, and books that explain the hardships Muslims face globally. This stage also prepares a potential member to move from passivity to action. Mashhur highlights four signs that prove this stage is completed before recruiters move to the next step: (1) becoming passionate and sympathetic with other fellow Muslims; (2) donating money to support Islamic causes; (3) becoming more active in relationships with family, friends, and the community; and (4) starting to preach and recruit other members. Mashhur assigns recruiters a number of al-Banna's epistles to help them incite the duty to work for Islam within the hearts of potential members. This stage is estimated to last one month, depending on the time needed to instill a greater sense of activism within the individual.

The fifth stage of the individual call is collective action. After explaining the importance of collective action in achieving the Brotherhood's ultimate objectives recruiters' main task is to persuade potential members to take part in the Brotherhood's campaign, including participating in demonstrations and elections. According to Mashhur, *du'ah* emphasize the importance of establishing an Islamic state as the ultimate goal for Muslims. However, Mashhur draws a subtle link between achieving this goal and joining the Brotherhood: "Since establishing the Islamic state is the duty of all Muslims, the only way to achieve it is through joining a movement or 'jama'a.'"[25] He also highlights five standards to which Brotherhood members should commit themselves: obedience, brotherhood, vigilance, sacrifice, and integrity.

The main objective at this stage is to create a self-disciplined member who will devote his life to the Brotherhood's cause. Mashhur's suggested readings at this point include Fathi Yakan's books, such as *What Does*

It Mean My Belonging to Islam?, Between Individuality and Collectiveness, and *The Path to the Brotherhood.*[26] This phase is estimated to last approximately one month.

The last stage of the individual call is to formally ask potential members to join the Brotherhood. Mashhur points out that the main goal of this stage is to convince the recruit that the Brotherhood is the only Islamic movement he should join:

> You [the recruiter] should convince potential members that the movement they should join is the one that exhibits six features: 1) follows the path of Prophet Muhammad and seeks to establish the Islamic state; 2) believes in the comprehensiveness of Islam; 3) has branches around the world; 4) has a global experience in dealing with major issues; 5) is moderate and peaceful; and 6) the one that has a well-established organization.[27]

To facilitate potential members' decision to join the Brotherhood, Mashhur recommends more of al-Banna's tracts, such as *The Horizons of the Teachings, The Fifth Conference Tract,* and *Brothers under the Banner of the Qur'an.*

By creating an intimate and personal connection between the movement and its potential members the individual call plays a vital role in enabling the Brotherhood to attract and recruit new members. Many interviewees stressed the role the individual call played in shaping their decision to join the Brotherhood. For instance, Sherif Ayman was recruited after he participated in activities the Brotherhood held in his neighborhood. He says, "The individual call creates a strong and faithful relationship between the movement and new members who behave as brothers."[28]

As Table 5.1 illustrates, the individual call follows a disciplined and complex system of communication and indoctrination that lasts months and can even last years. A few points are worth emphasizing. First, the time scale of these stages is not rigid and is determined by the response of potential members as well as the ability and skills of recruiters in convincing them to join the movement. Thus it can take a longer time for some individuals to become active members in the Brotherhood. Second, the stages of individual call are conducted gradually in order to acclimate potential members to the Brotherhood's ideology and regulations. Until they become members, targeted individuals are subject to regular and close observation that informs the strategy recruiters' follow. Third, and most

Table 5.1 Mashhur's Blueprint of the Individual Call

Stage	Goal	Tools	Time scale	The outcome
1. *Selection and acquaintance*	To detect potential members	Personal connection, gifts, home visits, phone calls, etc.	Three weeks	Familiarizing potential members with the Brotherhood's ideology
2. *Stimulating Islamic faith*	To create religious commitment and stimulate moral behavior in everyday life	Islamic videotapes, cassettes, leaflets, etc.	One month	Transforming behavior and attitudes toward the Brotherhood
3. *Instill the notion of Islamic comprehensiveness*	To implant Islamic ideology in the mindset of potential members	Islamic books about the comprehensiveness of Islam and gifts	One month	Following Islam in everyday life
4. *The duty to work for Islam*	To politicize potential members	Conferences, lectures, religious and public activities, etc.	Six weeks or more	Encouraging Islamic sentiment and connection with the Islamic cause
5. *Collective action*	To create a sense of responsibility and commitment among potential members	Demonstrations, elections, camps, etc.	One month	Reformulating the personality of potential members to become more disciplined and active
6. *Affiliating with the Brotherhood*	To encourage the potential member to join an Islamic movement	Weekly gatherings and meetings with senior leaders	One month	Becoming a full-fledged member in the Brotherhood

Based on data presented in Mustafa Mashhur, *The Individual Call*, at http://www.daawa-info.net/books1.php?parts=168

important, in many cases potential members do not know about these stages until they are full-fledged members. In fact they move from one stage to the next without realizing the difference between them. Fourth, the symbolic power of the Islamic call (*al-da'wa al-islamiyya*) inspires potential members and reinforces their religious commitment; therefore recruiters strive to align their behavior and activities with Islamic norms and teachings to gain potential members' confidence and ultimately convince them to join the movement.

In short, the individual call functions as a laboratory for potential members. It implants the movement's ideology and norms within recruits and prepares them to undertake the Brotherhood's social and political activities. As I explain in chapter 6, after being selected to join, new members undergo another process of identification to consolidate their new identity as *ikhwan*.

The Brotherhood's Social Networks

The importance of social networks in mobilizing and generating collective action is unquestionable. Social networks enable social movements to allocate resources, recruit new members, and generate collective action. According to Florence Passy, social networks have three key functions: (1) offering participation opportunities to individuals (structural function); (2) shaping preferences before an individual decides to join a movement (decision-shaping function); and (3) socializing and building individual identities (cultural function).[29] The Brotherhood capitalizes on different types of social networks—kinship, friendship, social gatherings, and religious occasions—to expand its constituency. It thrives in different venues: schools, universities, and mosques. As a massive social movement that targets individuals from different social strata, the Brotherhood adopts unique outreach and recruitment tactics and has different outreach committees for different social networks. For example, in each district there is a "buddy" (*bara'im*) committee that is responsible for attracting and recruiting young members. Abdurrahman Ayyash, a former young member of the Brotherhood, recalls that he was recruited at the age of eight by the "children's activities" committee in his neighborhood.[30] The Brotherhood also has an active section called Maktab al-Talaba (Students Office) that is responsible for recruiting students in high schools and universities. Sherif Ayman was recruited through the activities of the Students Office at his university,[31] and many others I interviewed affirmed the important role of the Student Office in recruiting new members. The Brotherhood uses different tactics to spread its message among university students, including distributing flyers and leaflets, providing financial assistance to poor students (particularly those from rural areas), and contesting student union elections.

Historically the Brotherhood expanded its network through this office during the 1930s and 1940s, particularly in Cairo and Alexandria. At that time universities were among the most active centers for protesting against British authorities and the Egyptian government. However, the Brotherhood's role at universities waned during the 1950s and 1960s as a result of Nasser's move to repress the movement. During the 1970s and 1980s the Brotherhood rebuilt its organization through its robust presence at universities. Many of its leaders, such as Abdelmoniem Aboul Fottouh,[32] Essam al-Erian, Helmi El-Gazar, Mohamed Habib, Abu El-Ela Madi, Essam Sultan, and Khaled Daoud, were active members in Egyptian universities during the 1970s.

The Brotherhood also capitalizes on family connections to recruit new members. Ammar El-Beltagi, a twenty-three-year-old and the son of the prominent Brotherhood leader Mohamed El-Beltagi, says he was born *ikhwan* like the rest of his family.[33] The Brotherhood also works to expand its family and kinship networks through intermarriage and personal links. In fact many of the leaders have family and intermarriage connections that strengthen their commitment to the movement. For example, Khairat al-Shater, the Brotherhood's strategist and a business tycoon, is the son-in-law of Mahmoud Ghozlan, the former spokesperson of the Brotherhood, and Mahdi Akef, the former general guide, is the son-in-law of Mahmoud Ezzat, the former secretary general of the movement.

The Brotherhood has created an extensive network of relatives and friends who build their relationships on ideology and personal linkages. For example, many members choose their spouse from *ikhwani* families.[34] Marrying a member of an *ikhwani* family can also achieve one of the Brotherhood's ultimate goals: creating an Islamic society. It reflects the ripple effect, which helps the Brotherhood expand its boundaries and widen its organizational and social networks. Sobhi Saleh, a senior leader in the Brotherhood, urges young members to marry sisters in the movement and avoid outside marriage. He argues that marrying outside the movement might negatively impact and delay achievement of the Brotherhood's objectives. According to Husam Tamamm, a prominent expert on the Brotherhood, the movement creates its own community through marriage and kinship relations. He argues that the Brotherhood is a society within the greater society when he states, "The Brotherhood creates its own community within society where a member can live, get education, make friends, get married, find a job, and become politically engaged fully in the Brotherhood's environment."[35]

Recruitment also occurs through kinship influence. Mohamed Ayoub, a thirty-two-year-old former member, says he joined the Brotherhood through his uncle, who was an active member in the movement. He describes his path to the Brotherhood as "a family business whereby my uncle used to accompany me to the mosque and introduce me to peers in my age group when I was twelve years old."[36]

However, the use of family ties for recruitment has significant drawbacks: it creates favoritism and nepotism whereby senior leaders can exploit their position in order to help their family; it raises questions about transparency within the Brotherhood and whether leaders can be held accountable; and it leads to legitimate concerns about the movement's promotion process. In fact it is not uncommon for members to leave the Brotherhood due to the lack of transparency and fairness in the promotion process. Mohamed Yussif, a twenty-six-year-old former member, says, "My leader was not so transparent when he sided with some members who were not as committed to the movement as I was, therefore I decided to leave the Brotherhood."[37]

Social networks create ample opportunities for the Brotherhood not only to recruit new members but also to reshape members' identity and worldview. Personal and family ties have a significant impact on the personality and perceptions of the movement's members. Moreover the intensive daily interactions and relations among members creates a subculture that facilitates the socialization and identification process within the Brotherhood. This subculture, Wickham points out, is the springboard of Islamist movements' activism.[38]

6

Tarbiyya *and Consolidating the Brotherhood's Identity*

Tarbiyya *lives with us from birth to death. It transforms our identity and personality to become real* ikhwan.

SHERIF AYMAN, former member of the Brotherhood, interview with author, March 26, 2012

A CONSOLIDATED IDENTITY is the lifeblood of a social movement. By internalizing the movement's ideology, norms, and objectives, members remain loyal and committed for the long haul. One of the most effective methods to this end is a socialization process that accustoms members to the movement's rules and regulations. Consolidating members' identity also depends on the extent to which the movement can intensify interactions among its members in everyday life. The more intense and frequent these interactions are, the more strongly the movement's collective identity is reinforced among its members. In this chapter I explore the Brotherhood's socialization process and investigate different tactics that reshape and consolidate members' identity. I integrate ideational and structural factors to develop an "incubation model," an intensive socialization process that transforms an individual's perceptions and views to align with the movement's ideology, norms, and objectives. In fact incubation is the vehicle that connects individuals with the movement, ideas with its practices, and norms with its structure. It stimulates a member's willingness to become more involved in the Brotherhood's collective action, regardless of any risks this might entail. Incubation also spearheads the identification process within the movement and imbues a sense of cohesiveness and solidarity among its members. The more that individuals align themselves with the Brotherhood's ideology, objectives, and norms, the more coherent their identity becomes.

The Brotherhood's Incubation Model

The Brotherhood's incubation model is based on integrating recruitment and socialization processes. Those who are recruited by the movement are subject to a lengthy, intensive process of indoctrination and socialization. In this model I build on insights from social psychology as well as social movement theory. Several scholars have attempted to integrate the insights of social psychologists with those of social movement sociologists in order to understand the process of identity construction and consolidation in Islamist movements.[1] I take this scholarship a step further by examining the socialization and identification process that occurs within the Brotherhood. In this respect I go beyond the two predominant arguments on identity construction—the rational calculations of individuals and the identification within social movements—to investigate the underlying factors underpinning these two processes. In doing so I consider recruitment and participation mechanisms (the structural factors) along with the identification process (ideational and transformational factors) in order to explain the Brotherhood's identity construction. On one hand, the Brotherhood's recruitment and mobilization tactics enable it to identify potential members, stimulate their desire to participate, and ensure their allegiance. On the other hand, the socialization process reformulates members' perceptions and worldview, enhances their identification with the movement's norms and regulations, and consolidates their identity. These two processes are intertwined, shaping a new identity for the Brotherhood and enabling it to generate and maintain its collective action.

The Brotherhood tends to incubate its members before granting them full-fledged membership. It uses a multitiered membership system that can last for years until members become sufficiently loyal and committed to the cause. This incubation enables the Brotherhood to achieve four key objectives. First, it accustoms new members to the movement's rules and regulations. For new members to become committed to the Brotherhood's ideology, their worldview and attitudes must be reshaped. This can happen only through a gradual yet intensive socialization program whereby members are exposed to the Brotherhood's rules, norms, and ideology. Second, it creates cohesiveness and unity between old and new members. As a massive social movement with individuals from different social strata, the Brotherhood uses the incubation process to mitigate internal differences and create a shared sense of solidarity among its members. Third, it allows the movement to maintain control over its rank and file. For members to advance from one level to the next, they must meet certain requirements and conditions that subject them to greater control by the leadership. Fourth, it helps the Brotherhood remain active under regime repression. By instilling an ethic of commitment and sacrifice among members, the Brotherhood can survive regime crackdowns and sustain its social and political activism. Ultimately the Brotherhood's incubation model depends on two chief mechanisms: an intensive socialization (*tarbiyya*) process and a disciplined, multilevel membership system.

The Socialization (Tarbiyya) Process in the Brotherhood

Socialization, or *tarbiyya*, is a central concept in the Brotherhood's ideology and structure. It refers to the process of reshaping an individual's identity through practice. Al-Banna viewed *tarbiyya* as the "rope that binds brothers together."[2] It is through *tarbiyya* that the Brotherhood can intensify its members' new identity and ensure their loyalty and commitment. As Abdelhamid El-Ghazali, one of the leaders, succinctly puts it, "The most important product which is expected from *tarbiyya* is that it provides us with members who adopt the movement's values in everyday life." That is, *tarbiyya* is the underlying process that reformulates members' worldview, perceptions, and behavior to align with the Brotherhood's norms and regulations. According to El-Ghazali, the main objective of *tarbiyya* is "to develop, mobilize, and prepare men who are able to shoulder the responsibility of spreading and informing the Call and establishing the project of the revival to achieve an honourable life based on Islam."[3] *Tarbiyya* is the cornerstone to accomplishing the Brotherhood's mission and objectives. Given its importance, the Brotherhood dedicates an entire division to supervise and conduct *tarbiyya* activities, called Qism al-tarbiyya, or the Socialization Department.

A prominent figure in the Brotherhood defines *tarbiyya* as "the proper way to influence individuals and to change them for the better."[4] For him it is about how the Brotherhood directs and guides its members in everyday life. Each member has gone through the *tarbiyya* process in order to comprehend its ideology and become accustomed to its norms and regulations. According to Mohamed Badie, the general guide of the Brotherhood and former head of the Qism al-tarbiyya, "*Tarbiyya* is a central concept in our project as it aims to rebuild individuals' personalities."[5]

Tarbiyya is a gradual process that continues as long as members are affiliated with the Brotherhood. Sherif Ayman explains, "*Tarbiyya* lives with us from birth to death. It transforms our identity and personality to become real *ikhwan*."[6] *Tarbiyya* is a fundamental part of an individual's identity formation. Therefore, in each stage of membership, members must embrace a certain set of norms and values in their everyday lives, such as obedience, confidence in leadership, loyalty, sincerity, sacrifice, and commitment. In other words, *tarbiyya* is a key tool that enables the Brotherhood to instill its norms and code of values in an individual's identity. It also has different dimensions and objectives. Amer Shemakh, a middle-ranking leader, highlights three overarching dimensions for *tarbiyya*: religious, social, and political. He further explains that *tarbiyya* should be based on five pillars: the oneness of God (*rabbaniyya*), integration and comprehensiveness (*al-takamul wa'l-shumul*), positive construction (*ijabiyyat al-bina'*), moderation and balance (*i'itidal wa-twazun*), and collective action (*jam'iyya*).[7] These concepts are internalized through distinct mechanisms during the socialization process. As mentioned in previous chapters, the Brotherhood's members are not merely religious or spiritual leaders; they are primarily social and political activists seeking to transform society.

Tarbiyya's objectives are threefold: ensuring members' religious self-purification, reinforcing their organizational commitment, and connecting members; thus it fulfills both their spiritual and their social needs. Al-Banna stressed the role of *tarbiyya* in "purifying individuals' ethics and practices to be sincere and truthful." He argued, "Each member should be physically strong, ethically committed, intellectual, self-sufficient, faithfully purified, organized, and keen to get the maximum benefit from his time."[8] Al-Banna wrote an important epistle that is taught as part of the *tarbiyya*'s curriculum called *Risalat at-Ta'alim* (The Teachings), which includes the code of norms and values that active members should follow and embrace in their everyday life.

Tarbiyya also enhances members' organizational commitment. During *tarbiyya* sessions members have to abide by the movement's norms and regulations. Members tend to follow the leadership and respect its commands not only to avoid marginalization but also to achieve promotion within the organization. Mohamed Hamza, a young member, asserts that the Brotherhood operates a sophisticated system of punishment and reward that members value and feel obliged to follow.[9] In addition *tarbiyya* aims to connect members to create a sense of solidarity among them.

According to a twenty-eight-year old member named Mohamed Yussif, "*Tarbiyya* is the main tool that binds Brothers together."[10] The weekly and monthly gatherings help members get to know each other better and act collectively to achieve the movement's objectives.

Tarbiyya is not limited to a particular level of membership. Senior leaders as well as lower-level members participate in *tarbiyya* sessions that suit their rank. Abdurrahman Mansour, a former Brotherhood member, confirms that all leaders, including the general guide, participate in *tarbiyya* sessions.[11]

Tarbiyya Venues and Tools

Tarbiyya is conducted in what are called *mahdin at-tarbiyya* (socialization incubators), the locations where Brotherhood members and leaders meet, communicate, and interact weekly or monthly to strengthen their relationships and internalize the Brotherhood's ideology. According to a mid-ranking leader, *mahdin at-tarbiyya* are the primary place for members to socialize and get to know each other: "A *mhaden* [singular of *mahdin*] is the primary means for members to deepen their relationship and coalesce their vision on different issues."[12] The incubator aims to create an intimate environment in which members come together, communicate, and exchange thoughts.

In addition *mhaden* serve as venues for religious purification and spiritual salvation. For example, they often include religious rituals, such as reciting the Qur'an and Sunna and performing prayers, as well as organizational activities. However, the most important role of *mhaden* is fostering the sense of commitment and solidarity among members. It provides a free space for them to discuss, debate, and build their views about the movement and the external world. Mohamed Mustafa, a forty-two-year-old, stresses the vital role of *mhaden* in consolidating collective identity. He describes his relationship with the movement as fundamental to his life: "I cannot feel anything other than part of the Brotherhood. To me, it is my family, home, and nation."[13] Clearly, for some members the Brotherhood is more than a social movement. According to Mohamed al-Qassas, who was first exposed to the Brotherhood as a middle school student, the relationship between the Brotherhood and members can be eternal: "The Brotherhood is more of an educational incubator for a Brother. You get introduced to the group at an early age and ultimately your formative years become tied to it."[14]

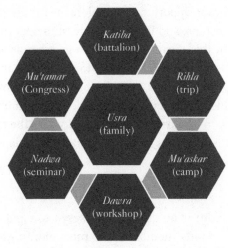

FIGURE 6.1 Venues of Socialization (*Tarbiyya*) in the Brotherhood

The main venues are divided into seven components: *usra* (family), *katiba* (battalion), *rihla* (trip), *mu'askar* (camp), *dawra* (workshop), *nadwa* (seminar), and *mu'tamar* (congress). These venues, which are illustrated in Figure 6.1, are connected and correspond with membership levels. While some venues, such as *usra and nadwa*, can include potential members and sometimes the general public, *katiba* and *mu'tamar* are exclusive to members only. The platform of socialization at each level is designed to meet the conditions and requirements set by the Brotherhood's rules and regulations.

Usra

Usra, or family, is the basic unit in the Brotherhood's structure. It consists of five or six members who meet weekly for religious, personal, and organizational purposes. The leader of the *usra* is called the *naqib* (captain) and is responsible for supervising the religious and ideological socialization of members and monitoring their behavior. Each member, including senior leaders, is placed in an *usra*, usually close to where he lives. *Usra* meetings typically take place in the *naqib*'s house and aim to achieve three key objectives: acquaintance (*ta'arruf*), understanding (*tafahum*), and solidarity (*takaful*).[15]

The *usra* plays a vital role in linking new members with the movement by familiarizing them with the movement's rules and regulations. It also gives new members an opportunity to explore the Brotherhood from within, build new relationships, and identify mentorship opportunities with leaders and cadres. In this regard *usra* gatherings serve as an orientation for new members. *Usra* meetings also work to achieve the movement's objectives by spurring the religious and ideological commitment of members and facilitating the movement's organizational communications and activities. According to Abdurrahman Ayyash, *usra* is "the main incubator of *tarbiyya*, as it binds members together through education and guidance."[16]

Katiba

The *katiba* (battalion) is an amalgam of seven to eight *usra*, or approximately thirty-five to forty members, who meet monthly for between three and four days.[17] These aim to strengthen members' religious and ideological commitment to the Brotherhood through an intensive program of indoctrination. In contrast to the more informal *usra* gathering, a *katiba* meeting is a "boot camp" for instilling and solidifying the Brotherhood's values within its members. According to Abdel Halim, *katiba* is the most important incubator of *tarbiyya* because it relies on direct communication between the educator and the educated. He points out that al-Banna emphasized the importance of educating and directing members through *kata'ib* (the plural of *katiba*) meetings to the extent that he founded a section called the Battalions Unit (Nizam al-kata'ib) to oversee its activities.[18]

Katiba has two main goals. The first is to reinforce the spiritual and religious preparation of members and instill norms of obedience, allegiance, and confidence in members and leadership. Therefore it includes a strict program of physical and mental training that members must undergo for three or four days. According to Salah Abdul Halim, *kata'ib* are designed primarily to increase the spiritual readiness of members. This preparation is manifested in night prayers, religious rituals, and lectures. Abdul Halim states, "*Kata'ib* help members achieve a high degree of spiritual purification and keep their hearts connected to God."[19]

The *katiba* additionally aims to prepare members physically and mentally. This happens through an intensive program of athletic activities, such as running and exercise. According to Ibrahim Saleh, a young member of the Brotherhood, *kata'ib* help members learn patience, attentiveness, and self-control.[20] The *katiba* is also a useful arena to evaluate a member's adherence and commitment to the Brotherhood's rules and regulations. During the course of the *katiba* each member must carry out certain duties and activities, such as memorizing Quranic chapters or abstaining from food and sleep for hours on end in order to gauge discipline and organizational capabilities.

Each *katiba* has a leader (*amir*) and an assistant who organize and supervise its activities. Members must comply with the *amir*'s commands and follow his guidance. The *amir* is usually the oldest and most religiously adept member in each *katiba*. The duties of members toward the *amir* include listening attentively, exhibiting proper decorum, and demonstrating obedience, respect, love, and a willingness to help.

Rihla

A *rihla* (trip) consists of ten to fifteen members marching together in the countryside or the desert. It is typically assigned to those with full membership in the Brotherhood, but can occasionally include potential members in order to evaluate their readiness to join. It can also include families; however, it always avoids mixing men with women. According to Mohamed Mustafa, during the *rihla* participants exercise, recite the Qur'an, and train to tolerate hunger and thirst.[21] *Rihla* takes place monthly for one day (from dawn to dusk).

The main objective of *rihla* is to imbue commitment, dedication, obligation, secrecy, and sacrifice in a member's personality and mindset. Like *katiba*, each *rihla* is overseen by an *amir* and his aides. The *amir* is typically the oldest member in the group and is responsible for supervising and guiding members during the *rihla* process.

Mu'skar

The *mu'skar* (camp) is a continuation of the scouts (*jawwala*) system that was founded by al-Banna in the 1930s. Its main purpose is to strengthen the physical and mental capabilities of members by supplementing the spiritual and intellectual activities of the movement.[22] According to Mahmoud, *mu'skarat* (the plural of *mu'skar*) have three chief objectives: grouping (*tajmi'*), socialization (*tarbiyya*), and exercise (*tadrib*).[23] To achieve *tajmi'*, the camp serves as a place for members to practice religious and physical activities. Those who attend are typically full members but can include potential members seeking a deeper understanding of the Brotherhood. The number of individuals in the camp is around 200 and the process usually lasts two to three weeks.

To ensure effectiveness and differentiation, the participants are grouped on four distinct levels. The first is open to the public, to anyone "eager to serve Islam and help other fellow Muslims." The second is for full members who belong to a particular district and come together to strengthen their relationship. The third is designed for senior members who gather to discuss different organizational duties and objectives. The final level is for members and leaders who come from different branches around the world. They convene to coordinate and discuss the Brotherhood's affairs and activities in their countries and to develop policies on how to deal with problems confronting the movement internationally.[24]

The second goal of the camps is intensifying members' *tarbiyya*. According to one mid-level leader, Mohamed Soliman, camps provide a pure Islamic life of worship, exercise, and brotherhood.[25] Abdul Halim asserts that camps are an important tool for self-education: "In camps, members learn three rules: to have self-restraint, to become accustomed to life's hardships, and to obey and be committed to leadership."[26] Furthermore members participate in discussions and readings that foster their loyalty and collective action.

The third objective of camps is exercise (*tadrib*). Camps are crucial for developing members' physical and mental training. These attributes are beneficial for the movement because it ensures members maintain good health and are able to participate in demonstrations and election campaigns and undertake other duties. Mahmoud explains that members receive athletic, sporting, and security training and also become more familiar with the Brotherhood's rules and regulations.[27] During the period of *mu'skar* members are expected to follow these rules and behave accordingly. As Ayman puts it, "Camps transform a member's entire life and reformulate his personality. In camps each member should behave according to the Brotherhood's norms and regulations."[28]

Each *mu'skar* has a leader (*amir*) and assistants. The *amir* must possess both leadership skills and a wide knowledge of religion in order to serve as a role model. He is responsible for supervising the camp and ensuring that members follow the Brotherhood's bylaws.

Dawra

The workshop, or *dawra*, is a study group where members gather for one to two days to attain more in-depth knowledge of specific issues. This study group is organized periodically for a select number of members and expert individuals and leaders who have sound and deep knowledge on these issues. According to Mahmoud, the main goal of the *dawra* is to create well-informed and capable cadres who are assigned to undertake more duties and responsibilities. The topics and issues covered during the workshop are of a political, social, and economic nature. The workshop is open to students, workers, peasants, and professionals alike.[29] Each workshop includes sports, preaching, and management. The schedule is set by middle-ranking leaders who guide and supervise members during the sessions.

Nadwa

Nadwa is a weekly symposium or seminar in which members meet with experts to discuss diverse topics, such as politics, religion, and women, or to resolve specific problems. It is not exclusive to the Brotherhood's members but is also open to the general public. According to Mahmoud, *nadwa* aims to enhance the intellectual skills of Muslims. Each *nadwa* is organized by a leader or manager who is responsible for selecting the topic and inviting speakers. The leader must possess sophisticated religious knowledge along with engaging oratory skills and has assistants who help with organizational and logistical procedures.

Mu'tamar

A *mu'tamar* is an annual large meeting of the Brotherhood's members who are invited to gather from across the country for a few days to discuss a set of topics and execute decisions on behalf of the movement. The nature of the congress varies; it can be regional, in which case it is assigned to a group of the Brotherhood's districts, or it can be national, where all members can attend. A *mu'tamar* can also be held to discuss private matters, including organizational changes and bylaws. The Brotherhood has convened many general congresses since its inception; however, the movement was banned from holding them during the 1950s and 1960s. It was not until after the 2011 uprising that the Brotherhood began holding its public congress again.

Membership in the Brotherhood

Historically al-Banna's writings were the source of membership criteria and requirements. The Brotherhood's first internal bylaw (*al-la'iha al-dakhiliyya*) outlined four degrees of membership. First is the assistant member (musa'id), a position that is open to any Muslim who declares an intention to join the movement, signs a membership card, and pays membership dues. Second is the associate member (muntasib), a level that can be achieved if the individual attends regular meetings, can prove he has mastered the movement's principles, and is fully obedient to the leadership. The associate member must be older than fifteen, receive recommendations from three members, and have his membership ratified by the Guidance Bureau (Maktab al-irshad). The third level is active membership ('amil). A member is deemed active when he meets the requirements of the previous levels and becomes fully involved in the Brotherhood's activities. He must also receive physical training, memorize a certain number of the Qur'an's chapters and hadith, and swear an oath of allegiance (bay'a) to the general guide.[30] The duties of active members include attending meetings, paying monthly fees, and executing specific missions. The fourth and highest degree of membership is mujahid.[31] This level is available only to those selected by the Guidance Bureau. Members at this level must follow a stricter program of socialization (tarbiyya) and be ready to sacrifice their wealth, time, and life for the sake of the movement.

The movement changed its membership system after clashes with the Egyptian government culminated in the assassination of al-Banna on February 12, 1949, and the dissolution of the movement. Instead of being based on the four degrees proscribed by al-Banna, the levels were reduced to two: provisional (taht al-ikhtibar) and active ('amil). The former refers to those who recently joined the Brotherhood and embraced its ideas but were still under scrutiny by the leadership. Provisional members were monitored for six months until they fulfilled their membership duties. The individual then pledged bay'a to the general guide to ratify his membership. Provisional members did not have the right to vote in the Brotherhood's internal elections. Active members were those who abided by the movement's regulations, fulfilled all the requisite membership duties and responsibilities, and gave bay'a to the general guide.[32] A Brother who did not meet his duties or abide by the regulations of the movement was subject to punishment and disciplinary action by the branch head, which included but was not limited to a warning, fine, suspension, or even expulsion.[33]

The Brotherhood's membership system has witnessed many changes since the foundation of the movement. The first version of the Basic Law (Al-qanun al-assasi) was issued in 1930, and the Internal Bylaws (Al-la'iha al-dakhliyya) were amended in 1932, 1935, 1944, 1945, 1948, 1951,

1982, 1994, and 2009. The amendments were an attempt to adjust to the changing internal and external environment. During this time three main changes have occurred to the membership categories. At the outset there were four degrees of membership, but in 1945 these were reduced to only two levels, tentative (*taht al-ikhtibar*) and active (*'amil*).[34] Since the return of the Brotherhood in the 1970s there have been five levels. For security reasons these membership levels have been removed from the Brotherhood's bylaws. Ironically these rules remain in place following the political recognition of the Brotherhood in the wake of the January 25 Revolution.

The five levels in the current membership system are *muhib* (sympathizer), *mu'ayyid* (supporter), *muntasib* (associate), *muntazim* (regular or registered), and *'amil* (active or operating member). These levels, which are illustrated in Figure 6.2, reflect how the Brotherhood intensifies and consolidates its members' identity.

Muhib

Members at the *muhib* (sympathizer or lover) level, according to Eslam Ahmed, start to become acquainted with other members and gradually participate in the Brotherhood's activities. The main goal of this level is to familiarize new members with the Brotherhood's rules and norms. The *muhib* joins the *usra* (family) in weekly meetings to gradually internalize the Brotherhood's ideology.[35]

Members at this level are not required to be involved heavily in organizational activities. According to Abdurrahman Ayyash, the main objective of the *muhib* level is to change an individual's morals and behaviors.[36] Also Eslam Ahmed explains that the Brotherhood does not set

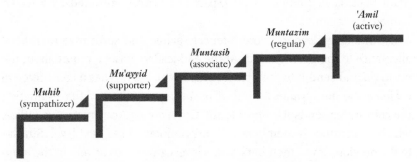

FIGURE 6.2 The Brotherhood's Multitiered System of Membership

hard conditions for members to fulfill at this point: "The Brotherhood facilitates membership at this level, and new members are not required to undertake major responsibilities."[37] However, members at this level can join any of existing committees that implement specific policies or tasks. It is also important to mention that members at this level are not eligible to run or vote in the Brotherhood's internal elections and are not required to pay dues.

This stage can last between six months to one year, during which time the leader of the *usra* (*naqib*) closely monitors the *muhib* and evaluates their fit with the movement. The *tarbiyya* program at this level is simple in order to encourage members and build a positive response to the movement. Each member is encouraged to study Islamic textbooks and readings as part of his socialization process. Ayyash says that books at this level include subject matter that is suitable to entry-level members.[38]

Mu'ayyid

At the *mu'ayyid* (supporter) level members become more committed to the Brotherhood's norms and standards. *Muhib* that demonstrate the requisite commitment to the movement and its duties are eligible for promotion to this level. At this point members still maintain an unofficial affiliation with the Brotherhood; hence they do not have voting rights or hold a formal organizational position. According to Mansur, *mu'ayyid* cannot attend any meeting above the *usra* level.[39]

The *tarbiyya* process at the *mu'ayyid* level is more intense than at the *muhib* level. Members are required to undertake more significant duties, such as memorizing chapters of the Qur'an, reading the Brotherhood's literature, and becoming engaged in local activities, such as providing social services and assistance to the poor or organizing literacy campaigns. The main book is *Fi rihab al-Islam* (Spaces of Islam), authored by a leader named Ali Laban.

At this stage leaders more intensely gauge and scrutinize members' allegiance to the Brotherhood. At the end leaders write a report about the *mu'ayyid* and send it to the district office, which convenes a committee to evaluate the *mu'ayyidun* (plural of *mu'ayyid*) members. After evaluation the committee sends its report to the Governorate Administrative Office, which determines if members will be promoted to the next level. Similar to the previous level, members at this level cannot run or vote in the internal elections and are not required to pay monthly fees.

Muntasib

Muntasib (associate) members are officially registered with the Muslim Brotherhood. However, their membership is not yet fully complete as they cannot hold official positions with the movement. According to Eslam Ahmed, "At the *muntasib* level, members become real Brothers."[40] They spend at least two years at this level before moving to the next. Ayyash says that some members stay for years at the *muntasib* level.[41]

The *tarbiyya* platform at the *muntasib* level is increasingly strict. Members must strengthen their commitment not just to the movement's ideology but also to its leadership. Ayman emphasizes the importance of loyalty and allegiance of each *muntasib* to his leader. As he puts it, "This level verifies members' commitment to leaders and the movement."[42] Members at this stage are required to increase their religious knowledge so they can lead religious sermons and talks on religious matters. They are also asked to undertake more organizational responsibilities and duties. According to Ayyash, *muntasib* can attend *shu'ba* (division) meetings.[43]

Promotion from the *muntasib* level occurs through the same process as from the *mu'ayyid*: a committee evaluates the member's performance, commitment, and adherence to the Brotherhood and sends a report to the Governorate Administrative Office, which is the final arbiter of whether or not that member should be promoted. It is worth mentioning that many members do not know their level until told by their leaders, who says Ammar El-Beltagi, tend to not reveal that information until a member's commitment and loyalty to the movement can be verified.[44] Members at this level are eligible to vote in the *shu'ba* (district) elections but not in the higher organizational elections. However, they can donate money to the Brotherhood and do pay dues.

Muntazim

If the *muntasib* evaluation report is satisfactory, the member can receive a promotion to the fourth level: *muntazim* (regular). This is the last level before full membership in the Brotherhood. The duties and requirements of members at this level are rigorous; they are subject to even more intensive monitoring of their behavior, morals, and organizational performance and must demonstrate total submission to their superiors.

The minimum time spent at this level is five years. However, as Mansur claims, some members stay at this level their entire life.[45]

The *tarbiyya* program at this level is characterized by religious and organizational duties. For example, a *muntazim* must memorize large sections of the Qur'an as well as the hadith. He should also be able to give a *khutba* (religious speech) and lead people in prayers. The curriculum at this stage includes a book by Mahmud Abu Ra'ia, *Anwar al-Islam* (The Lights of Islam), a selection of al-Banna's epistles, and some of Sayyid Qutb's writings.

In terms of organizational duties, all *muntazimin* (plural of *muntazim*) are eligible to join a division. They also can be elected to the executive board, though not as the head or deputy of the *shu'ba*. Members at this level can run for and vote in the *shu'ba* (division) and *mantiqa* (district) elections but not at the higher organizational levels. They are asked to donate money and contribute to the movement's local activities.

After a minimum of five years and a positive evaluation report, a *muntazim* can attend a workshop that prepares him for promotion to the final stage. At the promotion workshop each candidate has to fulfill certain duties and pass religious and psychological tests to prove his capabilities. If successful, he can be promoted to active member (*'amil*).

'Amil

'Amil (active) is the final level in the Brotherhood's membership system. Members reach this point after completing the duties and responsibilities of the previous four stages. According to Eslam Ahmed, all active members are equal in rights and duties.[46] Therefore they are eligible to run and vote in the internal elections at all levels, from the *shu'ba* (division) to the Maktab al-irshad (the Guidance Bureau).

Because of their important role in the Brotherhood, al-Banna wrote an exclusive epistle for active members called *Risalat at-Ta'alim* (The Teachings), which outlines their duties. The epistle stipulates that all active members should swear an oath of *bay'a* to the Brotherhood's leadership based on ten principles: *fahm* (understanding), *ikhlas* (sincerity), *'amal* (action), *jihad* (struggle), *tadhiyya* (sacrifice), *ta'ah* (obedience), *thabat* (perseverance), *tajarud* (devotion), *aukhwa* (brotherhood), and *thiqa* (trust).[47] These values should be internalized in an active member's identity and reflected in their manners and actions. In other words, active members fully embrace the Brotherhood's ideology in everyday life. They must also pay between 1 and 7% of their income for dues and subscription fees, which ranges depending on their ability to pay. Members pay dues as part of their religious duty toward the movement.

The *tarbiyya* program at this level is more comprehensive than at any of the previous levels. Members are fully exposed to al-Banna's literature, are required to deepen their religious knowledge by studying the history of Islam, and are expected to be knowledgeable about the hardships Muslims face around the world. In addition active members are asked to increase their religious duties through worship, night prayers, and fasting, among other activities. They should also engage in daily recitation and memorization of the Qur'an and hadith. *Risalat at-Ta'alim* teaches that members should demonstrate progress across the different skills and attributes attained at previous levels, such as having a strong and healthy body, possessing sound moral character, raising their intellectual capacity, and working hard to earn a living.[48]

Consolidating Identity through Membership

The relationship between the Brotherhood's membership system and identity consolidation is significant. Each level of membership requires socialization and indoctrination that suit the member's age, degree of commitment, and personality. For example, newcomers must follow a gradual platform that focuses on ethical and moral reform, and those who have spent more time in the Brotherhood are subject to stricter duties. In this respect the intensity of a member's identity depends on the requirements and duties of his membership level.

Tarbiyya is the main vehicle of membership promotion within the Brotherhood. As in any other movement, members must abide by the group's rules and regulations in order to receive promotion. The more they abide by the Brotherhood's code, the greater the chance that they will be promoted. In fact the Brotherhood's membership system is designed to spur a member's commitment, dedication, and allegiance. Members are subject to monitoring in order to ensure they follow the rules and regulations. It is through this system that the Brotherhood selects, scrutinizes, and consolidates a member's identity.

Ultimately the Brotherhood's system of membership enables it to reshape its members' worldview and behaviors. In fact the complexity and sophistication of this system reflect two key features of the Brotherhood: its vigilant and cautious character and the intensity of its members' identity. Operating in a repressive environment, the best way to ensure coherence and unity is by maintaining control over the membership process. This well-orchestrated system tightens the leadership's grip on the movement and enables them to avoid infiltration.

7

The Brotherhood's Organization, Structure, and Ideology

The organizational machinery of the Brotherhood is designed to realize its objectives. . . . All members, including senior leaders, follow this structure and abide by its rules and regulations.

MOHAMED MUSTAFA, middle-ranking member of the Brotherhood, interview with author, April 1, 2012

THE MUSLIM BROTHERHOOD'S organizational structure is potent and sophisticated. It has distinguished the Brotherhood from other prominent Islamist movements in recent decades and has enabled the movement to expand its social network and, more important, endure regime repression and maintain its activism, particularly during the Mubarak era. The Brotherhood's steadfast organization (*tanzim*) was a significant challenge to Mubarak, who failed to penetrate and dismantle it. Members take great pride in their organizational capabilities as a fundamental tool in their struggle to realize their objectives. Indeed Hasan al-Banna's brilliance lay in intricately weaving the movement's structure with its ideology and objectives, a foundational element of each brother's identity.

One of the key characteristics of the Brotherhood's organization is its elasticity and adaptability. The Brotherhood's structure has evolved over time in response to both internal and external factors, yet changes to the bylaws and its internal dynamics and regulations did not affect the dynamism and functionality of the movement, which remained effective and vibrant. The development of the organization reflects the movement's responsiveness to contextual changes. The movement deftly adapted and adjusted its structure and organizational tactics in order to remain relevant and active—it bent, but never substantially broke.

Furthermore the Brotherhood's broad and far-reaching ideology shapes its organizational strategy and tactics. The proselytizing character of this ideology requires a structure capable of carrying out the movement's message and reaching out to specific constituencies. And the Brotherhood's religious ideology has shaped its norms, regulations, and internal code of values. The movement's leaders and ideologues utilize these norms in order to enhance their positions and maintain control over the membership.

Previous scholarship on the Brotherhood provides detailed accounts of its organization and structure. The pioneering studies of Mitchell and Lia enlightened our understanding of the historical development of the Brotherhood's organization, particularly in the 1930s and 1940s.[1] Recent studies have also enhanced our knowledge of the Brotherhood's organizational dynamics.[2] This chapter contributes to the literature by exploring recent changes in the Brotherhood's organizational and internal dynamics. I investigate the impact of ideology on the movement's structure and the interplay between these elements in everyday life. I also examine the impact of repression on the Brotherhood's structure. Operating under an authoritarian regime, the Brotherhood developed a distinct pattern of hierarchy, structure, and leadership, enabling it to avoid repression and continue its activities. In fact the Brotherhood's quasi-clandestine character can be attributed to this environment, which significantly impacted the movement's internal dynamics and organizational strategy. However, before unpacking the Brotherhood's structure, we need to examine the relationship between organization and identity and situate this discussion within the literature on social movements.

Organization, Structure, and Identity

The bourgeoning literature on social movements enhances our understanding of the relationship between a movement's organization, structure, and ideology.[3] The seminal work of Della Porta and Diani shows that organization plays a vital role in helping social movements achieve a number of key functions, such as encouraging participation, defining organizational aims, managing and coordinating contributions, and collecting resources from the environment. Della Porta and Diani recognize the role of organization as a source of a movement's identity; however, they largely ignore the role of a movement's structure in reshaping its identity.

They posit, "For people committed to a certain cause, organizations are an important source of continuity, not only in terms of identity, but also in terms of action."[4] A second body of literature reveals the role organization plays in maintaining organizational unity and accommodating internal rifts and factionalism.[5] Mayer Zald and John McCarthy demonstrate that heterogeneity can cause splits within movements due to concerns over ideological and doctrinal purity.[6]

However, Melucci's pivotal work on collective identity provides the most persuasive analysis of the impact of an organization's internal structure on its identity and activism. He defines a social movement as "an actor engaged in a conflict directly or indirectly affecting the distribution of power within a society."[7] This definition illustrates the extent to which social movements seek to build complexity into their organization. The more the movement is involved in social and political conflicts, contests power, and defies the existing regime and other dominant groups, the more tight-knit its organization should be.

In addition the internal structure of a social movement is subject to various influences depending on its objectives, activities, size, and ideology. Thus the crucial question is not how a movement creates its organizational structure, but how it can ensure its efficiency. Melucci highlights three important, interrelated components of a movement's organizational structure: (1) a system of roles and the division of labor, (2) mechanisms and criteria for the distribution of costs and benefits, and (3) a structure of incentives. In this sense the key objective of a movement's internal structure is to pursue the group's goals, adapt to the environment it operates in, and maintain the unity and preservation of the movement as a whole.[8]

This chapter builds on Melucci's analysis of organizational structure in order to unpack the Brotherhood's organization and understand its impact on the identity formation process. I contend that the Brotherhood's organizational structure is deliberately tailored to create a unique pattern of identity. Its organizational norms and regulations create a frame of identity, *ikhwanism*, that dominates and directs individuals in their everyday lives. *Ikhwanism* is responsible for implanting the movement's objectives, governing its internal dynamics, and reshaping the identity of its members.

Also the type of organizational structure a social movement employs is instructive for understanding its identity construction process. It reflects the movement's objectives and ideology and also reveals its complexity, elasticity, and cohesiveness. Many studies stress the importance of an organization's typology in identifying its strategies, tactics, and internal structure. Zald and McCarthy, for instance, highlight the relationship between an organization's type and its activism. They believe that a social movement organization is a "complex, or formal, organization which identifies its goals with the preference of social movement or countermovement and attempts to achieve those goals."[9]

A social movement's organizational structure is manifested differently based on a variety of criteria. Dell Porta and Diani highlight the heterogeneity of organizational forms within social movements by illustrating three prominent archetypes. First is the "professional movement," referring to organizations that are characterized by clear leadership and a nonexistent membership base. Second is the "mass protest organization," which combines internal democracy with certain levels of formalization and organizational structures. Third is the "grassroots organization," which combines strong participatory orientation with low levels of formal structure.[10]

Melucci, however, maintains that "instead of thinking in *types of organizations*, one should use the dimensions relevant to the classification as *analytical tools* to make distinctions, to 'deconstruct' empirical unities, and to account for their complexity." He therefore provides vital criteria for analyzing an organization's forms. Expressive objectives refer to the satisfaction of the social and psychological needs of members through participation and solidarity; instrumental objectives are the attainment of specific external goods. Organizational structure can be built into affiliations and membership requirements, which can be divided into inclusive and exclusive organizations. The former, according to Melucci, do not apply rigid mechanisms for selecting members and expect only a low degree of commitment; the latter exercise rigid control over the selection and recruitment of members and require intensive identification, commitment, and total discipline. Moreover there are two forms of organizations based on power relations and democracy within the movement. The authoritarian form reflects a high level of monopoly of power within the movement, and the participatory form assumes members have more power in and access to the decision-making process.[11]

As a social movement the Brotherhood has a complex organizational structure that exhibits many of Melucci's analytical criteria. For example, as mentioned in chapter 4, the Brotherhood has two groups of objectives: expressive and instrumental. A key expressive objective, as articulated by al-Banna, is "to lead humanity towards the well-being under the banner of Islam." Instrumental objectives include liberating Islamic countries from foreign occupation, resisting the materialist and atheist wave that dominates Muslim societies, and reformulating the political, social, economic, educational, and judiciary systems to be based on Islamic principles.[12]

Chapter 6 demonstrated that the Brotherhood utilizes an exclusive membership system that requires a high degree of indoctrination and ideological socialization. Members must meet clearly defined conditions and prerequisites in order to receive full membership. Inside the movement is a centralized decision-making process dominated by the leadership and senior members. This structure can be partially explained by the authoritarian and oppressive environment within which the Brotherhood operates, a factor that exerts significant pressure on the group's meetings and deliberations. Nevertheless members at the lower levels have the right to select their leaders in internal elections.

The Structure of the Brotherhood

Al-Banna constructed a complex yet effective structure that he believed would enable the Brotherhood to achieve its objectives. Nathan Brown calls this structure "the most notable feature of the Muslim Brotherhood model." The Brotherhood follows a hierarchal structure that connects divisions and branches through a well-controlled system of administration. The internal system, chain of command and leadership, and norms and regulations are well defined in the bylaws and basic charter. Brown points out that Islamist movements that follow the Brotherhood's model strive to have "bylaws, clear criteria for various gradations of membership, regular arrangements, established procedures for selecting officers and determining policies and positions, collegial and consultative decision-making organs, and specialized bodies with clear function tasks."[13]

As an ideological movement keen to pursue its objectives and maintain the loyalty of its members, the Brotherhood is a tight-knit structure that can be divided into two chief axes. The vertical axis is the hierarchical and pyramidal structure, which is illustrated in Figure 7.1; it includes seven administrative levels: *usra* (family or cell), *shu'ba* (division or branch), *mantiqa* (district), *maktab idari* (administrative office), Majlis

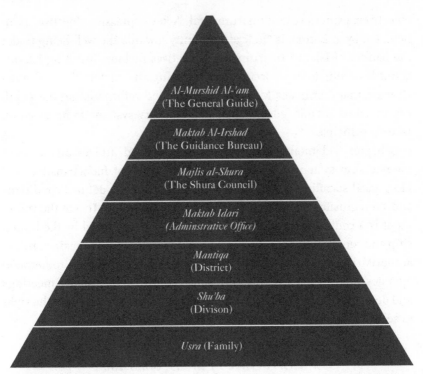

Al-Murshid Al-'am
(The General Guide)

Maktab Al-Irshad
(The Guidance Bureau)

Majlis al-Shura
(The Shura Council)

Maktab Idari
(Adminstrative Office)

Mantiqa
(District)

Shu'ba
(Divison)

Usra (Family)

FIGURE 7.1 The Vertical Structure of the Brotherhood

al-shura (the Shura Council), Maktab Al-Irshad (the Guidance Bureau), and *al-murshid al-'am* (the general guide). The horizontal axis, as illustrated in Figure 7.2, consists of three basic components: sections (*aqsam*), committees (*lijan*), and units (*wahdat*).[14] The main task of this axis is to facilitate the work of the Brotherhood's organizational bodies (the Guidance Bureau and Shura Council) and to enable them to achieve their assigned objectives. There are no specific instructions articulated in the Brotherhood's bylaws on how these components should be organized or function.

The Brotherhood's bylaws determine the responsibility and power of each organizational level and how they should interact and communicate with each other. Furthermore each level has its own bylaw that identifies and organizes its tasks. Importantly, both axes are set in a way that serves the chief objectives of the Brotherhood. Mohamed Mustafa, the head of a *shu'ba*, explains that the organizational machinery of the Brotherhood is designed to realize its objectives. All members, including senior leaders, follow this structure and abide by its rules and regulations.[15]

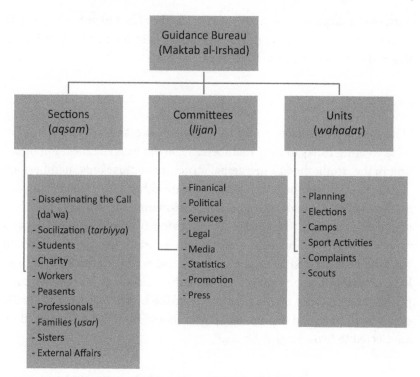

FIGURE 7.2 The Horizontal Structure of the Brotherhood

The composition, functions, and responsibilities of each organizational level are spelled out in the Brotherhood's current bylaws and charter.[16]

Usra

As discussed in chapter 6, the *usra*, or family, is the basic unit in the Brotherhood's structure. It consists of five to seven individuals who meet weekly to discuss different issues, ranging from religious to political matters. In the Brotherhood's early years the key task for *usra* was to familiarize and then indoctrinate members with the movement's ideology and objectives. However, in recent years the role and tasks of *usra* have become more organizational and political. For example, *usra* activities now include planning for political events such as elections and demonstrations and organizing social campaigns to provide social services in poor areas. *Usra* members now spend more time with each other during the week, particularly in daily prayers. Each *usra* includes a financial unit that covers and sponsors its activities and provides assistance for members in need. According to the bylaws, each *usra* must elect a *naqib*, or captain, who is usually the oldest member in the *usra*. Each member in the Brotherhood, including senior members, must join an *usra* and actively engage in its activities.

Shu'ba

The *shu'ba*, or division, comprises between five and six *usar* (plural of *usra*), totaling thirty to forty members.[17] The *shu'ba* is the most important unit in the Brotherhood's hierarchal structure because only members are eligible to join. Members who join *shu'ba* are either active (*'amil*), supporters (*mu'ayyid*), or associates (*muntasib*). Moreover the *shu'ba* is the chief organizational level responsible for achieving the Brotherhood's organizational, social, and political objectives in a certain geographical area. It runs the Brotherhood's *da'wa*, recruiting, and social activities through its local network. It also manages internal affairs, such as promotion, complaints, and financial matters. According to the bylaws, each *shu'ba* should elect a head (*rais*) and deputy (*naib*), who should be active members. Both are elected to two four-year terms.[18]

Mantiqa

The *mantiqa*, or district, is an amalgamation of three to four divisions (*shu'ab*) that meet regularly to discuss and implement the Administrative Office's plans. District members can be either active (*'amil*) or associated (*muntasib*), but they must have spent at least two years in the Brotherhood. The district's key task is to run the Brotherhood's activities in a designated geographical area and to provide recommendations to the higher organizational level, the Administrative Office. Districts are also responsible for supervising a *shu'ba*'s activities and resolving any organizational or institutional problems that arise at the lower membership levels. Each district has an elected office, headed by a chief and deputy who are directly elected and should be active members. Each governorate can have one district or more, depending on its population and the number of members in the region. Typically each governorate contains three to four districts.

Maktab Idari

The Maktab Idari (Administrative Office) constitutes the administrative authority at the governorate level. Each governorate has an Administrative

Office composed of districts and members who live in that region. The Administrative Office exemplifies the executive body of the Brotherhood on the governorate level. According to the bylaws, the Administrative Office is responsible for implementing the Brotherhood's plans in its governorate.

The Administrative Office holds two meetings each month to discuss and supervise the Brotherhood's organizational, social, and political activities in a designated geographical area. It has full authority over members in each governorate and it has jurisdiction to form technical committees that serve the Brotherhood's objectives, such as charity and political committees.

According to Article 29 of the Brotherhood's bylaws, the Administrative Office is required to provide an annual report on its activities to the governorate's Shura Council.[19] The Shura Council elects members of the Administrative Office to four-year terms, and they are eligible to be reelected for subsequent terms. Article 30, however, grants the Guidance Bureau the authority to suspend an Administrative Office or freeze its activities for thirty days until the governorate's Shura Council elects a new office.

Majlis al-Shura

The Majlis al-Shura (Shura Council) is the Brotherhood's legislative body and one of its most significant entities for governing. It consists of ninety members who are elected from the governorates' Shura Councils.[20] Each governorate has a quota of seats on the Shura Council depending on the number of members in that governorate. The Guidance Bureau has the authority to appoint members to the Shura Council, but this number is not to exceed fifteen, and can increase the quota of each governorate in the Shura Council. Members of the Shura Council must meet the following requirements: be at least thirty years old, have been an active member for at least five years, and be a member of their governorate's Shura Council. Each representative serves in the Shura Council for four years.

The general guide calls for the Shura Councils to meet twice a year. However, either the general guide or at least twenty members of the Council can call an emergency meeting, for example to deal with the arrest of senior leaders or a political crisis. Each Shura Council meeting is led by the general guide and, if he is absent, by either his first deputy or the oldest member of the Council. The Shura Council's decisions are made by a simple majority of attendees, unless there is a designated number for taking the vote on specific issues.

The Shura Council is responsible for discussing, outlining, and approving the Brotherhood's broad plans, policies, strategies, and budget. However, its most important function is electing the Guidance Bureau and the general guide, the highest executive in the Brotherhood. Therefore the Guidance Bureau is responsible before the Shura Council and is required to provide a detailed and comprehensive annual report on its activities during the previous year. It is also obliged to provide plans and policies for the coming year to be discussed and approved by the Shura Council. The Council can dismiss any member of the Guidance Bureau and choose his successor in secret voting.

Maktab al-Irshad

The Maktab al-Irshad (Guidance Bureau) is the Brotherhood's highest executive body. Its sixteen members are elected by the Shura Council in direct, secret voting and should reflect the Brotherhood's geographical distribution but without a specific quota. The Guidance Bureau can appoint three additional members through majority voting.[21] To be elected, a member should receive more than 50% of the total votes. If this threshold is not reached, a new round of voting is held between those who received the highest number of votes in the first round. If a seat becomes vacant, the person receiving the highest number of votes in the previous election is promoted. Members of the Guidance Bureau should be at least thirty years old,[22] be members of the Shura Council, and have been in the Brotherhood for at least ten years.[23]

Guidance Bureau members serve a four-year term, which can be extended by an additional term by the Shura Council. Moreover the Shura Council can renew the terms of Guidance Bureau members if it decides it needs more time to elect a new Bureau. This was the case during the Mubarak era, as the Brotherhood could not hold internal elections for security reasons. However, some members claim that the Guidance Bureau frequently abuses this rule for its own benefit.[24] The Shura Council can also terminate the membership of any member for health or other reasons in secret voting. The Guidance Bureau can also terminate the membership of any of its members if he does not exercise his membership for a six-month period.[25] The Guidance Bureau holds regular meetings, usually weekly, but the general guide or at least five members can call an emergency meeting. The meetings are held in Cairo unless the general guide or a majority of the Guidance Bureau's members choose another location. Guidance Bureau meetings are led by the general guide or his deputy if he is absent; if both are absent, the most senior member of the Bureau leads the meeting. The Bureau's decisions are by a majority vote of those in attendance. The Guidance Bureau also has the authority to form an emergency committee of four members headed by the general guide and his deputy to make decisions in urgent matters.

The key function of the Guidance Bureau is to execute the plans and policies of the Brotherhood relating to its organizational, political, social, and religious activities. It is also responsible for making urgent decisions, such as dealing with the arrest of its members or with regime repression. It has the power to form technical committees to aid the implementation of its plans and objectives. The Bureau is responsible before the Shura Council and the general guide. As mentioned, it provides a comprehensive annual report to the Shura Council highlighting its achievements and future plans and strategy.

Al-murshid al-'am

Al-murshid al-'am, the general guide,[26] is the head of the Brotherhood and presides over its executive and legislative bodies. He is elected by the Shura Council in secret voting and must be at least forty years old and an active member in the Brotherhood for at least fifteen years. After being elected the general guide receives *bay'a* (allegiance) from the Brotherhood's members. He should be totally free to serve the Brotherhood and should not hold any other position or have any other professional, financial, or economic commitments.[27] The general guide can select one or more deputies form the Guidance Bureau and delegate any of them to head the meetings of the Shura Council or the Guidance Bureau. In the case of the absence of the general guide, his first deputy assumes the role. If the absence is permanent due to death or dismissal, the deputy assumes the role of the general guide until the Shura Council elects a new general guide. Theoretically the Shura Council can also remove the general guide if he violates the rules or falls short of achieving expected objectives, which has never happened. The general guide serves for two terms of six years.[28]

The general guide is responsible for supervising the Brotherhood's institutions and representing the movement in society. He is also responsible for ensuring that those at the lower levels of the Brotherhood's structure follow the rules and strive to achieve the movement's objectives. He has the power to call the Guidance Bureau or the Shura Council for meetings and to question any of their members. All plans, policies, and strategies have to be presented before the general guide and receive his approval before they are implemented. Put simply, the general guide is the highest position in the Brotherhood, with far-reaching powers over the movement. However, the general guide's authority is neither absolute nor unchecked. As mentioned earlier, he is responsible before the Shura Council, which can remove him if he doesn't abide by the movement's rules and regulations.

Decision Making in the Brotherhood

The Brotherhood is a centralized movement; however, it has a two-pronged decision-making mechanism: a centralized decision-making process and decentralized implementation. Decisions are made by a small, exclusive circle of leaders at the top, and the lower- and middle-ranking leaders and members at the bottom implement the decisions For example, if the leadership decides to contest parliamentary or municipal elections, the local offices and middle-level leaders are responsible for running the electoral campaign, reaching out to the constituency, and propagating candidates' slogans and platforms. They thus have freedom and authority to do whatever they think can help achieve the main objective of winning the elections.

The Brotherhood's centralization corresponds with the hierarchal and disciplined structure whereby the general guide and the Guidance Bureau preside over the organization and control its structure. According to the bylaws, the Guidance Bureau and Shura Council vote on key strategic decisions such as participating in elections, negotiating with the regime, and protesting. In reality, however, the general guide and Guidance Bureau have the final word. Furthermore, as a result of regime repression in recent decades, the Guidance Bureau has wielded overwhelming power in decision making at the expense of the Shura Council, which could not convene its regular meetings. This led to an imbalanced relationship between these institutions and created a problem of asymmetric information that led to a power struggle within the Brotherhood.

Yet the decentralization of the Brotherhood serves its broad objectives and extensive network. The local branches and offices exercise relative freedom in running the movement's activities according to current circumstances and needs without needing to confer with the leadership. Mustafa claims that the districts (*shu'ab*) and administrative offices enjoy a high degree of independence and have the ability to craft local policies, organize events, and oversee social activities.[29] Furthermore decentralization provides ample opportunities for young members to receive training and gain managerial and organizational experience. By managing local activities, implementing the movement's plans, and following its strategy, young members are exposed to collective action and advance their leadership and organizational skills. This learning experience also qualifies them to be promoted within the Brotherhood and facilitates their rise to leadership roles. Indeed one of the key objectives of the Brotherhood's organizational machinery is to produce new leaders capable of managing the movement, particularly in the absence of senior leaders. This was evident after the July 2013 coup that ousted President Morsi and excluded the Brotherhood. Despite brutal repression against the Brotherhood, whereby many of its senior leaders were either arrested or in exile, the movement was able to survive and continue its activities, particularly in rural areas, thanks to younger leaders stepping forward.[30]

Ideology and Organization

Ideology plays an important role in molding a social movement's structure and norms—whether it is centralized or decentralized, democratic or authoritarian, and reflects its worldview and system of beliefs.[31] Unlike some scholars who undervalue the role ideology plays in shaping a social movement's actions and decisions,[32] I contend that a movement's ideology imbues it with certain norms and values and also ensures members' allegiance to these norms and values. Furthermore the relationship between ideology and structure is reciprocal. Whereas its ideology determines the breadth and complexity of the organization, its structure enables the movement to implant its ideology and code of norms in members. Ideology identifies the type of objectives (expressive or instrumental), worldview (rigid or elastic), and normative reference; structure translates these abstract elements into reality.

As discussed in chapter 4, the Brotherhood's ideology is broad, comprehensive, and to some extent vague. This affects the movement's structure, code of norms, and everyday practices. From the highest level of the general guide to the lowest level of ordinary members, all are connected by an inclusive ideology and structure that surrounds them and shapes their identity. The real impact of ideology on the Brotherhood's organizational structure, however, stems from formulating the movement's norms and code of values, such as allegiance, obedience, commitment, solidarity, and loyalty. These norms play a fundamental role in pairing ideology with structure, members with leadership, and objectives with strategy. Ironically al-Banna established the Brotherhood's structure before he fully articulated its ideology. He astutely blended the organizational structure (*tanzim*) with its ideology (*al-fikra al-islamiyya*) in a robust but flexible formula.

In addition ideology is a key source of the Brotherhood's political programs, statements, and actions. Leaders and members utilize the broadness of this ideology to articulate ideas, form policies, and outline their strategy. The long-standing mantra of the Brotherhood, "Islam is the solution," stems from the comprehensive character of its ideology. As Nathan Brown observes, "Islamist movements modeled on the Muslim Brotherhood are indeed highly ideological. And their ideologies do inform their actions. But their ideologies are also fairly general and allow considerable flexibility not on merely tactics but also on strategy and especially on the question of elections and even on democracy."[33]

The religious aspect of the Brotherhood's ideology also impacts its structure. Several of the ideologues and leaders consider organization a fundamental tool to disseminate the movement's ideology. For them building a robust and disciplined organization is a religious necessity because it promulgates Islam and achieves the goals of *da'wa*. For example, Said Hawwa, a prominent leader of the Syrian Muslim Brotherhood during the 1970s and 1980s, writes, "Building an organization is a necessity in order to reach Islamic objectives and disseminating Islam." Hawwa asserts that Islamists should articulate what he calls an "Islamic organizational theory" capable of saving the Muslim *umma* from "intellectual disarray." This theory should be based on Islamic ethics, good manners, and clear objectives. To this end he believes Islamist movements should have comprehensive bylaws, clearly delineated hierarchal structures, and consistent membership systems.[34] Fathi Yakan, one of the most influential Islamist ideologues and the founder of the Lebanese Islamic Action Front, reiterates the need for Islamist movements to build robust organizational structures. In fact Yakan goes a step further, identifying organizational structure as a religious duty: "Islamic *manhaj* should be based on an organizational system that can guide Muslims in everyday life."[35]

An effective organizational structure is crucial for the Brotherhood to manage the full range of its activities. Its tight-knit structure enables it to reach out to its expansive constituency. Munson explains that the Brotherhood's structure helps it allocate resources, expand its social network, and disseminate its ideology among different social strata. For example, he points out that the Brotherhood's federated structure facilitated its penetration into urban and suburban areas in Egypt during the 1930s and 1940s.[36]

Ideology also impacts the Brotherhood's decision-making process by helping leaders legitimize, and sometimes sanctify, their decisions and actions. Essam al-Erian declares, the Brotherhood's former head of Political Bureau, "Our decisions are made for the sake of *da'wa*, not the organization."[37] Moreover the leadership occasionally utilizes the vagueness of the Brotherhood's ideology to manipulate members and maintain control over the organization.

Importantly ideology also helps the Brotherhood maintain organizational cohesion and unity. The movement utilizes its members' religious and ideological commitment to ensure their allegiance to the leadership and to diminish internal opposition. As I explain in chapter 9, the more conservative members succeeded in marginalizing the reformists by discrediting and sometimes demonizing their ideological and religious stance.

Sometimes, however, the Brotherhood's leaders perceive ideology differently. For example, leaders give different meanings to the slogan "Islam is the solution." While some view it as a reflection of the Brotherhood's comprehensive ideology, others treat it as a pragmatic platform that can be implemented. It is also important to stress that despite the vagueness of the Brotherhood's ideology, its plans and platforms are specific and clearly defined. As Brown explains, "Movements based on the Muslim Brotherhood model have only vague ideology texts, and their leaders are generally highly practical people rather than ideologues or intellectuals."[38] In fact this broad ideology allows leaders and members to adapt their strategies to fit different contexts.

The Institutionalization of the Brotherhood: An Appraisal

The Brotherhood's structure and hierarchy reveal a high degree of discipline and institutionalization, which has shaped the Brotherhood as a vigorous and resilient organization capable of surviving crises and coexisting with different political regimes. The chain of command and the flow of orders, decisions, and instructions from one level to another is governed by the bylaws and follows specific procedures that are respected and followed by all members. As Brown aptly observes, "The movements not only work hard to follow formal procedures; they take great pride in doing so."[39]

However, the complexity of this structure has turned it into a highly bureaucratic movement. On paper the roles, tasks, and powers of each organizational level are clearly defined, and the bylaws determine the hierarchical relationship between these levels and specify the regulations, rules, and procedures and the punishment in cases of violation. Yet the picture is not as clear in practice. First and foremost is the lack of separation of power between institutional bodies, particularly the Guidance Bureau and the Shura Council. In fact the relationship between these two bodies is confusing and imbalanced. For example, while the Guidance Bureau is accountable to the Shura Council, it has more power and clout over the Brotherhood than the latter. Not only does the Guidance Bureau possess exceptional power in governing the Brotherhood's affairs alongside the general guide, but it also dominates the decision-making process, particularly on key issues such as political participation, negotiating with the regime, and administering the budget. Several Shura Council members have expressed dissatisfaction with the increasing power of their counterparts in the Guidance Bureau and the prestige these roles carry. Sayyid El-Melegi, a former member of the Shura Council, claims the Guidance Bureau controls the Shura Council and took over many of its powers, particularly those relating to the budget and financial resources of the Brotherhood. He also claims the Guidance Bureau suffers from nepotism and corruption.[40]

Second, the Brotherhood's institutions are subject to power struggles. Like any other organization, the Brotherhood comprises individuals and factions who debate, argue, and squabble over interests, influence, and privileges. Membership in the Guidance Bureau, for instance, is subject to intense debate within the Brotherhood. Most significant, the differences between the movement's conservatives and reformists overshadowed the movement itself throughout the past two decades. The Brotherhood may have been able to accommodate and manage these disputes in the short term, but it proved incapable of preventing them from having lasting impacts in the long run. There are also disputes between generations that have undermined the movement's organizational structure in recent years. Divisions between the old guard and youth over strategy, political and ideological stances, and the relationship with the regime have become commonplace.

Third is the relationship between the general guide and the Brotherhood's institutions, which is highly imbalanced and leans in favor of the former. Unlike other religious movements where the chief leader's power is limited to the spiritual sphere, the general guide has both spiritual and operational authority over the movement. As mentioned, the bylaws give the general guide comprehensive power over the movement's legislative and executive bodies. Not only does this place him above the Guidance Bureau and the Shura Council in practice, but it also gives him the right to amend the movement's bylaws and the charter. Also the general guide has significant moral power over the Brotherhood's members who revere and respect him as the highest figure and symbol of the movement. On many occasions he has utilized his moral power to influence members to behave in a certain way, to resolve internal problems, and to pass certain decisions. This was particularly palpable during the reign of the first three general guides (Hasan al-Banna, Hasan al-Hudaybi, and Omar al-Tilmisani), who had far-reaching power and remain highly respected among the rank and file. Over the past three decades, specifically since the fourth general guide, Mohamed Hamed Abu al-Nasr, and the absence of a charismatic leadership, the position has become akin to an arbitrator among factions. True, the general guide still possesses far-reaching power, but he has to consider the balance of power within the movement to avoid splits or fissures.[41]

Fourth is the stagnation and inertia in the organization. The Brotherhood's pyramidal and disciplined structure came at the expense of its internal vibrancy and vitality. Its determination to ensure the unity and integration of its organization affected internal dynamics and reduced the chances of fostering a healthy organizational environment. In addition the procedures of internal mobility and promotion lack transparency and do not follow a merit-based system but are instead based on members' allegiance and obedience.[42] In this respect the organizational culture of the Brotherhood has actually created a largely subservient and submissive membership who are not willing to risk losing their membership or being marginalized by challenging the leadership. Moreover the rigidity of the Brotherhood's structure and norms affect the decision-making process, which in recent years has become sluggish and sometimes irrelevant. In fact some scholars have criticized the Brotherhood for treating the organization, *tanzim*, as an objective per se.[43] In contrast other scholars, such as Husam Tammam, a prominent Egyptian analyst of the Brotherhood, believe it has built a robust organization similar to the state, which seeks to replace it.[44]

Fifth, the Brotherhood's organization is male-centered, with no representation of women (sisters) in the movement's institutions, particularly the Guidance Bureau and Shura Council. Although it is true that there is a section for women called the Muslim Sisters (Qism al-akhwat al-muslimat), which was founded by al-Banna in the early 1930s,[45] it does not have real power or authority. And there is no direct communication between the Sisters and the general guide; rather all communication takes place at the Administrative Office level. According to Omayma Abdel-Latif, "In each bureau, one male member is in charge of women's activities (al-Nashat al-Nisaaee) and acts as liaison between the Sisters' division in each governorate and district movement headquarters in Cairo."[46] Despite Sisters undertaking some organizational tasks, such as participating in protests and charity activities, they are not entitled to the same rights as men. The marginalization of women within the structure reflects the movement's patriarchal view of women and their role in public life, which its leaders believe should be complementary to men.[47] Abdel-Latif points out that some Sisters have been vocal about this disenfranchisement and have called for more inclusive practices. She notes, "The majority of women activists interviewed view integration as crucial in ending the marginal status of the women's movement inside the Muslim Brotherhood."[48]

Sixth, some scholars describe the Brotherhood's structure as totalitarian and lacking internal democracy.[49] The missionary character of the movement, the chain of command, and the decision-making process are reflective of a closed organization. Some members expressed dissatisfaction with the rigidity of the Brotherhood's structure because it does not foster a culture that encourages dissenting opinions or opposition to the leadership. According to them, the order to "listen and obey" denies egalitarianism and hinders accountability.[50] Haitham Abu Khalil attributes the despotic character of the Brotherhood's structure to the unlimited powers of the leadership: "The extraordinary powers of the leadership and the absence of accountability or oversight from members turned it into a despotic authority."[51]

Nevertheless, while it is true that the Brotherhood's strict structure affects its internal dynamics, the movement has made several changes that enhance its internal democracy and accountability. Since 2004 it has routinely conducted internal elections on all organizational levels, from *shu'ba* (district) to the Guidance Bureau. Active members can be nominated, vote, and select their representatives at different levels, who serve for specific and fixed terms. The recent changes in the bylaws enhanced internal procedures of accountability and responsibility. These new mechanisms were created after the media exposed the Brotherhood's internal problems. The Brotherhood established a committee to hear complaints that has the power to investigate and punish members who violate the rules.

Notwithstanding the previous observations on the Brotherhood's structure, it is quite important to situate them within the broader context of the relationship between the Brotherhood and the regime. The repressive environment wherein the Brotherhood operates can explain, among other factors, the strictness of its organization. For example, the Mubarak regime's repressive and exclusionary policies toward the Brotherhood pushed it inward and crippled its internal dynamics. Tammam notes that during times of repression the Brotherhood tends to focus on maintaining internal unity at the expense of openness and transparency.[52] Furthermore the Brotherhood's paranoia about infiltration by state elements has made it even more sensitive to organizational openness. In fact the regime bears some responsibility for the stagnation of the Brotherhood. Not only has repression made the Brotherhood more focused on safeguarding its organizational integrity, but it also played into the hands of the conservative elements that came to control the organization at the expense of the reformists. During repression the Brotherhood's priority becomes how to protect and defend the organization at all costs, not how to reform and modernize it.

8

Ikhwanism

THE BROTHERHOOD'S CODE OF IDENTITY

*After spending some time in the Brotherhood, members
start to feel that they not only live within the Brotherhood,
but also that the Brotherhood lives within them.*

SHEIKH ABDUL KHALIQ AL-SHERIF, head of the *Da'wa*
Division, interview with author, April 5, 2012

THE MUSLIM BROTHERHOOD has a unique code of identity that distinguishes it from other Islamist movements. This code reflects the interplay of the movement's organizational norms, structure, and ideology in everyday life. The Brotherhood's regulations, values, hierarchy, patterns of leadership, and social interactions impact its members' perceptions and shape their worldview. The intensity of organizational dynamics creates a subculture that dominates and guides individuals throughout their lives. This unique subculture plays a fundamental role in articulating the Brotherhood's identity and delineates its character and practices. It also defines power relations, organizational roles, membership and affiliation rules, and the structure of incentives that foster collective action.

I call the Brotherhood's code of identity *ikhwanism*. As a socioreligious movement that aims to change the views, perceptions, and behaviors of its members, the Brotherhood constructs its own ideological and organizational framework for identity that enhances its cohesion and engenders social and political activism. It instills a sense of differentiation and distinctiveness within its members and ensures their loyalty to the movement. This code of identity is constructed and reinforced through everyday interactions, organizational rules and regulations, and ideological identification processes. It reflects the interaction of ideology with structure, norms with behaviors, and strategy with reality. In fact *ikhwanism* is not a mere ideology or slogan but a way of life. To be an *ikhwani* is to think, live, and behave as a committed and obedient member. In other words, *ikhwanism* embodies the identity that signifies the uniqueness and distinctiveness of the Brotherhood as a social movement. As I will explain, the norms of obedience, allegiance, commitment, and loyalty are the backbone of *ikhwanism* as a form of identity.

The Brotherhood's Organizational Norms

To ensure cohesion, integration, and competence, social movements tend to construct a set of norms and regulations that enable them to control members, organize their activities, and generate collective action. Members must abide by these clearly articulated standards in order to avoid marginalization and punishment. Moreover organizational norms enhance a movement's coherence and unity by establishing an unshakeable commitment to the movement's objectives, leadership, and ideology.

Melucci defines norms as "the point at which operational needs (the allocation of resources) come together with the needs of integration and control (power)." Norms and regulations articulate the relationship between leadership and members, define membership rules and procedures, distribute power within the movement, and determine the structure of incentives. Melucci highlights four roles norms can play within an organization: (1) governing the relationship between the organization and members; (2) regulating the relationship between different components of the organization; (3) articulating the relationship between the movement and society; and (4) specifying the objectives and means of collective action.[1]

The Brotherhood's organizational norms and interactions create a unique identity that is largely characterized by obedience and submissiveness. As discussed earlier, these traits are encouraged and maintained through the indoctrination (*tarbiyya*) and ideological identification processes. The reach of the movement's norms and interactions are extensive; leaders and members alike must adhere to them at all times. They enable the Brotherhood not only to organize its structure and activities but also to ensure members' loyalty and obedience. Thus adhering to these behaviors is compulsory and nonnegotiable. Those found violating these standards are punished in order to maintain the legitimacy of the movement's indoctrination processes. In turn these norms decrease the likelihood of fragmentation and the emergence of a legitimate opposition. And the hierarchal order of the Brotherhood utilizes a top-down approach that does not allow space for serious splits or cleavages in the structure. However, it should be noted that the Brotherhood's norms and regulations are not static or rigid but are more akin to a dynamic code of conduct that reflects social interactions within the organization.

Ikhwanism *as a "Frame" of Identity*

From the movement's inception al-Banna was deeply cognizant of the value of creating an impermeable internal culture that could preserve the Brotherhood and differentiate it from the plethora of organizations emerging around the same time. In many of his epistles he stressed the necessity of setting clear rules and regulations that connect members with the movement. In *Risalat at-Ta'alim* (The Teachings) he identified the norms and code of values members should follow and honor in everyday life. This text is the keystone of the Brotherhood's indoctrination and identification processes.

The Muslim Brotherhood is well known for its organizational coherence. In recent decades it has developed a code of norms and practices that are institutionalized and engrained in the movement's structure—*ikhwanism*. In fact *ikhwanism* reflects the development of the Brotherhood's organizational structure over time. If al-Banna was the leader who sowed the seeds of *ikhwanism* in the Brotherhood's ideology, it was his successors who implanted it within the organizational structure.

Ikhwanism is not a rigid set of sacred ideas, however, but a constellation of social norms and organizational values that stems from the internal dynamics and interactions within the movement. It is a frame of identity that guides members in everyday life. It gives meaning to their practices and connects them with the movement. Furthermore *ikhwanism* does not negate the fact that the Brotherhood's members can maintain their personal, social, or professional identities; being an *ikhwani* does not mean that one cannot work as a lawyer, doctor, or teacher. Indeed what distinguishes the Brotherhood from other Islamist movements is the multiple layers of identity that facilitate the dissemination of the Brotherhood's ideology in wider society.

Ikhwanism revolves around five basic norms: *bay'a* (allegiance), *ta'ah* (obedience), *thiqa* (trust), *iltizam* (commitment), and *intima* (loyalty). The Brotherhood tends to blend these norms with Islamic teachings and principles to preserve their symbolic power and influence. These norms are implanted in the Brotherhood's structure through the intensive socialization and incubation process highlighted in chapter 5. As a result these norms penetrate the hearts and minds, in fact the very essence of each member.

Bay'a

Bay'a (allegiance) is a central norm and one of the first procedures undertaken when joining the Brotherhood.[2] The ritual has its roots in the Islamic traditions and signifies a contract or pledge between the ruler and the ruled to serve Islam.[3] According to Ella Landau-Tasseron, *bay'a* is commonly interpreted as "an oath given by a subordinate to a leader as a token of allegiance."[4] At the Brotherhood's inception al-Banna emphasized the religious character of *bay'a* by invoking Quranic verses and emulating the Prophet Muhammad, who took the oath from new converts to Islam in the early years of his message.[5] Al-Banna took *bay'a* from the first six members who, along with him, established the Brotherhood in 1928. He writes in his memoirs:

> One evening of March 1928, six brothers came to my house and asked to work together for the sake of Islam and the interests of the nation (*watan*). I said; let us exchange pledges with Allah (fa-l-nubayi' allah 'ala ...) that we shall be soldiers in the service of the Call to Islam (or, the Cause of Islam, *da'wa*), for the life of the homeland and the glory of the [Islamic] community depend upon [this call/cause].[6]

Al-Banna linked *bay'a* to himself as a leader and, more important, to the Brotherhood's cause and ideology.[7] He implanted the concept of *bay'a* within the Brotherhood's structure by establishing it as a compulsory procedure for joining the movement, and he linked *bay'a* with other values and norms such as obedience and commitment. In *Risalat at-Ta'alim*, al-Banna identified ten pillars of *bay'a* (*arkanu al-bay'a*) that should be adopted in order to attain full membership: understanding, sincerity, action, jihad, sacrifice, obedience, perseverance, devotion, brotherhood, and trust.[8] He provided a detailed explanation for each of these pillars and urged members to memorize them and put them into action.

The implications of *bay'a* for the Brotherhood's organizational structure are considerable.[9] On the procedural level, members cannot receive membership without giving *bay'a* to the leadership. As discussed in chapter 6, the multitiered system of membership spells out certain requirements and conditions that individuals must meet before becoming fully fledged members. Despite the fact that there is no fixed statement or formula for *bay'a*, the common pledge stipulates that each member should give the following oath:

> I pledge with God to abide by the rules of Islam and jihad for Allah's sake, and to fulfil and commit myself to the conditions and obligations of the Muslim Brothers, and to listen and obey its leadership whether willingly or not (*fi'l-manshat wa'l-makrah*) as long as he succumbs to Allah. I swear by God on that and he is the witness on my pledge.[10]

According to the Brotherhood's bylaws,[11] the oath of *bay'a* should be given to the general guide (*al-murshid al-'am*); however, due to the fear of security surveillance, the oath can be taken before any other leader at the provincial level who subsequently relays it to the general guide. This practice was particularly common during the Mubarak regime when the Brotherhood was subject to high levels of repression and surveillance.

Members perceive *bay'a* in different ways. While some stress the importance of giving *bay'a* in connecting them to the organization, others view it as merely a symbolic gesture. For example, Ammar El-Beltagi highlights the role of *bay'a* in ensuring a member's commitment and loyalty to the Brotherhood,[12] while Abdurrahman Ayyash plays down the importance of *bay'a*, saying, "Giving *bay'a* is a symbolic procedure, not an actual one, therefore I did not give *bay'a* literally."[13] However, both individuals assert that members should embrace the ten pillars of *bay'a* and put them into practice to become a full member.

On a more practical level, *bay'a* reveals the pattern of the relationship between members and leaders, which tends to be based on submission and adherence. *Bay'a* implies that members should obey and follow the leadership at all costs because the leadership is working toward achieving the movement's objectives. Members are therefore expected to respect and follow orders from their superiors even if they disagree with them. In this regard by pledging *bay'a* members renounce their individual desires and devote their lives entirely to the will of the movement.

Although members justify their allegiance as a reflection of their organizational discipline and commitment, the religious thrust and character of *bay'a* should not be discounted. Members perceive *bay'a* as a religious duty, not just an organizational norm. According to Mohamed Mustafa, *bay'a* is a sign of a member's religious devotion: "*Bay'a* is a contract between me and God, who will hold me accountable for this hereafter."[14] He ardently defends the importance of *bay'a* in strengthening the relationship between members and the Brotherhood as a whole. In fact *bay'a* fosters strong commitment among the movement's members. Landau-Tasseron observes, "By choosing the term *bay'a*, al-Banna expressed all at once the ideology, the modes of its implementation, and the commitment to both."[15] Some members believe that violation of *bay'a* is religiously prohibited (*haram*).[16]

Bay'a is a fundamental tool for promotion within the Brotherhood. It reflects the extent to which members adhere to the movement's rules and regulations. According to the bylaws, a member cannot attain the highest level of membership (*'amil*) without first giving *bay'a*.[17] Therefore, to be allowed to give *bay'a*, members must demonstrate an unshakeable dedication to the Brotherhood's ideology and leadership.

Bay'a imposes certain duties and responsibilities that should be carried out by each member, and violation of *bay'a* rules can result in punishment, such as suspending membership or marginalization. According to Karim Radawan, a member of the Brotherhood's Shura Council, any violation of *bay'a* leaves members subject to penalties.[18] *Bay'a* implies that members are fully responsible for their actions and practices not only to the leadership but also to God, making it both a symbolic and a practical exposition of power.

The organizational aspect of *bay'a* is palpable. Members perceive *bay'a* as a mutual contract with the leadership, who serve as responsible representatives of the movement. This became clear after the amendments in the General Bylaws (Al-la'iha al-'ama) introduced in 1982, which clarifies that the general guide is responsible before members and must also give *bay'a*. In accordance with the bylaws, the general guide is obliged to pledge *bay'a* to the Shura Council (Majlis al-shura al-'am), the legislative body of the Brotherhood, which is responsible for electing the general guide and the Guidance Bureau. The general guide recites the following pledge: "I give my word to *Allah* and the *Sunna* of His messenger as far as I am able to abide by the platform of the Brotherhood and its basic law, thereby performing the resolution of the Society regarding myself even if they differ from my opinion. Allah is my witness." The bylaws also stipulate that the general guide be held accountable for his decisions and actions if he violates the rules and regulations of the Brotherhood or is incapable of carrying out his duties.

The Brotherhood's opponents have criticized the submissive character of *bay'a* and the blank check it grants the leadership. In its defense, the Brotherhood's leaders differentiate between general *bay'a* (*al-bay'a al-ama*) and special *bay'a* (*al-bay'a al-khasa*).[19] Abdurrahman al-Barr, a member of the Guidance Bureau and the mufti of the Brotherhood, explains that citizens should give general *bay'a* to the leader of the nation (the *imam*) who rules according to Islamic teachings and principles and should obey him as long as he obeys Allah. The special *bay'a*, however, is a pledge or oath among people who agree to work for the sake of Islam. In this case when the leader takes *bay'a* from the group, the *bay'a* is binding only within that group, not society as a whole. The Brotherhood, al-Barr maintains, employs special *bay'a*, not general *bay'a*.[20]

Despite the religious and symbolic character of *bay'a*, members who oppose the leadership can still abandon the movement without breaking the *bay'a* oath. The multiple interpretations of *bay'a* enable members to contest the leadership. Some argue that the oath is not given to individuals but to the ideology and principles of the movement, which members can embrace even if they leave.[21] Landau-Tasseron maintains that members can reject the leadership's decisions without annulling their *bay'a*.[22] Unsurprisingly *bay'a* has been a contested subject within the Brotherhood. Some members, particularly those adopting reformist views, criticize the misuse of *bay'a* as a tool to suppress opponents. They believe *bay'a* should be limited to the religious and spiritual sphere and not extend to the Brotherhood's organizational structure. A former member named Mohamed Ayoub believes some leaders politicize *bay'a* and use it to exclude their opponents.[23]

Members can boycott weekly meetings or freeze their membership for a period of time to protest certain decisions. They can also use *bay'a* to delegitimize the leadership. For example, the senior leaders Mohamed Habib, Abdelmoniem Aboul Fottouh, and Ibrahim al-Za'farani did not give *bay'a* to Badie to protest the way he was elected.

Bay'a can best be described as an agreement between members and leadership based on mutual commitment and responsibilities. As Landau-Tarreson puts it, "*Bay'a* is both a concept and practice.... As such it has always been broad and flexible."[24]

Ta'ah

Ta'ah, or obedience, is the flip side of *bay'a*, whereby members submit to the movement's regulations and rules. Like *bay'a*, *ta'ah* is derived from

Islamic traditions.[25] Thus the religious and symbolic effect of obedience is significant. It enables the Brotherhood's leaders to maintain control over the organization and its members. Not surprisingly al-Banna emphasized *ta'ah* as one of the main pillars of *bay'a* by persistently stressing its role in achieving the Brotherhood's objectives.[26]

The oath of *bay'a* states that members should listen and obey whether or not they are willing, which instills the concept of obedience within the Brotherhood's structure. As Landau-Tasseron notes, al-Banna aptly blended *bay'a* and *ta'ah* to create the Brotherhood's credo.[27] The leaders view the link between *bay'a* and *ta'ah* as inseparable. Accordingly the motto "Listen and obey" has become one of the key features of the movement. However, this slogan has been controversial and casts the Brotherhood as an authoritarian organization. Therefore the leaders and ideologues differentiate between two types of *ta'ah*: blind obedience (*ta'a 'am'iya*) and sighted obedience (*ta'a mubsra*). According to Amer Shemakh, a mid-ranking leader, blind *ta'ah* refers to following leaders without questioning their decisions or actions, which he believes does not exist in the movement.[28] Sighted *ta'a*, on the other hand, allows members to express their views even if they disagree with the leadership. Some members contend that *ta'ah* should be contingent upon the leadership's ideological commitment to work for the sake of Islam.[29]

In practice differentiation between blind and sighted *ta'ah* remains vague and controversial. Many of the Brotherhood's youth have repeatedly criticized the application of *ta'ah*. They accuse leaders of abusing the norm to impose certain decisions or justify the Brotherhood's stance on certain issues. Over the past decade the Brotherhood has experienced vocal dissent coming from its youth elements due to the political stances and internal decisions taken by the leadership. Some of these youth claim the Brotherhood exhibits an "absolute" form of *ta'ah* that leaves no space for debate or criticism. A former member named Ahmed Samir al-Koumi claims the Brotherhood does not allow members to voice their opinions freely; they must obey the leadership's commands blindly and without discussion.[30]

There are four primary ways in which *ta'ah* impacts the Brotherhood's identity. First, it reinforces the pattern of subordination and submission within the movement. The top-down hierarchy makes it difficult for members at the lower levels to influence the decisions and policies of the Brotherhood as a whole. The relationship between members and leaders is characterized by obedience more than equality. Members in branches and districts cannot hold their leaders accountable, not only because of the movement's rules but also due to the symbolic power of *ta'a*, which hinders real accountability.

Second, *ta'ah* is employed by the leadership to accommodate, and sometimes suppress, demands for reform and change. Mustafa al-Naggar, a former member, claims the Brotherhood always manipulates members' calls for change. He criticizes the leaders and code of norms, which he believes made the Brotherhood an autocratic organization. In one of his blogs, al-Naggar states, "When people hear words like obedience, allegiance, battalion, trust, etc. they start to believe that the Brotherhood has a secret and quasi-militant organization."[31]

Third, *ta'ah* is utilized to maintain the internal coherence of the Brotherhood. Islamist movements, particularly the Brotherhood, have been accused of internal stagnation and inertia, for which critics blame *ta'ah* as the primary factor responsible. Those who disobey the leadership's decisions are frequently marginalized and sometimes even demonized. Mohamed Hamza, a mid-level member and prominent blogger, asserts that the Brotherhood does not tolerate dissenters who challenge the leadership. He points out, "The 'Listen and obey' motto is a mere weapon used by leaders to maintain unity of the organization and avoid cleavages."[32] Moreover the Brotherhood employs the religious and symbolic character of *ta'ah* to delegitimize opposition. According to Ayyash, those who defy the Brotherhood's leadership are portrayed as deviants (*munharifin*) from the path: "If you confront your leader, he will, indirectly, smear and discredit you among members."[33] Operating in a repressive environment makes the Brotherhood especially sensitive to criticism and strengthens the force of its blows when responding to these existential threats. The Brotherhood strives to contain internal disputes in order to maintain its image as a unified movement. Therefore, instead of questioning dissenters, the Brotherhood isolates and marginalizes them. Not surprisingly many dissenters have left the movement without much protest from those remaining.[34]

Fourth, like allegiance, *ta'ah* is an influential instrument for promotion. Those who follow the rules are likely to be promoted. Indeed leaders use obedience as an indicator of a member's devotion and loyalty. Ayyash says, "The more you 'listen and obey,' the higher position you will achieve."[35]

The promotion procedures in the Brotherhood are a subject of great importance and debate. On one hand, members merit promotion because of their loyalty and obedience. The more they obey the leadership, the more they will be trusted and promoted. According to Ayman Ashraf, a former member of the Brotherhood, the only way to become a *naqib* (captain), a leader of an *usra*, is to "listen and obey."[36] On the other hand, some members believe the promotion procedures are subjective and unfair. They express dissatisfaction with the nepotism and bias inherent in this structure. Hamza argues that promotion criteria focus mainly on a member's religious obedience and devotion rather than his skills or competence.[37] A mid-ranking member named Anwar Hamed also criticizes the subjectivity of the promotion process; he claims that several qualified members left the Brotherhood because they were less "submissive and obedient to the leadership."[38]

Thiqa

Thiqa (trust) is the third pillar of *bay'a* articulated by al-Banna in *Risalat at-Ta'alim*. Unlike the previous two pillars it addresses the commitment of members to the movement's ideology rather than to the leadership structure itself. Al-Banna asserts that relations between leaders and members should be similar to those "between soldiers and their leader."[39] Though soldiers must obey their leaders, the comparison intends to evoke an allusion to the greater cause driving the struggle. The concept of *thiqa* is predominant within the Brotherhood's literature and among its members. As with the other norms, the leadership tends to blend *thiqa* with religious symbolism. According to a mid-ranking member named Mohamed Hamed Eliwa, *thiqa* is "a matter of belief and faith." He reinforces the connection with religion when he states, "*Thiqa* is part of our inner belief that connects members with Allah."[40]

The Brotherhood treats *thiqa* as a fundamental tool in solidifying and enhancing its internal structure. In his explanation of *thiqa*, a member named Emad Ghanim highlights five aspects. The first is trust in the movement's approach (*manhaj*), which is derived from Islamic teachings. The second is trust in the organization and collective action, which, according to Ghanim, should be for the sake of Islam and *da'wa*. Ghanim urges members to believe the Brotherhood is the only "trustworthy" organization worth following. The third is trust in the Brotherhood's decisions, which he believes should be followed and implemented by members. The fourth is trust in the leadership and submission to its commands, which Ghanim links to the leadership's piety and willingness to follow *shura* (consultation in decision making). The fifth is trust in God's assistance. Following these aspects in everyday life, Ghanim maintains, would strengthen members' commitment and loyalty.[41] The vast majority of the Brotherhood's members perceive *thiqa* to be a religious obligation and a reflection of their commitment to the Brotherhood and its leadership. For many of them, trusting the leadership is crucial to achieving the Brotherhood's objectives. According to Mustafa, trust is the only way to measure a member's commitment and loyalty: "The more members succumb to the leaders and follow their commands, the more cohesive our organization will be."[42]

In addition *thiqa* significantly impacts the organization of the Brotherhood. The relationship between leaders and members is shaped by trust and obedience, as members tend to submissively trust the leadership's decisions and actions as part of their duty and commitment. Moreover membership conditions and promotion prospects are fundamentally built on trust more than skill; the more members trust and follow their leaders, the more likely it is they will be promoted.

However, like *ta'a*, the rigid application of *thiqa* is a source of dissatisfaction among young members. According to Hamza, some leaders seek "blind trust" from members and refuse any rejection or questioning of their decisions or actions.[43] Therefore youth occasionally protest by refusing to follow their leaders' commands. Abdurrahman Mansour, a former member of the Brotherhood, claims leaders misuse trust to avoid any critique of their decisions or behavior.[44] This abuse of trust eliminates accountability and transparency. A young member named Amr Soliman, for instance, believes some leaders use trust not to make rational decisions but to suppress opponents. As he explains, "Trust is a double-edged sword. On one hand, it strengthens the relationship between leaders and members, but on the other hand, it undermines the responsibility and accountability of the leadership."[45]

Iltizam

Iltizam (commitment) is a central concept in social movement theory. According to Burke and Stets, social movements seek to create a sense of commitment among members in order to sustain their collective action. They define commitment as "a binding tie between an individual and some other social entity, whether an identity, another individual, a group or organization, or an exchange relationship."[46]

Islamist movements foster religious and organizational commitment among members by blending Islamic values with organizational duties in order to ensure their allegiance. Therefore *iltizam* is one of the defining features of the Brotherhood's identity; it is treated as both a tool and an outcome. The Brotherhood uses *iltizam* as a tool to strengthen its internal coherence. The movement invests in the religious leanings and piety of its members to generate a sense of commitment that goes beyond the self. It perceives *iltizam* as an outcome because it seeks to reshape members' behavior to make them pious and religiously committed (*multazimin*). For the Brotherhood's leaders, creating a sense of religious commitment is an objective per se.

As Melucci notes, commitment to a movement is based on solidarity and strong identification with the goals of the organization.[47] The incubation and socialization process (*tarbiyya*) play a vital role in fostering members' commitment not only to the movement's ideology but also to its leadership. Sustaining commitment, however, requires a movement to intensify its socialization and habituation process.[48] As chapter 6 illustrates, *tarbiyya* venues such as camps, seminars, and workshops play an influential role in reinforcing an individual's religious and organizational commitment.

Accordingly the impact of *iltizam* on the Brotherhood's organization should not be underestimated. Those I interviewed listed four types of commitment within the Brotherhood: commitment to the movement's objectives and cause, commitment to the movement's rules and regulations, commitment to leaders, and commitment to fellow members. These constitute a fundamental part of the indoctrination process.

Upon joining the movement members are indoctrinated to be committed to the movement's objectives and cause. The Brotherhood tends to keep members connected with its ideology through the notion of Islamic project (*al-mashrou' al-islami*). According to Salah Ghorab, a mid-level leader in the Brotherhood, "Commitment is not merely words but actions and deeds for the sake of Islam and the *jama'a*."[49] The oath of *bay'a* underpins individual commitment; once members give the oath, they are expected to become self-committed and work tirelessly to pursue the Brotherhood's objectives. Mohamed al-Naggar, a young Brotherhood member, views commitment as a fundamental component of his membership. He explains, "My commitment to the Brotherhood's cause is unshakable; it is part of my identity."[50]

Members express their commitment by respecting the Brotherhood's rules and following its bylaws. Sherif Ayman explains that following the rules of the movement is an essential part of a member's commitment. He believes that "to be a committed brother [akh multazim], one should devoutly follow the movement's rules and regulations and act upon them."[51]

Commitment and respect for the leadership's decisions is an important norm in the Brotherhood organization. Similar to thiqa and ta'ah, iltizam is rooted in the religious ideology of the Brotherhood, and members treat it as a duty that should be fulfilled. Abiding by the rules, following the leadership, and implementing the movement's decisions are key manifestations of members' commitment. A mid-ranking member named Sayyid Shoa'iyb agrees that trust in and obedience to the leadership are signs of members' commitment.[52] Furthermore members' commitment strengthens the personal and social bonds in the Brotherhood. Members adopt the notion of brethren (ukhwwa) as a mechanism for communication and interaction. As Mohamed Sarahn, a Brotherhood member, says, "I do not feel that I belong to the Brotherhood until I interact and communicate with my fellow brothers."[53]

Intima

Intima (loyalty) is one of the most tangible features of the Brotherhood's identity. It indicates the adherence and dedication of members to the Brotherhood's ideology and leadership. From the movement's early years, al-Banna prioritized loyalty in the Brotherhood's ideology and structure. In one of his epistles, Da'watuna (Our Call), he calls upon members to demonstrate loyalty to the da'wa and al-fikra al-islamiyya. He identifies seven ways for members to foster their loyalty: (1) believe in the movement's objectives and cause; (2) become a principled believer in and preacher of the Brotherhood ideology; (3) possess a strong willingness to work for the greater good of the movement; (4) serve as a good example to others; (5) adopt secrecy in activities; (6) firmly believe and trust in the leadership; and (7) abide by the laws and regulations of the Brotherhood.[54]

Loyalty is closely related to commitment. Indeed commitment is considered the most visible manifestation of a member's loyalty. Members tend to demonstrate their loyalty by aligning their views and practices with the movement's code of norms and regulations. Moreover the religious foundation of loyalty is evident, and the movement's ideologues and leaders link loyalty to a member's religious adherence. Fathi Yakan wrote a famous tract titled *What Does My Belonging to Islam Mean?* in which he identifies loyalty to the movement's ideology and cause and loyalty to its leadership. He asserts that those who seek to work for Islam must possess a firm belief in the movement and its objectives.[55]

Members perceive loyalty to be part of their religious commitment. According to Shoa'iyb, a member's loyalty to the Brotherhood reflects his belief that Islam should be a central part of his daily life: "Belonging to the Brotherhood is belonging to Islam as understood by the movement."[56] The construction of loyalty and reinforcement of its value are key goals of the socialization processes in the Brotherhood. Weekly meetings and religious rituals aim to strengthen a member's sense of belonging and loyalty to the movement. Mohamed Sarhan proposes that loyalty is a duty for members to fulfill when he states, "Loyalty to the Brotherhood is not something to know but to practice in everyday life."[57]

Establishing loyalty is also central to solidifying the Brotherhood's organizational structure. By securing loyalty the Brotherhood ensures control over the organization. Loyalty helps the Brotherhood uphold its coherence and unity. Since the loyalty of members is measured by adherence and commitment to the movement's ideology and leadership, dissenters are marginalized. Ayyash points out that committed members obey their leaders even if they disagree with them. "Loyalty is above personal opinions," he asserts. [58]

Loyalty also helps the Brotherhood maintain control over its members. As mentioned, members prove their loyalty to the leadership by obeying commands. They ardently obey their leaders as part of their religious commitment. Mohamed al-Naggar claims, "Obeying my leader is part of my commitment towards the movement and the *da'wa*."[59]

The Brotherhood employs members' loyalty in disseminating the movement's ideology and expanding its network. Members express their loyalty by recruiting new members and spreading the Brotherhood's message throughout society. Ayman explains, "Attracting new members is part of our loyalty as a duty." [60]

Loyalty operates as a bulwark against regime repression and security penetration. The brutal policies enacted by the Mubarak regime forced the Brotherhood to adopt a strict, semiclandestine structure based on the loyalty and adherence of its members. Without ensuring their loyalty and commitment, the Brotherhood could have become more vulnerable to security suppression and even disintegration.

These five norms constitute the core values of the Brotherhood and guide members' behavior and actions in everyday life. These norms are not abstract or hypothetical ideas but practical and operational tools that enable the Brotherhood to maintain its organization and consolidate its identity. The relationship between these norms is not clear-cut or fixed; they are mutual and intertwined. Members do not treat them as discrete concepts but as connected and sometimes as similar. These norms are constructed, created, and internalized through socialization mechanisms discussed in chapter 6. They also play a key role in the promotion process; the more a member can follow and abide by them, the better his chances to be promoted and gain a higher position in the organization. Therefore members are keen to honor and apply these norms in everyday life.

Institutionalization of Ikhwanism *in the Brotherhood*

Ideological social movements have a complex and disciplined organization. One method of addressing this complexity is by institutionalizing or routinizing the movement's norms and regulations among members. Organizational norms and regulations provide the Brotherhood with a cognitive map that can preserve the movement from internal cleavages and external infiltration. As Melucci points out, institutionalizing norms is crucial to maintaining a movement's coherence and integration.[61] The degree of institutionalization necessary relies upon the complexity of the organization and the relationship between members and leadership. The Brotherhood operates in a hostile environment, which places significant pressure on its organizational structure. Without institutionalizing the norms of allegiance, obedience, trust, commitment, and loyalty, it would be significantly more difficult for the movement to survive.

The Brotherhood's organizational structure institutionalizes its norms and regulations through its bylaws and internal charter. Since its inception the Brotherhood has been governed by bylaws that are widely respected by members. The Brotherhood has embraced a structure of moral and material incentives that supplement the bylaws by fostering a sense of commitment and loyalty among members. However, the most important mechanism for institutionalizing *ikhwanism* is socialization (*tarbiyya*). Many interviewees said that members exemplify the Brotherhood's norms and values in their behavior and everyday practices. They act not as individuals but as committed members—as *ikhwan*. Salah Ghorab is one who emphasizes that individuals behave as fully committed and responsible members once they join the movement.[62]

The *ikhwanization* of social norms, values, and practices is the Brotherhood's strategic goal—not only to ensure the Islamization of members' identity but, more important, to guarantee their commitment and loyalty to the organization. Members are surrounded by symbolic images and meanings that shape their worldview and attitudes. It is the organizational structure rather than just the ideology that keeps them connected with the leadership and their fellow members. With time *ikhwanization* is internalized as a social reality that members seamlessly incorporate into their everyday lives. This thorough permeation of social norms, values, and practices marks the defining moment when a member becomes an *ikhwan*.

Unlike other social movements in which members have a transient identity, the Brotherhood's norms and values create a resilient and permanent identity for its members. Husam Tammam, a renowned Egyptian expert on the Brotherhood, concludes that the Brotherhood creates a parallel community for members that reinforces their commitment and loyalty: "The Brother, *al-akh*, lives, gets education, makes friends, finds a job, and gets married, all through the *ikhwan* network."[63] With time *ikhwanism* becomes the foundation of the Brother's identity. The Brotherhood's organization plays a chief role in constructing this cognitive identity framework. The processes of indoctrination, ritualization, and institutionalization reshape an individual's identity and foster self-identification. The result is that an individual's identity is dissolved and absorbed into that of the movement. The statement by Abdul Khaliq Al-Sherif that opened this chapter encapsulates this process.

In addition the Brotherhood's organizational structure reinforces the relationship between individual members. The regularity of internal activities (e.g., seminars, battalions, camps) helps members interact, communicate, and homogenize. Mustafa stresses the importance of weekly and monthly meetings in fostering collective identity, particularly in rural and suburban areas: "Camps [*mu'askarat*] help members interact and socialize with other fellow members and generate a sense of brotherhood."[64] These interactions are particularly important for those living outside urban areas because it is not as likely that they will interact with other members in their everyday lives.

The organization allows leaders to orchestrate and sometimes manipulate the identity of its members. The Brotherhood's chain of command, hierarchy, and multitiered membership system enable leaders to dominate and reshape individuals' perceptions and behaviors. Hamza underscores the strong influence of these factors on the identity of its members: "The general guide and other senior leaders constitute a role model [that members] attempt to emulate and follow."[65]

The top-down style of the Brotherhood affirms the impact of the leadership on each individual's identity. This particular structure creates a distinct identity that tends to be more submissive and obedient to the leadership. As mentioned, members are required to abide by the rules and bylaws of the organization and also by its norms and standards. Obedience is mostly voluntary, as a manifestation of their religious and moral commitment to the movement.

This analysis of the Brotherhood's norms and regulations unpacks the key factors in the identity formation process. Chiefly *ikhwanism* provides members with the symbolic code of everyday values and standards that reinforce their sense of loyalty and commitment to the movement. The Brotherhood's structure connects norms with behavior, bylaws with values, and members with leadership. It also intertwines the norms of allegiance (*bay'a*), obedience (*ta'a*), trust (*thiqa*), commitment (*iltizam*), and loyalty (*intima*), which dominate the thoughts and actions of members and guide them in their everyday lives. These norms have played a pivotal role in enabling the Brotherhood to preserve its internal coherence and avoid fragmentation despite the tumultuous events that have befallen it in recent decades.

9

Enforced Coherence

THE BROTHERHOOD UNDER REGIME REPRESSION

IN THE PAST few decades the Muslim Brotherhood has been subject to significant regime repression, surveillance, and exclusion. Yet the movement not only survived but was able to build upon its activism, unity, and coherence. In fact it utilized regime repression to become stronger. The movement operated in a hostile and restrictive environment that requires a high degree of discipline and cohesiveness. The political environment is the arena within which resources, potential members, adversaries, and the target audience exist. It also contains opportunities, as well as threats and constraints that impact the calculus of political and social movements. A repressive environment limits a movement's ability to allocate resources, recruit new members, and generate collective action, but its most important effect is its impact on the movement's unity and coherence. Contrary to conventional wisdom, which assumes political actors have little space within an authoritarian environment, the Brotherhood flourished and became more politically and socially influential under the Mubarak regime. The movement altered its strategy and tactics in order to adapt to changing circumstances. It dealt with repression as a tool, not a threat, that can bind together its members and fosters their allegiance and solidarity. In response to repression, a movement's survival becomes its chief priority and self-preservation overrides internal divisions. The Brotherhood's leadership was able to contain its internal differences. This strategy was the Brotherhood's primary safeguard from fracturing and dissolving under Mubarak.

Regime repression did impact the balance of power within the Brotherhood. Specifically it enhanced the position of the so-called conservatives, the hardliners, at the expense of the reformists. The conservative faction took advantage of regime repression to avoid accountability and delegitimize calls for internal reform. Conservatives tend to utilize repression to justify their decisions, adopt specific political or ideological stances, and undermine and sometimes demonize their internal opponents and rivals. While scholars tend to assume repression is a curse for social and political agents, I argue that it can be a viable tool that enables them to strengthen their cohesiveness.

Social Movements under Authoritarian Regimes

Literature on semi-authoritarianism suggests that regimes tend to manipulate the opposition with competitive yet meaningless elections, decorative representation in government, restricted access to the media, and other mechanisms.[1] Andreas Schedler explains, "Electoral authoritarian regimes neither practice democracy nor resort regularly to naked repression. By organizing periodic elections they try to obtain at least a semblance of democratic legitimacy, hoping to satisfy external as well as internal actors."[2] Moreover elections can strengthen an authoritarian regime's legitimacy and justify its actions. Lisa Blaydes echoes this sentiment when she writes that the "authoritarian regime [of Mubarak] in Egypt has endured *not* despite competitive elections, but, to some degree, *because* of these elections."[3]

The relationship between the political environment and social movements is of great importance. As Melucci notes, "The environment of an organization is made up of the wider society in which the movement is situated and from which it draws its support base."[4] Social movements seek to adapt to the changing environment in order to avoid regime repression and maintain their collective identity. The environment is composed of the state (or the political regime) and social actors, including supporters as well as adversaries. As Hanspeter Kriesi points out, "The configuration of political actors at any given point in time is partly determined by the structures of the political context."[5] Several scholars contend that social movements can be viewed as a product of their "structural" environments.[6]

Under relentless waves of oppression and exclusion some movements, particularly those that are highly ideological and ideational, tend to focus inward in order to preserve their unity. Over time they develop a more defensive identity that preserves their coherence. Manuel Castells notes that defensive or resistant identity is the byproduct of regime hegemony and repression. He maintains that *identity of resistance* leads to the formation of communes or communities as it constructs "forms of collective resistance against otherwise unbearable oppression, usually on the basis of identities that were, apparently, clearly defined by history, geography, or biology, making it easier to essentialize the boundaries of resistance."[7] In highly ideological movements such as the Brotherhood, regime repression heightens the indoctrination and socialization process. Therefore the greater the repression, the more intense the identification process. Within this environment the movement's primary goal is to *survive* rather than *participate*. Over time the sense of self-preservation becomes more visible and influential among members seeking to avoid divisions within the movement.

Under the Mubarak regime the Brotherhood exhibited an unusual degree of unity and resilience compared with other political forces in Egypt.[8] Although it is true the Brotherhood experienced a number of quarrels, divisions, and sometimes splits, particularly between the older and younger generations, these disagreements never reached the point where they threatened the disintegration of the organization. In fact the Brotherhood took advantage of its circumstances to develop a narrative of adversity and affliction (*mihna*), which helped members overcome the consequences of repression in the short run. The leaders employed this narrative to ensure members' commitment; while members perceived regime repression as adversity (*mihna*), leaders viewed it as a tool to maintain solidarity.

From Accommodation to Confrontation

Until his downfall in February 2011, Hosni Mubarak presided over one of the most notorious and durable semi-authoritarian regimes in the Third World.[9] Since taking power following the assassination of Anwar Sadat in October 1981, Mubarak sought total domination over the political scene. After a short honeymoon period with the opposition, during which he launched a series of limited and cosmetic reforms in pursuit of legitimacy,[10] Mubarak turned against the opposition and attempted to undermine its leaders. By empowering his party, the National Democratic Party (NDP), Mubarak solidified his grip on power and secured his rule from the 1980s until 2011.

After taking power, Mubarak's most significant threat was Islamist movements, particularly those espousing radical and violent ideologies. He realized it would be risky to fight on two fronts at the same time and decided to pick his battles wisely. So while he sought to eradicate extremists belonging to al-Jama'a al-Islamiyya and the Jihad Movement, he adopted a softer, more accommodating approach toward the Brotherhood.

The Brotherhood astutely seized the new opportunities created by Mubarak's limited openness in the 1980s to expand its social network and enhance its political clout. It took the plunge into electoral politics and achieved major success running independent candidates in the 1984 and 1987 parliamentary elections. The Brotherhood also made substantial gains in professional syndicates and university unions, establishing a robust presence in fields such as medicine, pharmacy, and engineering.[11] By the end of the 1980s the Brotherhood had emerged as the most prominent opposition movement in Egypt, with an expansive social network and political sway it had not held since the 1950s. Moreover the Brotherhood witnessed the birth of a new political generation that would lead the movement over the next two decades; this new crop would shape its ideological and political discourse to become more pragmatic and open than ever before.[12]

The rewards of political participation encouraged the Brotherhood to invest heavily in politics during the 1980s. However, Mubarak realized that the expansion of the Brotherhood came at the expense of his legitimacy and could undermine his rule. By the beginning of the 1990s confrontation between the two sides was inevitable. During the 1990s the Mubarak regime carried out the most devastating state crackdown on the Brotherhood since the 1950s and 1960s.[13] In response the Brotherhood attempted to delegitimize the regime and discredit its political party, the NDP. To this end it boycotted the parliamentary elections in 1990 and sought to renew its alliance with other political forces. It also sought to replace its political activism with more social activities and an expanded network.

In the mid-1990s the relationship between Mubarak and the Brotherhood reached an impasse. As Wickham records, "After more than a decade of toleration, the government launched a major counteroffensive against the Muslim Brotherhood, arresting many of its most dynamic leaders and hammering away at its reputation by condemning it as an 'illegal organization with ties to extremist groups.'"[14] In addition the regime resorted to military trials to jettison the Brotherhood's active leaders; many were prosecuted and imprisoned for more than five years. As Al-Awadi observes, the period from 1995 to 2000 witnessed the regime's strongest dependence on coercion as a response to the Brotherhood's growing political and social influence.[15]

If the 1990s the decade of adversity, as a noted Brotherhood leader dubbed them,[16] the 2000s can best be described as a subtle confrontation between Mubarak and the Brotherhood or, as Nathan Brown puts it, a cat-and-mouse game.[17] After a decade of outright confrontation, Mubarak and the Brotherhood became more attuned to the rules of the game and unconsciously shifted positions. During the first half of the decade Mubarak caved to international pressure and changes in regional dynamics and assumed a more defensive posture; this created more spaces for the Brotherhood, which was emboldened to expand its influence. The Brotherhood reached out to secular, liberal, and leftist forces and launched an unprecedented initiative for political reform in March 2004 that unequivocally advocated for a civil and democratic state.[18] The initiative served as both a pragmatic and a symbolic step to turn the regime's claims that the Brotherhood was regressive back against itself. To observers the Brotherhood's initiative was a hallmark in the ideological and political development of the movement and was its most comprehensive platform to date.[19] By the end of 2004 the Brotherhood had developed strong relationships with both Nasserists and liberals, particularly after the emergence of the Kefaya (Enough) movement,[20] which became the umbrella group for political opposition against Mubarak.

The relationship between the United States and Egypt become strained after the reelection of George W. Bush in 2004. The Bush administration adopted a freedom agenda that sought to promote democracy and political reform throughout the Middle East. This complicated the relationship between the United States and its long-standing authoritarian allies in the region, including Mubarak. In order to preserve Egypt's strategic alliance with the United States, Mubarak implemented a limited number of reforms, all cosmetic. For example, he amended Article 76 of the Constitution to create a more competitive presidential election for the first time in Egypt's modern history. While the official media celebrated the change as a significant step toward real democracy, opposition leaders, particularly within the Brotherhood, viewed it as a sign of the Mubarak regime's growing weakness. Hence they seized the opportunity to push for more political gains.

In 2005 the Kefaya movement, along with groups of judges, university activists, and workers, launched large-scale protests against Mubarak. The Brotherhood shrewdly capitalized on the momentum that was generated and, for the first time since its return to politics in the 1970s, joined the protests against the regime. The Brotherhood's persistent pressure against Mubarak resulted in startling success in the 2005 elections, winning eighty-eight parliamentary seats (around 20% of the total) despite brutal repression by the security forces. The Brotherhood's electoral success posed more than an existential threat for Mubarak and jeopardized the NDP's domination. Mubarak realized that only more overwhelming repression could stop the Brotherhood and undermine its electoral success. As a result the regime unleashed an unprecedented campaign against the Brotherhood's leaders and targeted the lifeblood of its organization: its social and business activities. In addition the startling success of Hamas, the Palestinian offshoot of the Brotherhood, in the Palestinian parliamentary elections in 2006 and the easing of international pressure for democracy in the Middle East encouraged Mubarak to repress the Brotherhood more brutally. In 2007 approximately forty senior leaders were sentenced to between three and ten years in a military prison; they included Khairat al-Shater, deputy general guide, and Hasan Malek, the Brotherhood's business tycoon. Between 2008 and 2010 the Mubarak regime tightened its grip and targeted the Brotherhood's social and economic activities. Security forces arrested many middle-ranking members across the country, shut down the Brotherhood's offices, confiscated their belongings, and banned them from leaving the country. The Brotherhood won no seats in the parliamentary elections of 2010, and its political gains over the previous two decades were completely lost.

The Brotherhood's Response to Regime Repression

Islamist movements respond differently to regime repression. Some become radicalized and react violently; others respond more peacefully and attempt to tolerate regime repression to the best of their ability. An influential body of literature suggests that by including Islamist parties regimes can motivate tangible changes in their ideology, behavior, and organization.[21] This strand of scholarship belongs to what has become widely known as the "inclusion-moderation" hypothesis. The main premise is that antiregime movements tend to shift their position and discourse once they are integrated into the political game. Changes in a movement's ideology and behavior, the thesis maintains, is conducive to their participation in the political process. Hence great political opportunities and rewards result in more moderate movements. However, several scholars contest the inclusion-moderation thesis because of the vague and controversial nature of the concept of moderation and because the responses of Islamist movements to inclusion are not identical.[22] Some do become more moderate when they participate in the political process; others do not. And some movements, such as the Tunisian Ennahda Party and the Muslim Brotherhood in Syria and Egypt, were not radicalized despite regime repression from the 1980s until the Arab Spring.

Although I concur with the broad criticism of the inclusion-moderation thesis, I am not concerned with the impact of inclusion or exclusion on the behaviors or ideologies of movements. Rather I focus primarily on the effects of repression on a movement's internal dynamics. In other words, instead of emphasizing the external outcomes arising from regime repression (i.e., moderation or radicalization), I believe it is more useful to explore the internal impacts of repression on the movement's structure and dynamics. Therefore, instead of examining the responses of an Islamist movement to repression, I focus on the utilization of this repression within the movement.

The Brotherhood utilized regime repression in order to foster solidarity among its members. This took two main forms: a pattern of enforced coherence by constructing a narrative of victimization, or *mihna* (adversity), and an intense balance of power within the movement between different factions.

Constructing the Mihna *Narrative*

The question of why the Brotherhood did not fracture is significant and instructive. The movement had experienced different waves of repression over the past decades, yet it was able to survive and maintain its unity. In fact it turned repression into a source of solidarity rather than anguish. This occurred because of what can be called the "adversity narrative," or *mihna*, the sense of victimization that prevails among the Brotherhood's members because of regime repression. This sense is rooted in the movement's literature and socialization process. It originates from the movement's memories of torture and its malaise under Nasser's regime (the 1950s and 1960s). Nasser's brutal attempt to wipe out the Brotherhood left a significant physiological impact on the movement's leaders, who repeatedly invoke these images in order to create solidarity among members and ensure the movement's unity. These images foster identification with the movement because they solidify members' shared history. Over time the *mihna* narrative has become an integral component of the Brotherhood's indoctrination and socialization process. It helped the Brotherhood accommodate repression and avoid internal schisms over the past decades.

The sense of shared tribulations is frequently evoked in the Brotherhood's internal discourse. Its literature is filled with *mihna* connotations and stories. Notions like patience (*sabr*), test (*ibtila*), and sacrifice (*tadhiyya*) are predominant in the Brotherhood's statements and are regularly invoked during times of crisis, accompanied by religious connotations. For instance, Mohamed Mustafa points out that tribulation is a test of members' faith and beliefs and that prisons are venues where members can be tested and endure oppression. Strikingly he calls upon his fellow members to be ready to sacrifice their freedom for the sake of the Brotherhood and the *da'wa*.[23]

Repression also boosts the Brotherhood's appeal among the public. The movement tends to portray itself as a victim of the regime, a role that enables it to attract and recruit new members who are also disenfranchised by oppression. According to Mahmoud Ezzat, deputy general guide, the Brotherhood gains from repression and torture more than it loses: "It is remarkable that after each tribulation supporters and members of the Brotherhood increase. People always show sympathy and support with the families of those who are arrested."[24]

Furthermore the suffering of members enhances their position within the organization because it demonstrates their level of sacrifice. Therefore those who have been frequently arrested or tortured tend to employ their oppression to reach leadership positions in the movement and gain respect from the rank and file. This does not imply that members seek to be arrested or tortured; it illustrates how regime repression can sometimes benefit members materially and organizationally.

The indoctrination and socialization process deepens the salvation and emancipation narrative, which the Brotherhood employs to accommodate repression. Leaders and members view oppression as a signpost for their cause. As Ezzat says, "Regime repression is the glue that binds us together and reflects that we are on the right path."[25] Surrendering to regime repression is employed by leaders to reinforce members' commitment and adherence to the Brotherhood. A former member named Islam Lotfi expressed his astonishment at the Brotherhood's reaction to repression. He writes in one of his blogs, "After the verdict of many Brotherhood leaders, I received several comments and messages from young members who seemed thrilled by the verdict and the imprisoning of the leaders as they view it as a sign of God's promise of victory and salvation."[26]

During times of repression the Brotherhood typically focuses inward in order to maintain internal unity. As Melucci observes, "With regime repression, self-preservation and group solidarity become the sole goal of the movement."[27] Mohamed Mustafa puts it this way: "The chief priority of the movement during repression is to keep members connected and ensure their solidarity. This can only happen through intensifying the identification and socialization process."[28] In addition repression prompts the Brotherhood to change its bylaws; for example, to protect members from police harassment, the Brotherhood omitted aspects of its membership procedures after the 1990s. It was the first time since the foundation of the movement that the levels of membership (*muhib, muntasib, muntazim,* etc.) were not included. Moreover the bylaws were not made available to ordinary members or to the general public until recently.[29] Only leaders and high-ranking cadres were able to access them.

Another factor that can explain the Brotherhood's coherence is the absence of viable political alternatives. The lack of political space in Egypt under Mubarak discouraged many members from leaving the Brotherhood. Mohamed Hamza explains that despite his dissatisfaction with the Brotherhood's policies, he felt he could not leave it because there was no other option.[30] Abdurrahman Ayyash puts the point more succinctly: "We are stuck between the bad and the ugly."[31] Reformist figures are caught in the crossfire between regime repression and the Brotherhood.[32]

A final factor that can explain the Brotherhood's resilience is its ability to marginalize dissenting members without creating major rifts. One of the key features of the Brotherhood as a social organization is its ability to undermine dissenting voices and push them to the sidelines. The movement rarely dismisses members who criticize it or defy its leadership. Instead it demonizes their cause and ostracizes them. In fact the Brotherhood has developed internal norms that delegitimize calls for reform. Dissenting members are confronted with two uneasy options: leave the Brotherhood or remain without the ability to express their views.

Managing Divisions

Since its foundation the Brotherhood has experienced different types of divisions. As noted earlier, the Brotherhood is an umbrella organization that encompasses different factions, trends, and generations who debate ideology, discourse, and the political stance of the leadership, though these disagreements rarely lead to major splits within the movement. As Brown demonstrates, the Brotherhood's followers and leaders quarrel endlessly; however, it is usually over short-term tactical and organizational issues, and not more serious ideological or religious points.[33] Although I agree with Brown on the Brotherhood's ideological coherence, I believe divisions can go beyond organizational and tactical issues. For instance, the dividing lines between conservatives and reformers are chiefly ideological and religious in nature, which can lead to serious clashes and rifts in the Brotherhood. Moreover organizational and tactical issues, such as promotion procedures, generational relationships, and accountability, can also lead to significant divisions. Members of the Al-Wasat Party, as I explain later, left the Brotherhood due to ideological and political differences with the leadership as well as organizational stagnation.

The history of divisions within the Brotherhood dates back to its early days under al-Banna's leadership, when a group of zealous members who adopted a more radical ideology called for using force against the British occupation. This group was called Muhammad's Youth and split from the Brotherhood in 1939. The second division under al-Banna was led by a close friend of his, Ahmed al-Sokkary. Al-Sokkary was the first secretary general of the Brotherhood but openly criticized al-Banna for governing the movement in a despotic fashion and accused some members of corruption and nepotism. For his efforts Al-Sokkary was expelled from the Brotherhood in 1947.[34] Divisions continued under al-Banna's successor, Hasan al-Hudaybi, when some leaders of the movement's armed wing, the Special Apparatus (Al-tanzim al-khas), tried to take over the movement and isolate al-Hudaybi because of his close relationship to Nasser. This split was more serious than previous episodes because of the movement's vulnerability in the aftermath of al-Banna's death.

Despite relative openness under Sadat, the Brotherhood maintained the *mihna* narrative to rebuild its organization and retain solidarity. Under

Mubarak, however, the Brotherhood experienced increasing division. With its growing politicization came different opinions regarding its political and ideological stances. For example, a group of *ikhwan* at al-Azhar University led by an Azharite named Mohamed Rushdi decided to leave the Brotherhood in protest against what he perceived as "deviation from the righteous path of Islam."[35]

After a decade of political success and social expansion, internal tensions increased during the early 1990s. Emboldened by its political success, a group of middle-ranking leaders who emerged during the 1970s and 1980s pressed the leadership to take a clear stance on controversial issues, such as establishing a political party, women's and Christians' rights, and political pluralism. In 1994 the Brotherhood issued a bold statement defining its position on these issues. The statement, titled "Shura and Party Pluralism in Muslim Society," recognized for the first time the political rights of women and Christians and emphasized that democracy is the only viable political system. The Shura statement was a byproduct of the fervent debate between the older and younger generations. It aimed to make a clear break from the ambiguous and ambivalent stance of the older generation on the issues raised by the statement.[36] More important, the statement was published a few months after the Mubarak regime launched a renewed crackdown on the Brotherhood.

In the mid-1990s the Brotherhood faced one of its most critical crises during the Mubarak era when a group of middle-ranking members led by Abul 'Ela Madi and Esam Sultan decided to end the history of on again–off again political activity and long-standing legislation that banned the Brotherhood. When they failed to persuade the leadership to establish a political party, they decided to take the initiative and do so themselves, establishing the Al-Wasat Party. Wickham notes that in its early days the Al-Wasat Party was perceived by the regime as a front to shield the Brotherhood.[37] As a result Madi and several other members of the party and the Brotherhood were arrested. Madi described the Al-Wasat Party as an attempt to thaw the frozen relationship between the Brotherhood and the Mubarak regime that sought to circumvent the Brotherhood's apparatus entirely.[38] The Brotherhood leadership under Mustafa Mashhur, the fifth general guide, and his deputy, Ma'mun al-Hudaybi, did not tolerate the Al-Wasat Party and forced its members to resign from the Brotherhood. Moreover Mashhur and al-Hudaybi threatened Brotherhood members who joined the Al-Wasat Party with expulsion.[39] The Al-Wasat crisis reveals how the Brotherhood treats those who defy its leadership.

Despite the organizational consequences of the crisis, the Brotherhood was able to weather the storm and maintain its integrity; in fact the leadership utilized the crisis to enhance internal coherence and delegitimize Al-Wasat's dissidents. In this case the Brotherhood improved its unity not by transforming its own brand, but by clearly articulating what they would not stand for. Further, Mubarak's refusal to recognize the Al-Wasat Party as a legitimate political entity strengthened the position of the Brotherhood and discouraged others from leaving the movement. Not surprisingly the Brotherhood has not witnessed serious internal splits since then.

The Balance of Power within the Brotherhood

Scholars of Islamist politics tend to divide Islamists into two camps, calling them conservatives and reformers, hawks and doves, or moderates and radicals. Regardless of the accuracy of these classifications, factionalism within Islamist movements is undeniable. Like other movements they suffer internal power conflicts between different elements. They fight over position, interests, and strategy. They also seek to dominate and shape the power structure to work in their favor.

The Brotherhood is no exception; it experienced its own power struggle between conservative and reformist elements. These currents coexisted, disputed, and clashed—their relationship a constant ebb and flow. By conservatives, I am referring to leaders who adopt strict ideological and religious beliefs and are preoccupied mainly with the organization's existence and survival. They focus on *da'wa, tarbiyya,* and social services more than politics. They also prefer to operate under the umbrella of the Brotherhood as a religious movement, not a political party. This group is usually dubbed *al-tiyyar al-tanzimi* (the organizational current) because they focus on organizational unity as the Brotherhood's chief priority. In contrast reformists adopt a progressive religious and ideological position and seek to integrate the Brotherhood in the political process. They focus on political activity, building cross-ideological alliances with liberal and secular forces, and contesting elections. They also call for internal changes and reform of the Brotherhood's structure to be more democratic and transparent. They are usually called *taiyyar al-'aml al-'am* (the public activity current).

The balance of power between these two currents has vacillated since the 1970s and has leaned toward the conservatives since the 1990s. As mentioned earlier, regime repression played a key role in this shift, which ironically strengthened the position of the conservatives at the expense of the reformists. To start with, during the 1970s and the 1980s the reformist current was influential. After the political return of the Brotherhood in the 1970s, a new generation of activists and politicians emerged. The core of the reformist current was Abdelmoniem Aboul Fottouh, Esam al-'Aryan, Abul 'Ela Madi, Helmi al-Gazzar, and Ibrahim al-Za'farani. They sought to rebuild the Brotherhood after two decades of fragmentation and anguish under Nasser. They benefited from the relative political openness under Sadat, who used Islamists to counterbalance his chief adversaries: leftists and Nasserists. This generation rebuilt the institutional structure of the Brotherhood and pulled it out of its political isolation to become integrated and more politicized. They pushed the Brotherhood toward electoral politics and pressed the leadership to develop clear ideological and religious views. This reformist element flourished in urban centers such as Cairo and Alexandria, as well as in Upper Egypt, particularly in Assuit and Al-Minya. It was backed by Omar al-Tilmisani, the third general guide, who embraced moderate views and was determined to politicize the Brotherhood.[40] If the 1970s witnessed the birth of this current, the decade of the 1980s was its heyday, reaching its peak in the 1984 and 1987 parliamentary elections. This current also strengthened the presence of the Brotherhood in professional syndicates and universities across Egypt and reshaped the Brotherhood's ideology and discourse to be more politicized, moderate, and pragmatic. Under al-Tilmisani's leadership the Brotherhood renounced violence, became politically active, and built coalitions with liberal, leftist, and secular forces.

The death of al-Tilmisani in 1986 was a major blow to the reformist current, as many of its leaders were alienated afterward. Abulfotouh recalls, "The departure of al-Tilmissani was a big loss to the movement and the reformist wing."[41] According to Madi, al-Tilmisani was not only a genuine supporter of reformists but also a bulwark that protected them from the domination of the old guard.[42] Esam Sultan, a former leader and the cofounder of the Al-Wasat Party with Madi, points out that al-Tilmisani maintained a balance between the conservatives and the reformists. He states, "By the death of al-Tilmissani, the balance between the generation of the Special Apparatus [*al-tanzim al-khas*] and the reformists ended in favor of the former."[43]

After the death of al-Tilmisani the balance of power shifted incrementally in favor of the Brotherhood's older leaders, who had left the country under Nasser and Sadat and returned in 1980s.[44] Three of these leaders,

Mustafa Mashhur, Ma'mun al-Hudaybi, and Mahdi Akef, would go on to become the fifth, sixth, and seventh general guides.[45] At the same time, another group of conservative leaders emerged and sought to counterbalance the reformists. Among them were Mohamed Badie, who would become the eighth general guide; Mahmoud Ezzat, who would become secretary general; and Khairat al-Shater, the Brotherhood's business tycoon and its most powerful leader in the twenty-first century.

The shift in the balance of power between the conservatives and the reformists became more visible under the tenure of the fourth general guide, Mohamed Hamed Abu al-Nasr (1986–1996). A veteran member who spent more than twenty years in prison under Nasser, Abu al-Nasr was less progressive than his predecessor, al-Tilmisani, and his weak leadership created space for the conservatives to become powerful and dominate the organization.[46]

During the first half of the 1990s the conservative current solidified its grip on power by dominating the Guidance Bureau, the Shura Council, and the Administrative Offices. In fact Mubarak's repression helped enable this shift. In 1992 regime security forces raided an electronics company, Salsabil, owned by al-Shater and Hasan Malek, accusing them by plotting against the state. The documents seized by the police titled "The Empowerment" ("Al-tamkin"), which the regime said contained a detailed plan for the Brotherhood to take over the country and establish an Islamic state.[47] The Salsabil case revealed the conservatives' attempt to control the Brotherhood after the death of al-Tilmisani. It also accentuated the role of al-Shater, who would later become the movement's chief strategist and most influential leader.

A second incident the regime exploited to repress the Brotherhood occurred when the Shura Council convened in January 1995 to select the sixteen members of the Guidance Bureau. This was the first time since the 1950s the Shura Council would select the Guidance Bureau. But the regime arrested dozens of the Brotherhood's members and accused them of attempting to overthrow the government. These members were subsequently sent to military trials for the first since the Nasser era.[48]

In conjunction with the waning influence of the reformists, a new line of conservatives began consolidating its power over the Brotherhood. After the death of al-Nasr in January 1996, the conservatives chose one of their own to become the new general guide. In a strong show of power, a small group of the conservative leaders declared Mustafa Mashhur the fifth general guide immediately after al-Nasr's burial, in what became widely known as the "cemetery pledge of allegiance" ("bay'at al-maqabir").[49] El-Ghobashy describes the moment: "A tight-knit circle led by Guidance Bureau members Ma'mun al-Hudaybi and Mashour himself essentially anointed Mashour to the highest executive post without election or consultation with Shura Council members, citing as justification the security clampdown on the last Shura Council meeting in 1995."[50]

Mashhur's inauguration was a declaration of the shift in power toward the conservatives and paved the way for conservatives to control the Brotherhood in the following years. Under Mashhur's tenure, which was dominated by his bold deputy, Ma'mun al-Hudaybi, the conservatives adopted an uncompromising stance toward the reformists, resulting in the Al-Wasat crisis. The ideological and religious development of the Brotherhood was stalled and unenforceable. Mashhur, for example, declared that Copts should pay *jizya* (a poll tax) instead of serving in the army.[51] By the end of the 1990s the Brotherhood had come under the control of the conservatives, who did not tolerate calls from reformists to implement reforms or share power.

The Power Center of al-Shater and Ezzat

By the turn of the new millennium the Brotherhood's reformist current was on the precipice of fading away. Only Abulfotouh remained on the Guidance Bureau, which was otherwise dominated by the conservatives. Other reformist figures, such as al-'Aryan, Mohamed Habib, Gamal Heshmat, and Ibrahim al-Za'farani, were sidelined. The new conservative power center was primarily led by Khairat al-Shater and Mahmoud Ezzat, who is currently serving as deputy general guide.

The tale of al-Shater's rise within the Brotherhood proves that allegiance and loyalty are key credentials for promotion. Born in 1951 to a middle-class family in the rural area of El-Mansoura, al-Shater depicted himself as a strong advocate of the Brotherhood's survival. Ironically he began his political career as a socialist and was arrested in high school after participating in protests against Nasser in 1968. During his time working in academia in the early 1970s he became attached to the emerging Islamic trend dominating Egyptian universities, leading him to join the Brotherhood in 1974. There he was influenced by two hardcore conservative leaders, Sheikh Sabri Arafa and Mohamed Al-Adawy, both veteran members of the Brotherhood. Both belonged to what was known as the generation of the 1960s,[52] men who were in prison during the 1960s and were profoundly impacted by Sayyid Qutb's ideology. Many of them were freed by Sadat and became influential in the Brotherhood. During the 1980s al-Shater spent seven years in exile in Yemen, Saudi Arabia, Jordan, and the United Kingdom to avoid regime repression in the aftermath of Sadat's assassination in 1981. During his travels he made a large fortune from his extensive business networks that allowed him to become a key player in the Brotherhood. In 1992 he was arrested and imprisoned for one year following the Salsabil case, which brought him to the attention of the Brotherhood's leadership. A businessman with strategic and outstanding managerial skills, al-Shater proved himself unflinchingly loyal to the Brotherhood's ideology and leadership. In 1995 he became a member of the Guidance Bureau, which was then dominated by elderly and veteran conservative members.

Between 1995 and 2000 al-Shater solidified his position in the Brotherhood by controlling most of its financial assets and running its business operations. As a banned movement, the Brotherhood was not allowed to invest or accumulate money, and its leaders could not publicly run its business without the state threatening that it would be confiscated. The movement was surviving financially because of its membership dues and donations. (According to several interviewees, dues are paid based on income. Lower-income members pay 1 to 2% of their income; medium-income members pay 3 to 5%; and higher-income members pay 5 to 7%.[53]) Accordingly the organization needed someone with a relatively low political profile and with business experience and skills; above all else the individual had to be trustworthy. Al-Shater fit the bill precisely and was chosen to manage business operations. According to a former member of the Brotherhood named Haitham Abu Khalil, al-Shater's main role was to boost the Brotherhood's wealth and business.[54] To this end he created and supervised many small and medium-size businesses that served as fronts for the Brotherhood's financial activities without drawing the regime's attention.[55] Over time al-Shater became a key player within the Brotherhood in the following decade due to his financial and organizational capabilities.[56]

The other influential leader in the Brotherhood who helped al-Shater create the conservative power center was Mahmoud Ezzat, the former secretary general, one of three current deputy general guides, and a member of the Guidance Bureau. Ezzat is considered one of the Brotherhood's most conservative hardliners. He joined the Brotherhood at an early age and was heavily influenced by Sayyid Qutb, as he spent around nine years, between 1965 and 1974, in prison under Nasser. After he was released in the early 1970s Ezzat became an active member in the Brotherhood and played an important role in rebuilding the organization alongside Mashhur, al-Hudaybi, and Ahmed Hassanin, and other conservative leaders. He fled to Yemen when he found out about Sadat's harsh campaign in September 1981 and returned to Egypt in 1986.The turning point came when he was selected as a member of the Guidance Bureau in 1995. Since then he has consolidated his position by taking responsibility for the Students Section (Qism al-talabah), which is responsible for recruiting new members from the universities, and the Socialization Section (Qism al-tarbiyya), which is responsible for helping members internalize the Brotherhood's ideology. Ezzat grew even more influential after being selected secretary general in 2004, a post he held until 2010. Like al-Shater, Ezzat was promoted primarily due to his loyalty and dedication to the Brotherhood's ideology and leadership. His position as secretary general enabled him to control the organizational structure, as he was responsible for supervising the Administrative Offices and Shura Councils. He also had a profound impact on the Shura Council's members and influenced their decisions, particularly during internal elections.[57] Not surprisingly domestic media have always portrayed Ezzat as the Brotherhood's "iron man."[58]

Ezzat and al-Shater first met in Yemen in the early 1980s after fleeing from Sadat. They grew closer when they met again in England while both were pursuing their postgraduate studies. Since then they have been close allies and have worked together to enhance the role and position of the Brotherhood's conservative elements. When al-Shater was in prison, Ezzat was the person he most trusted to run Brotherhood activities. Some accounts highlight Ezzat's participation with al-Shater in establishing the Salsabil company in the late 1980s, highlighting his arrest in 1992 with al-Shater and Malek.[59]

The death of Ma'mun al-Hudaybi in 2004 helped al-Shater and Ezzat become even more powerful within the Brotherhood. Together they became the vanguard of the new conservative bloc. According to Abu Khalil, these two control the Brotherhood, the former through his financial capabilities, and the latter by his organizational clout.[60] After al-Hudaybi's death the Brotherhood selected Mohamed Mahdi Akef as the seventh general guide. Under Akef's tenure (2004–2010) the alliance of al-Shater and Ezzat became more visible. Akef was seventy-six, a veteran leader who had joined the Brotherhood in 1940, and was sentenced to death in absentia before the ruling was commuted to life imprisonment. He was a continuation of the conservatives' leadership, albeit with a more accommodating propensity. His tenure was more inclusive than his predecessors' and he tried to reengage the reformers in order to counterbalance the hardliners. To this end he appointed Mohamed Habib as his first deputy and maintained a cooperative relationship with Abulfotouh, al-'Aryan, al-Za'farani, and other young reformers.

However, al-Shater and Ezzat, who played a crucial role in selecting Akef, undermined his new policies. Thanks to his financial and organizational capabilities, al-Shater became the second deputy to Akef, a position that had not existed previously. In this role he sought to strengthen the new conservative power center in three ways. First, he put in place plans to restructure the organization to become more active and dynamic. To accomplish this he rebuilt the Brotherhood's media section and promoted many young leaders in different organizational sections, such as the Students Section. Second, he engaged with the regional and administrative offices across the country and supported some of their leaders to become members of the Shura Council and the Guidance Bureau. Third, and most important, he became the mediator between the Brotherhood and the regime during the 2000s.[61] According to Abu Khalil, al-Shater created a parallel organization within the Brotherhood that was loyal to him over anyone else, including the General Guide.[62] However, al-Shater could not have amassed so much power without the help of Ezzat, who controlled the Brotherhood's organizational capabilities. Ezzat, who was Akef's brother-in-law, utilized his strong position in the Brotherhood to promote his subordinates and followers in the regional offices.[63]

Al-Shater and Ezzat as Kingmakers

The influence of al-Shater and Ezzat became evident during the second half of the 2000s, when they became the kingmakers of most of the Brotherhood's senior and middle-ranking leaders. This influence manifested itself in two crises that the Brotherhood faced between 2008 and 2010. The first was the election of new members to the Guidance Bureau, and the second was the succession following the resignation of Mahdi Akef.

In May 2008 five new members joined the Guidance Bureau, the first time new members ascended to these positions since 1995.[64] According to the Brotherhood's bylaws, the Shura Council, which consists of 105 members (ninety by election and fifteen by appointment from the Guidance Bureau), is responsible for electing the Guidance Bureau's sixteen members. The selection of new members revealed the powerful role of the al-Shater–Ezzat bloc, as they all were entrenched within the conservative current. The five members were Mohamed Sa'ad al-Katatni, who by that time was the head of the Brotherhood's parliamentary bloc and had previously been the head of the Administrative Office in Al-Minya; Sa'ad al-Husseini, a member of Parliament and the head of the Brotherhood's Administrative Office in al-Mahalla; Mohei Hamed, the head of the Administrative Office in al-Sharqia and a very close associate of Ezzat; Osama Nasr, the head of the Administrative Office in Alexandria and a close friend of al-Shater; and Mohamed Abdel Rahman, deputy in the Administrative Office of al-Daqahiyya. The selection of these five members sparked outrage in the Brotherhood. The Shura Council's members protested the results of the elections, calling them illegal. Some media reports claimed Akef threatened to resign if al-'Aryan was not promoted—a reflection of his dissatisfaction with the conservatives.[65] However, Akef denied these reports and stated he only delegated his powers to his deputy, Mohamed Habib, and did not resign.[66] Habib sought to use the crisis to strengthen his own position. Initially he attempted to exercise some of Akef's powers and sought to defuse the crisis by suggesting that new elections to the Guidance Bureau could be held in six months, that is, in June 2010. However, the conservatives, led by Ezzat, rejected Habib's proposal and campaigned for immediate elections. They interpreted Habib's suggestion as an attempt to take over the Brotherhood and install himself as the de facto general guide. They planned to remove him from his post as deputy general guide and from the Guidance Bureau altogether.

The second crisis was the resignation of Mahdi Akef. As noted in chapter 7, the Brotherhood's bylaws specifies the general guide's service as two six-year terms. Akef took the post in January 2004 but announced in March 2009 that he would step down after his first term in January 2010 because of his old age.[67] Akef's decision took many by surprise, including the senior leaders, not only because it was the first time a general guide decided to leave office before finishing his term but also because of his timing. The relationship between the Brotherhood and the Mubarak regime was intense, and the movement suffered several security blows, which led to the arrest of many of its senior leaders. Moreover internal quarrels were mounting, which required strong leadership to manage. Still Akef was determined to step down, no matter the consequences.[68]

The Brotherhood was divided over who should succeed Akef and how the succession should take place. The conservatives, led by Ezzat and al-Shater (who was in prison at that time), called for immediate elections to the Guidance Bureau and a new general guide. But Mohamed Habib, Akef's first deputy, rejected their suggestion and instead called for postponing the elections until June 2010. The only way to resolve this conflict was through the Shura Council, which was responsible for choosing the general guide and the Guidance Bureau. After a few weeks of internal squabbles, the Shura Council, which was entirely under the control of Ezzat, decided to hold immediate elections for general guide. Habib rejected the decision and threatened to resign from the Brotherhood. Moreover he accused Ezzat, al-Shater, and Mohamed Morsi of staging a coup against him.[69]

At the end of December 2009 the Brotherhood announced that the Shura Council had elected a new Guidance Bureau; it was dominated by conservatives, with the exception of al 'Aryan, and excluded Habib and Abulfotouh. While the latter remained silent, Habib reacted furiously and accused Ezzat of manipulating the Brotherhood and abusing its bylaws and rules.[70] Al-Za'farani rejected the elections and sent a petition to the leadership calling for the formation of a committee to investigate the election results and to reform the bylaws.[71]

On January 26, 2010, the Brotherhood announced that Mohamed Badie had been elected to serve as its eighth general guide.[72] At the press conference where the announcement was delivered, Akef told journalists that Badie was "chosen by consensus by members of the consultative council."[73] A veteran member and a hard-line conservative, Badie took office amid a cruel power struggle within the Brotherhood. His selection was a declaration that the conservative current had solidified its control and that the reformists had lost the battle decisively. Not surprisingly, after the downfall of Mubarak most of the reformists left the movement and have not looked back since.

10

Conclusion

I BEGAN WRITING this book when the Brotherhood was the key opposition group in Egypt under Mubarak. The book covered the period between 1981 and 2011, before Mubarak was toppled in the aftermath of the popular uprising of January 25, 2011. However, the course of events in the following years cannot be overlooked. Not only have Egypt's politics turned upside down in recent years, but the Brotherhood's political status and strategy have also dramatically changed. After the removal of Mubarak on February 11, the Brotherhood became the chief political force in Egypt with a unique political history and unmatched social and organizational capabilities. With the enormous political vacuum left by the collapse of Mubarak's regime and the National Democratic Party, the axiomatic question became whether the Brotherhood would be able to fill this space. For the first time the Brotherhood's rhetoric about democracy, freedom, and human rights was brought to the fore and could be tested. The euphoria from the demonstrations in Tahrir Square boosted the hopes for democracy and freedom in Egypt after decades of authoritarianism. The Brotherhood's ability to live up to those hopes and translate them into reality was a key challenge to the movement. Furthermore its willingness to collaborate with and accommodate other ideological and political forces was questioned closely. The relationship between the Brotherhood and secular forces after the uprising was subject to widespread suspicion and mistrust. Not to be overshadowed, the post-uprising era witnessed the rise of new "religious" adversaries to the Brotherhood, such as the Salafis, who rushed into the political arena after decades of shunning it and aspired to gain political clout in order to advance their ideological agenda.

The Brotherhood after the Uprising

During the January 25 uprising the Brotherhood maintained a low profile in an attempt to assuage fears of its political ascendance. The behavior it adopted at this stage can best be characterized as one of caution and self-restraint. This behavior is consistent with the gradualism of the *jama'a* paradigm, which recognizes that the Brotherhood's aims can be achieved only in a steady progression of phases. For example, the Brotherhood announced it would not seek to dominate Parliament, recalling its long-standing slogan "Musharka la mughalaba" (Partnership, not domination), and that it would not contest presidential elections. The movement's leadership remained adamant that they would not advocate for applying *shari'a* or curbing personal rights in the post-Mubarak era. This emphasis on respecting the rights of all Egyptians is consistent with the Brotherhood's 1994 statement "Shura and Party Pluralism in Muslim Society," which was intended to position the movement as progressive and signal its ability to maintain cohesion despite initial disagreement. However, after the uprising the lure of power overshadowed the Brotherhood's rhetoric and progressive position. A few months after the removal of Mubarak, the movement decided to contest nearly half of the seats in Parliament and fielded a presidential candidate. As expected, the Brotherhood won a majority of seats in the first post-uprising parliamentary elections, and its presidential candidate, Mohamed Morsi, became the first freely and democratically elected president in Egypt's modern history. After more than eighty years in the shadows, the Brotherhood had thrust itself into the spotlight by demonstrating an explicit aspiration to move to the center of the political stage. From this position the movement played a fundamental role in shaping Egypt's nascent transition. Along with its Salafi allies, the Brotherhood drafted and passed the first constitution in the post-uprising era. Much to the discontent of the uprising's key forces (particularly the youth), the Brotherhood also attempted to accommodate state institutions such as the military, police, and judiciary. The beginning of the Brotherhood's downfall came when Morsi issued a controversial constitutional decree in November 2012 that granted him sweeping powers transcending judicial and institutional oversight. The decree sparked outrage among the opposition, which formed a unified bloc (the National Salvation Front) and challenged Morsi's legitimacy to lead Egypt's transition. The Brotherhood attempted to reach out to other political and ideological forces, but it was too little, too late—the gulf of mistrust had become unbridgeable.

The Brotherhood after the Coup

The Brotherhood's performance in power was astonishingly poor and disappointing. During its short reign the movement's leaders and cadres demonstrated a lack of key governance skills and failed to adopt a consensual model of government capable of including other political forces. It was not a surprise, therefore, that these forces turned against the Brotherhood after only one year and campaigned for its removal. The Brotherhood's actions once in a position of political power validated the narrative spun by its critics, which viewed its calls for steadiness and moderation as nothing more than a political play. After only one year in power there were massive protests against the Brotherhood, calling the military to step in and remove Morsi. The Brotherhood's reign was over.

Along with the Brotherhood's mismanagement and political miscalculations, one cannot disregard the role of the "deep-state" in hampering Morsi's presidency. The old regime institutions—the military, police, judiciary, and businessmen—had nothing in common but their contempt and fear of the Brotherhood. Either directly or indirectly they worked hard to remove Morsi from power. The army generals, despite attaining an exceptional status in the 2012 Constitution, treated the Brotherhood as a potential threat. Morsi's dismissal of Field Marshal Mohamed Hussein Tantawy, the former minister of defense, and his chief of staff, Sami Anan, in August 2012 enhanced this sentiment among the generals. Police officers, who had repressed the Brotherhood under Mubarak, could not politically or psychologically tolerate the new reality of being commanded by their former victim. They refused to collaborate with Morsi's government despite his willingness to appease and accommodate them. Likewise Morsi's attempt to restructure the judicial system was seen by many judges as an attempt to purge them and undermine their social status and privileges. And Mubarak's businessmen were suspicious of the Brotherhood's economic policies and procedures. While the Brotherhood did not adopt a different economic policy from that of Mubarak, wariness and uncertainty overshadowed the relationship between the old guard and the new.

On July 3, 2013, Minister of Defense Abdel Fattah al-Sisi deposed Morsi, suspended the Constitution, and dissolved Parliament. Capitalizing on public frustration with and distrust of the Brotherhood, the al-Sisi regime used a heavy hand to deal with the movement. In one day hundreds of the Brotherhood's supporters were gunned down by police responding to sit-ins at Rab'a and al-Nahda. These killings marked one of Egypt's worst massacres in modern history, according to Human Rights Watch. The Brotherhood's senior leaders and figures have been sentenced to life in prison; some have even received death sentences. Among them are General Guide Mohamed Badie and several members of the Guidance Bureau and the Shura Council. Furthermore the movement's businesses and financial assets were frozen, and the government has taken over its social and charity institutions. Much of the social capital that the movement assiduously built over decades was lost in a little more than one year's time.

The Brotherhood's Coherence

Since the coup the Brotherhood has spiraled into a state of disarray. It now lacks a clear vision, which affects its coherence and unity. It returned to its historical playbook in responding to regime repression in order to improve its image and regain public sympathy. This invocation of the *mihna* (affliction) narrative was also intended to preserve the Brotherhood's internal cohesiveness. At the same time, the Brotherhood experienced internal disputes over its vision and strategy in the months following the coup. These disputes were primarily between the older and younger generations and revolve around three key issues: leadership, vision, and strategy. The older generation, particularly those in exile or hiding in Egypt, such as acting general guide Mahmoud Ezzat and Secretary General Mahmoud Hussein, have struggled to maintain their control over the movement. As a result the younger, mid-level leaders have gained more control over the past three years. This group includes Guidance Bureau member Mohamed Kamal, the new spokesman Mohamed Montasser, and Shura Council members Essam Talimah and Yehia Hamed, among others. The younger generation believes the older leadership is responsible for the damage to the Brotherhood's internal cohesion and external image and that it is the time for them to let others lead. They also argue that because the youth have paid a high price, even sacrificing their lives, to preserve the movement's survival, they should play a more central role in the leadership moving forward.

The older generation has adopted a passive stance for dealing with the al-Sisi regime and generally tolerates its repression. Having experienced the waves of repression under the Mubarak regime, they believe the current wave is only temporary and that the Brotherhood should play the long game for its resurgence. Therefore they call upon members to practice self-restraint and nonconfrontation. This disciplined response is rooted in the *tarbiyya* process, which strengthens the membership's mental fortitude and reinforces the primacy of the movement above the individual. The underlying force at work during this process is the Brotherhood's social constructivist approach to identity building. During times of repression the movement's socialization process serves as a lifeline for individuals to grab on to and that reinforces the desire for a shared bond. The older leaders' call for restraint also reveals that they perceive the current crisis as no different from the myriad crises the movement has faced throughout its history; they consider repression under al-Sisi to be analogous to repression under Nasser and Mubarak.

The younger generation, however, believes the Brotherhood should be more defiant toward regime repression. They aim to remove the al-Sisi regime and change the rules of the game in their favor. The appeal of the younger generation's platform is their shared disenfranchisement after Morsi's governance failures and regime violence such as the Rab'a massacre. Viewed together the visions of the older and younger generations represent polar opposite characterizations of how the movement should respond to its current predicament. Throughout the Brotherhood's history, its identity construction and reinforcement processes have managed to contain internal divisions, ranging from the emergence of Muhammad's Youth in 1939 to the Al-Wasat crisis of the mid-1990s. Yet the Brotherhood's recent rise and fall is unique, for the movement ascended to its highest level of power only to fall into complete disarray after one year. Given this swift reversal and the al-Sisi regime's crackdown on many of the older generation's key leaders, the rise of the younger leadership provides a potent challenge to the movement's balance of power and its ability to maintain internal cohesion.

The older leadership also adheres to its reformist and gradualist strategy. In their view this tried and true method is the only way to sustain the movement and improve its image among the public in the long run. Abandoning this strategy in response to the downturn in the post-coup era is perceived as myopic. They believe it may lead only to continued violence and a further degradation of the Brotherhood's public image. However, the younger generation believes the reformist strategy is obsolete after the coup and that the movement must adopt a more revolutionary strategy. In order to turn the tide, this group advocates for weekly protests and agitating against the al-Sisi regime in any way possible. Driven by frustration and despair, the Brotherhood's youth have lost faith in formal politics and view it as a waste of time. After almost three years since the removal of Morsi, the Brotherhood maintains its weekly protests and organizational meetings (*usra, shu'ba,* etc.) and mobilizes its supporters. The protests occasionally lead to low-intensity violence that members justify as self-defense against regime brutality. Although the Brotherhood denounced violence decades ago, the brutality of the al-Sisi regime and the movement's current state of humiliation renewed internal debates over the utility of using violence to counter repression. While the movement's leadership remains committed to peaceful means, some of the youth have considered using what they call "tactical" violence against the state. This resort to violence is driven by frustration, perceived injustice, and a desire for immediate retribution. Young members seem to have concluded that power does not necessarily stem from the ballot box but can be attained by defiance and rebellion. In other words, this sort of violence is more political than religious and is largely the youth's reaction to regime repression. The fact that the youth have consistently defied the leadership's calls for self-restraint undermines the old guard's narrative of resiliency through gradualism. Moreover the generational divide presents a serious challenge to the Brotherhood's cohesion if the passage of time necessitates a passing of the torch to the younger, more revolutionary strain. The political and security pressure against the Brotherhood has put the movement's leadership in a tough position against its youth, who are dissatisfied with the leaders' willingness to accommodate regime repression. Clearly the Brotherhood's youth are on a collision course with the old guard and the regime that is redefining the movement's image and long-term prospects.

Yet despite the internal divisions, the Brotherhood still operates as a unified movement. Even if these divisions lead to rifts and splits in the future, this will not affect the nature of the movement. As I explained in chapter 9, the Brotherhood withstood many attempts on its existence over the course of its history, but this did not stop it from continuing its activism.

The Future of the Brotherhood

The Brotherhood is at a crossroads. Before the January uprising it was at its height despite regime repression. As I have showed, the key challenge for the Brotherhood has been to survive and maintain its activism. Since the uprising and particularly after the coup, the movement has grappled with many challenges and problems. First, the Brotherhood has come full circle over the past few years as it moved from opposition to power and vice versa. Its members seem to be torn between moving back to the old days, when the movement was a domesticated and compromising force, and being a revolutionary and confrontational group. Even if they decided to become the latter, they would need to rethink their ideology, strategy, and tactics. Simply put, the Brotherhood will not be the movement we used to know.

Second, the Brotherhood's experience in power exposed many of its weaknesses concerning how to govern and how to deal with other ideological forces. It failed to deliver socially and economically, and it could not move beyond its ideological boundaries to include other forces. True, Morsi's tenure was short and ended abruptly, but it was clear that he was not acting as a statesman but as a member of the Brotherhood. Third, the Brotherhood's image and credibility were severely damaged over the past few years. It could not live up to the uprising's hopes and aspirations, and the project of "renaissance" it had long advocated was nothing but a mirage. The post-coup regime has demonized the Brotherhood and designated it a terrorist organization, which affected its image and led to isolation. Fourth, the Brotherhood is facing a brutal campaign of repression it has not experienced since the 1960s. Al-Sisi's regime seems to be determined to wipe out the movement and end its political existence. And even if al-Sisi failed to do so, which is very likely, it is going to take the Brotherhood a lot of time and effort to rebuild its social network and improve its image. Fifth, the Brotherhood must rethink the relationship between its political and religious activities. The amalgamation of both spheres hindered the movement and exposed its weaknesses. Sixth, for the Brotherhood to regain its former status as a potent and influential societal force, it must rethink its ideology, structure, and organization and adapt to the post-uprising environment. The Brotherhood may not vanish or disappear; however, its influence and future will remain uncertain unless it can solve these challenges.

Notes

CHAPTER 1

1. Craig Calhoun, ed., *Social Theory and the Politics of Identity* (Cambridge, MA: Wiley-Blackwell, 1994), 13.
2. Alberto Melucci, *Challenging Codes: Collective Action in the Information Age* (Cambridge, UK: Cambridge University Press, 1996), 77, 4.
3. Alberto Melucci, *Nomads of the Present: Social Movements and Individual Needs in Contemporary Society* (Philadelphia: Temple University Press, 1989), 35.
4. Melucci, *Challenging Codes*, 77.
5. The literature on identity and collective action is vast. See, for example, Francesca Polletta and James M. Jasper, "Collective Identity and Social Movements," *Annual Review of Sociology* 27 (2001): 283–305.
6. Melucci, *Challenging Codes*, 317.
7. There are different accounts of this issue, but the prevalent one is that Mustafa el-Nahhas Pasha's government threatened to dissolve the Brotherhood if al-Banna ran in the elections; hence he had to withdraw. However, in 1944 al-Banna and some other members ran in the elections; when they did not win they accused the government and the British authorities of rigging the elections. For more see Mahmoud Abdel Halim, *Al-ikhwan al-Muslimun: Ahdath San'at al-tarkih* (The Muslim Brotherhood: Events That Made History) (Alexandria: Dar al-Da'wa, 1979).
8. On August 14, 2013, the police forces brutally dispersed the Brotherhood's sit-ins in Rab'a al-'Adawiyya and al-Nahda squares, leaving at least eight hundred people dead and dozens injured. For more see Human Rights Watch, "All According to Plan: The Rab'a Massacre and the Mass Killings of Protesters in Egypt," August 12, 2014, http://www.hrw.org/sites/default/files/reports/egypt0814web_0.pdf.
9. According to Wiki Thawra, an independent survey in Egypt, the number of political prisoners since Morsi's ouster ranges between 20,000 and 40,000, and most of these belong to the Brotherhood. See Abdelhalim Abdallah, "Over 40,000

Arrests Related to Political Turmoil since Morsi's Ouster: Wiki Thawara," *Daily News Egypt*, May 25, 2014, http://www.dailynewsegypt.com/2014/05/25/40000-arrests-related-political-turmoil-since-morsis-ouster-wiki-thawra/.

10. Roisin O'Connor, "14 Muslim Brotherhood Members Sentenced to Death in Egypt," *Independent* (UK), March 16, 2015, http://www.independent.co.uk/news/world/africa/14-muslim-brotherhood-members-sentenced-to-death-in-egypt-10112297.html.

11. Steven Brooke, "Egypt's Crackdown on Islamist Charities," *Foreign Policy*, December 27, 2013, http://foreignpolicy.com/2013/12/27/egypts-crackdown-on-islamist-charities/#sthash.7f0TCw46.S3hQRKly.dpbs.

12. Peter Berger and Thomas Luckmann, *The Social Construction of Reality: A Treatise in the Sociology of Knowledge* (London: Penguin Press, 1967), 249, 250.

13. M. Hakan Yavuz, *Islamic Political Identity in Turkey* (Oxford: Oxford University Press, 2003), 20.

14. Vivien Burr, *Social Constructivism* (London: Routledge, 2003), 7.

15. Bert Klandermans and Dirk Oegema, "Potentials, Networks, Motivations, and Barriers: Steps towards Participation in Social Movements," *American Sociological Review* 52 (August 1987): 519–531; Hank Johnston and Bert Klandermans, *Social Movements and Culture* (Minneapolis: University of Minnesota Press, 1995); John Drury and Steve Reicher, "Collective Action and Psychological Change: The Emergence of New Social Identities," *British Journal of Social Psychology* 39 (December 2000): 579–604.

16. On this point I rely on the lucid works of Bernard Simon and Stefan Stürmer on politicized identity. See Bernard Simon and Bert Klandermans, "Politicized Collective Identity: A Social Psychology Analysis," *American Psychologist* 56 (April 2001): 319–331; Stefan Stürmer and Bernd Simon, "Collective Action: Towards a Dual-Pathway Model," *European Review of Social Psychology* 15 (2004): 59–99.

17. Juliet Corbin and Anselm Strauss, *Basics of Qualitative Research: Techniques and Procedures for Developing Grounded Theory* (New York: Sage, 2007), 10.

CHAPTER 2

1. For a more detailed discussion on the disagreement among scholars of Islamism see Jillian Schwedler, "Why Academics Can't Go beyond Moderates and Radicals," *Washington Post*, February 12, 2014, http://www.washington-post.com/blogs/monkey-cage/wp/2015/02/12/why-academics-cant-get-beyond-moderates-and-radicals/.

2. I define *Islamism* as a political ideology and project carried out by social actors who seek to instill and activate religion (Islam in this case) in everyday life for political purposes.

3. Khalil al-Anani, "ISIS-ification of Islamist Politics," *Washington Post*, January 30, 2015.

4. Salwa Ismail, *Rethinking Islamist Politics: Culture, the State and Islamism* (London: I. B. Tauris, 2006), 1.

5. For decades proponents of secularism have predicted that religion would fade away as an inevitable consequence of modernity. They tended to view religion as an "irrelevant" phenomenon that should withdraw into the private sphere with no role in everyday public life. This view was proven false after the resurgence of religion and religious movements around the globe. For more on this issue see José Casanova, *Public Religions in the Modern World* (Chicago: University of Chicago Press, 1994).

6. Max Weber, *The Sociology of Religion* (Boston: Beacon Press, 1993), 20–31.

7. Emile Durkheim, *The Elementary Forms of Religious Life* (New York: Oxford University Press, 2001), 160–161.

8. For disagreement and division among social theorists on how to study religion see, for example, James A. Beckford, *Social Theory and Religion* (Cambridge, UK: Cambridge University Press, 2003).

9. Richard C. Martin, *Approaches to Islam in Religious Studies* (Tucson: University of Arizona Press, 1985), 3.

10. See, for example, Emmanuel Sivan, *Radical Islam: Medieval Theology and Modern Politics* (New Haven, CT: Yale University Press, 1990); Youssef M. Choueiri, *Islamic Fundamentalism* (London: Pinter, 1990).

11. James P. Piscatori, *Islam in the Political Process* (Cambridge, UK: Cambridge University Press, 1993), 8.

12. John L. Esposito, *The Future of Islam* (New York: Oxford University Press, 2010), 11.

13. See, for example, Nazih Ayubi, *Political Islam: Religion and Politics in the Arab World* (London: Routledge, 1993).

14. See, for example, Shabbir Akhtar, *Islam and Political Religion: The Future of an Imperial Faith* (London: Routledge, 2011).

15. Samuel P. Huntington, *The Clash of Civilizations and the Remaking of World Order* (New York, Simon & Schuster, 1996).

16. Bernard Lewis, *What Went Wrong? The Clash between Islam and Modernity in the Middle East* (London: Weidenfeld & Nicolson, 2002).

17. Bassam Tibi, *Islam's Predicament with Modernity: Religious Reform and Cultural Change* (London: Routledge, 2009).

18. Daniel Pipes, *In the Path of God: Islam and Political Power* (New York: Basic Books, 1983).

19. Edward W. Said, *Covering Islam: How the Media and the Experts Determine How We See the Rest of the World* (New York: Pantheon Books, 1981), 38

20. See, for example, Bassam Tibi, *Islam between Culture and Politics* (New York: Palgrave Macmillan, 2001).

21. See, for example, Bernard Lewis, *What Went Wrong? The Clash between Islam and Modernity in the Middle East* (New York: Oxford University Press, 2002).

22. Daniel Pipes, *In the Path of God: Islam and Political Power* (New York: Basic Books, 1983).

23. Ayubi, *Political Islam*, 1, 3.

24. Asef Bayat, *Making Islam Democratic: Social Movements and the Post-Islamist Turn* (Stanford: Stanford University Press, 2007), 2.

25. In Asef Bayat, "Islamism and Social Movement Theory," *Third World Quarterly* 26, no. 6 (2005): 894.

26. Michael C. Hudson, *Arab Politics: The Search for Legitimacy* (New Haven, CT: Yale University Press, 1977), 2. See also Nazih Ayubi, *Overstating the Arab State: Politics and Society in the Middle East* (London: I. B. Tauris, 1996).

27. Ali E. Dessouki, ed., *Islamic Resurgence in the Arab World* (Westport, CT: Praeger, 1982), 183.

28. Laura Guazzone, ed., *The Islamist Dilemma: The Political Role of Islamist Movements in the Contemporary Arab World* (: Ithaca Press, 1995), 3.

29. François Burgat and William Dowell, *The Islamic Movements in North Africa* (Austin: University of Texas Press, 1997), 48.

30. Yvonne Haddad, "Islamists and the 'Problem of Israel': The 1967 Awakening," *Middle East Journal* 46, no. 2 (1992): 266–285.

31. Lisa Anderson, "Fulfilling Prophecies: State Policy and Islamist Radicalism," in John L. Esposito, ed., *Political Islam: Revolution, Radicalism, or Reform?* (Boulder, CO: Lynne Rienner, 1997), 25.

32. Gudrun Krämer, "Cross-Links and Double Talk? Islamist Movements in the Political Process," in Guazzone, *The Islamist Dilemma*, 20.

33. Ayubi, 44.

34. Mark Tessler, "The Origins of Popular Support for Islamist Movement," in John Pierre Entelis, ed., *Islam, Democracy, and the State in North Africa* (Bloomington: Indiana University Press, 1997), 93–95.

35. Saad Eddin Ibrahim, *Egypt, Islam, and Democracy: Critical Essays* (Cairo: American University Press, 2004), 60.

36. Dirk Vandewalle, "Breaking with Socialism: Economic Liberalization and Privatization in Algeria," in Iliya Harik and Denis Sullivan, eds., *Privatization and Liberalization in the Middle East* (Bloomington: Indiana University Press, 1992), 190.

37. Tessler, "The Origins of Popular Support for Islamist Movement," 113.

38. Ismail, *Rethinking Islamist Politics*, 14.

39. The advocates of this trend include Samuel Huntington, Daniel Pipes, Bassam Tibi, P. J. Vatikiotis, and Emmanuel Sivan. Most of their work on Islam tends to essentialize Islam and Muslim societies. They look at Islam through "radicalism and extremism" lenses without giving much attention to the political context or the socioeconomic circumstances where religion is interpreted and instrumentalized.

40. M. Hakan Yavuz, *Islamic Political Identity in Turkey* (New York: Oxford University Press, 2002), 16.

41. Tibi, *Islam between Culture and Politics*, 4, 3.

42. Bassam Tibi, *Islam's Predicament with Modernity: Religious Reform and Cultural Change* (London: Routledge, 2009), 11.

43. Pipes, *In the Path of God*, 168.

44. Ibid., 111.

45. Peter L. Berger, *The Desecularization of the World: Resurgent Religion and World Politics* (Grand Rapids, MI: Wm. B. Eerdmans, 1999), 2–3.

46. Dale F. Eickelman and James Piscatori, *Muslim Politics* (Princeton, NJ: Princeton University Press, 2004), 23.

47. Fred Halliday, *Islam and the Myth of Confrontation: Religion and Politics in the Middle East* (London: I. B. Tauris, 1996), 14, 118.

48. Bobby S. Sayyid, *A Fundamental Fear: Eurocentrism and the Emergence of Islamism* (London: Zed Books, 1997), 138.

49. Akbar S. Ahmed, *Postmodernism and Islam: Predicament and Promise* (London: Routledge, 1992), 27.

50. Olivier Roy, *The Failure of Political Islam* (London: I. B. Tauris, 1994), 7.

51. This trend has grown remarkably in the post-9/11 era as a response to the limitations of other theoretical and analytical frameworks. See, for example, Ziad Munson, "Islamic Mobilization: Social Movement Theory and the Egyptian Muslim Brotherhood," *Sociological Quarterly* 42, no. 4 (2001): 487–510; Carrie Rosefsky Wickham, *Mobilizing Islam: Religion, Activism, and Political Change in Egypt* (New York: Columbia University Press, 2002); Yavuz, *Islamic Political Identity in Turkey*; Quintan Wiktorowicz, ed., *Islamic Activism: A Social Movement Theory Approach* (Bloomington: Indiana University Press, 2004); Bayat, "Islamism and Social Movement Theory."

52. Mohammad M. Hafez, *Why Muslims Rebel: Repression and Resistance in the Islamic World* (Boulder, CO: Lynne Rienner, 2003), 21, 19.

53. Jeff Goodwin and James Jasper, "Caught in a Winding, Snarling Vine: The Structural Bias of Political Process Theory," *Sociological Forum* 14, no. 1 (1999): 28.

54. See, for example, Sidney Tarrow, *Power in Movement: Social Movements and Contentious Politics* (Cambridge, UK: Cambridge University Press, 1994); Doug McAdam and David A. Snow, eds., *Social Movements: Readings on Their Emergence, Mobilization, and Dynamics* (Los Angeles: Roxbury, 1997); Doug McAdam, John D. McCarthy, and Mayer N. Zald, eds., *Comparative Perspectives on Social Movements: Political Opportunities, Mobilizing Structures, and Cultural Framings* (Cambridge, UK: Cambridge University Press, 1996).

55. Tarrow, *Power in Movement*, 86.

56. Wiktorowicz, *Islamic Activism*.

57. Yavuz, *Islamic Political Identity in Turkey*, 25.

58. Goodwin and Jasper, "Caught in a Winding, Snarling Vine," 31.

59. Munson, "Islamic Mobilization," 496–497.

60. On framing see, for example, David A. Snow, E. Burke RochfordJr., Steven K. Worden, and Robert D. Benford, "Frame Alignment Processes, Micromobilization, and Movement Participation," *American Sociological Review* 51, no. 4 (1986): 464–481; Robert D. Benford and David A. Snow, "Framing Processes and Social Movements: An Overview and Assessment," *Annual Review of Sociology* 26 (2000): 611–639.

61. Snow et al., "Frame Alignment Processes, Micromobilization, and Movement Participation," 467.

62. Wiktorowicz, *Islamic Activism*, 19.

63. Eickelman and Piscatori, *Muslim Politics*, 12.

64. Ismail, *Rethinking Islamist Politics*, 17.

65. Yavuz, *Islamic Political Identity in Turkey*.

66. Beckford, *Social Theory and Religion*, 161.

67. Richard P. Mitchell, *The Society of Muslim Brothers* (London: Oxford University Press, 1969).

68. Brynjar Lia, *The Society of the Muslim Brothers in Egypt: The Rise of an Islamic Mass Movement 1928–1942* (: Ithaca Press, 1998).

69. Barbara Zollner, *The Muslim Brotherhood: Hasan al-Hudaybi and Ideology* (London: Routledge, 2009).

70. Munson, "Islamic Mobilization," 496–497.

71. Abdullah Al-Arian, *Answering the Call: Popular Islamic Activism in Sadat's Egypt* (New York: Oxford University Press, 2014).

72. Wickham, *Mobilizing Islam*, 8.

73. Gilles Kepel, "Islamists versus the State in Egypt and Algeria," *Daedalus* 124, no. 3 (1995): 109–127.

74. Hesham Al-Awadi, "Mubarak and the Islamists: Why Did the 'Honeymoon' End?," *Middle East Journal* 59, no. 1 (2005): 75.

75. Wickham, *Mobilizing Islam*, 3.

76. Tarek Masoud, *Counting Islam: Religion, Class, and Elections in Egypt* (New York: Cambridge University Press, 2014), 5.

77. Nathan Brown, *When Victory Is Not an Option: Islamist Movements in Arab Politics* (Ithaca, NY: Cornell University Press, 2012), 2–3.

78. Mona El-Ghobashy, "The Metamorphosis of the Egyptian Muslim Brothers," *International Journal of Middle East Studies* 37, no. 3 (2005): 374.

79. Bruce K. Rutherford, "What Do Egypt's Islamists Want? Moderate Islam and the Rise of Islamic Constitutionalism," *Middle East Journal* 60, no. 4 (2006): 726.

80. El-Ghobashy, "The Metamorphosis of the Egyptian Muslim Brothers," 374.

81. Brown, *When Victory Is Not an Option*, 160.

82. This notion is widely overlooked in the literature on Islamist movements, particularly from the social movement theory perspective. The focus is always on Islamists as collective actors, without paying much attention to individuals and the configuration of their personal identity.

CHAPTER 3

1. Marilynn B. Brewer, "The Many Faces of Social Identity: Implications for Political Psychology," *Political Psychology* 22, no. 1 (2001): 115.

2. Zygmunt Bauman, *Identity: Conversations with Benedetto Vecchi* (Cambridge, UK: Polity Press, 2004), 10–11.

3. George Herbert Mead and Charles W. Morris, *Mind, Self and Society from the Standpoint of a Social Behaviorist* (Chicago: University of Chicago Press, 1934), 130, 154, 172.

4. The literature on interactionism is burgeoning. See, for example, Sheldon Stryker, *Symbolic Interactionism: A Social Structural Version* (: Blackburn Press, 2003); Sheldon Stryker and Richard T. Serpe, "Commitment, Identity Salience, and Role Behavior," in William Ickes and Eric Knowles, eds., *Personality, Roles, and Social Behavior* (New York: Springer-Verlag, 1982), 199–218; Sheldon Stryker, "Exploring the Relevance of Social Cognition for the Relationship of Self and Society," in Judith Howard and Peter L. Callero, eds., *The Self-Society Dynamic: Cognition, Emotion, and Action* (Cambridge, UK: Cambridge University Press, 1991), 19–41; Jan E. Stets and Peter J. Burke, "Identity Theory and Social Identity Theory," *Social Psychology Quarterly* 63, no. 3 (2000): 224–237.

5. Sheldon Stryker and Peter J. Burke, "The Past, Present, and Future of an Identity Theory," *Social Psychology Quarterly* 63, no. 4 (2000): 286.

6. Michael A. Hogg, Deborah J. Terry, and Katherine M. White, "A Tale of Two Theories: A Critical Comparison of Identity Theory with Social Identity Theory," *Social Psychology Quarterly* 58, no. 4 (1995): 256.

7. Stryker and Burke, "The Past, Present, and Future of an Identity Theory," 285–286.

8. Peter L. Callero, "Role-Identity Salience," *Social Psychology Quarterly* 48, no. 3 (1985): 204.

9. Hogg et al., "A Tale of Two Theories," 256.

10. Hogg et al., "A Tale of Two Theories," 257.

11. For more on self-identity see, for example, George J. McCall and Jerry Laird Simmons, *Identities and Interactions: An Examination of Human Associations in Everyday Life* (New York: Free Press, 1978); Sheldon Stryker, Timothy Joseph Owens, and Robert W. White, eds., *Self, Identity, and Social Movements* (Minneapolis: University of Minnesota Press, 2000). For more on social identity see Stryker et al., *Self, Identity, and Social Movements*; Stets and Burke, "Identity Theory and Social Identity Theory."

12. Charles Taylor, *Sources of the Self: The Making of the Modern Identity* (Cambridge, MA: Harvard University Press, 1989), 36, 27.

13. Mark R. Leary and June Price Tangney, eds., *Handbook of Self and Identity* (New York: Guilford Press, 2005), 91.

14. See, for example, Henri Tajfel, *Human Groups and Social Categories* (Cambridge, UK: Cambridge University Press, 1981); John C. Turner, *Rediscovering the Social*

Group: A Self Categorization Theory (Oxford: Blackwell, 1987); Dominic Abrams and Michael A. Hogg, *Social Identifications: A Social Psychology of Intergroup Relations and Group Processes* (London: Routledge, 1988).

15. Stets and Burke, "Identity Theory and Social Identity Theory," 225.

16. Stryker and Burke, "The Past, Present, and Future of an Identity Theory," 284.

17. Rogers Brubaker and Frederick Cooper, "Beyond Identity," *Theory and Society* 29, no. 1 (2000): 6–8.

18. Stryker and Burke, "The Past, Present, and Future of an Identity Theory," 286.

19. Stryker et al., *Self, Identity, and Social Movements*, 28.

20. Callero, "Role-Identity Salience," 203.

21. Stryker and Burke, "The Past, Present, and Future of an Identity Theory," 286.

22. See, for example, Karen A. Cerulo, "Identity Construction: New Issues, New Directions," *Annual Review of Sociology* 23 (August 1997): 385–409; Lory Peek, "Becoming Muslim: The Development of a Religious Identity," *Sociology of Religion* 66, no. 3 (2005): 215–242.

23. Taylor, *Sources of the Self*, 36.

24. Hank Johnston and Bert Klandermans, eds., *Social Movements and Culture* (Minneapolis: University of Minnesota Press, 1995).

25. Verta Taylor and Nancy Whittier, "Analytical Approaches to Social Movement Culture: The Culture of the Women's Movement," in Johnston and Klandermans, *Social Movements and Culture*, 172.

26. William A. Gamson, "Commitment and Agency in Social Movements," *Sociological Forum* 6, no. 1 (1991): 27–50.

27. Taylor and Whittier, "Analytical Approaches to Social Movement Culture," 172–173.

28. Gamson, "Commitment and Agency in Social Movements," 41.

29. Alberto Melucci, *Challenging Codes: Collective Action in the Informative Age* (Cambridge, UK: Cambridge University Press, 1996), 75.

30. Francesca Polletta and James M. Jasper, "Collective Identity and Social Movements," *Annual Review of Sociology* 27 (August 2001): 285.

31. Scoot A. Hunt, Robert D. Benford, and David A. Snow, "Identity Fields: Framing Processes and the Social Construction of Movements' Identities," in Enrique Larana, Hank Johnston, and Joseph R. Gusfield, eds., *New Social Movements: From Ideology to Identity* (Philadelphia: Temple University Press, 1994), 185.

32. See, for example, Alain Touraine, *The Voice and the Eye: An Analysis of Social Movements* (Cambridge, UK: Cambridge University Press); Alberto Melucci, John Keane, and Paul Mier, eds., *Nomads of the Present: Social Movements and Individual Needs in Contemporary Society* (Philadelphia: Temple University Press, 1989); Craig Calhoun, *Social Theory and the Politics of Identity* (Oxford: Blackwell, 1994).

33. Touraine, *The Voice and the Eye*, 81, 96.

34. Melucci et al., *Nomads of the Present*, 35.

35. Calhoun, *Social Theory and the Politics of Identity*, 12, 14.

36. Jean Cohen, "Strategy or Identity: New Theoretical Paradigms and Contemporary Social Movements," in "Social Movements," special issue, *Social Research* 52, no. 4 (1985): 707, 673.
37. Polletta and Jasper, "Collective Identity and Social Movements," 284.
38. Johnston and Klandermans, *Social Movements and Culture*, 5, 12.
39. Donatella Della Porta and Mario Diani, *Social Movements: An Introduction*, 2nd edition (Oxford: Wiley-Blackwell, 2006), 73.
40. Melucci, *Challenging Codes*, 77.
41. Cerulo, "Identity Construction," 387.
42. Peter L. Berger and Thomas Luckmann, *The Social Construction of Reality: A Treatise in Sociology of Knowledge* (New York: Anchor Books, 1967), 194.
43. M. Hakan Yavuz, *Islamic Political Identity in Turkey* (New York: Oxford University Press, 2002), 20.
44. Melucci, *Challenging Codes*, 20.
45. Olivier Roy, *Globalized Islam: The Search for A New Ummah* (New York: Columbia University Press, 1994).
46. Yavuz, *Islamic Political Identity in Turkey*, 23.
47. Melucci, *Challenging Codes*, 67, 76.
48. Ervin Goffman, *Frame Analysis: An Essay on the Organization of Experience* (Cambridge, MA: Harvard University Press, 1974), 21.
49. Robert D. Benford and David A. Snow, "Framing Processes and Social Movements: An Overview and Assessment," *Annual Review of Sociology* 26 (2000): 614.
50. Hasan al-Banna, *Majmou't Rass'il Al-Imam Al-Shahid Hasan al-Banna* (A Collection of Hasan Al-Banna Tracts) (Cairo: Dar Al-Da'wa, 2002), 15, 20, 22.
51. Yavuz, *Islamic Political Identity in Turkey*, 27–31.
52. Melucci, *Challenging Codes*, 315.
53. Ibid., 315.
54. Della Porta and Diani, *Social Movements*, 126.
55. Melucci, *Challenging Codes*, 323.
56. Ibid., 325.
57. The relationship between repression/radicalization and its antithesis, inclusion/moderation, is controversial and has recently become a subject of wide disagreement among scholars. Despite this I believe that the relationship in both theses is not linear or mechanical and that the environment still has a significant impact on movements' ideology, strategy, and tactics. For more on this debate see, for example, Gunes Murat Tezcur, "The Moderation Theory Revisited: The Case of Islamic Political Actors," *Party Politics* 16, no. 1 (2009): 69–88; Jillian Schwedler, "Can Islamists Become Moderates? Rethinking the Inclusion-Moderation Hypothesis," *World Politics* 63, no. 2 (2011): 347–376; Shadi Hamid, *Temptations of Power: Islamists and Illiberal Democracy in a New Middle East* (Oxford: Oxford University Press, 2014).
58. Melucci, *Challenging Codes*, 74.
59. Ibid., 75.

CHAPTER 4

1. See, for example, David Commins, "Hasan al-Banna (1906–1949)," in Ali Rahnema, ed., *Pioneers of Islamic Revival* (London: Zed Books, 1994); Gudrun Krämer, *Hasan al-Banna* (Oxford: One World, 2010). For Arabic resources see Jamal al-Banna, *Khitabat Hasan al-Banna al-Shab ila abihi* (The Young Hasan al-Banna's Letters to His Father) (Cairo: Dar al-Fikr al-Islami, 1990); Ibrahim El-Bayoumi Ghanim, *Al-fikr assiyasi Lil'imam Hasan Al-Banna* (The Political Thought of Hasan Al-Banna) (Cairo: Dar al-Shorouk, 1992).

2. There are many verses in the Qur'an that call Muslims to be united and avoid disputes or divisions. One verse stipulates, "Believers are indeed brothers" (Al-Hujurat, verse 10), and another verse asks Muslims to avoid disputes and differences: "Adhere to the Bond of Allah, together, and do not be divided" (Al-Imran, verse 103).

3. Richard Mitchell, *The Society of Muslim Brothers* (London: Oxford University Press, 1969), 1.

4. Ghanim, *Al-fikr assiyasi lil'imam Hasan Al-Banna*, 140, 141.

5. Ghanim attributes al-Banna's decision to his desire to avoid the strict regulations of the traditional educational system at al-Azhar (ibid., 143).

6. Although al-Banna embraced Sufism in his early years, he later criticized Sufi groups for their quietist and apolitical approach. For more on this see Hamada Ismail, *Hasan Al-Banna and the Society of Muslim Brothers between Religion and Politics 1928–1949* (Cairo: Dar el-Shorouq, 2010), 36.

7. Hourani provides a compelling analysis of the social and educational background of this debate. He asserts that it was a mere result of the social and economic transformations that occurred in Egypt during the rule of Mohamed Ali and his dynasty. Albert Hourani, *Arabic Thought in the Liberal Age, 1798–1939* (Cambridge, UK: Cambridge University Press, 1983), 138–144.

8. According to Hourani, modernists were those who had had a Western-style education, (e.g., Taha Hussein, Qasim Amin, and Ahmad Lutfi al-Sayyid), and Islamic revivalists were those who received a traditional and religious education at al-Azhar (e.g., Jamal al-Din al-Afghani, Mohamed Abdu, Rashid Rida). For more see Hourani, *Arabic Thought in the Liberal Age*, 242.

9. For more on the debate between modernists and Islamic revivalists see Hourani, *Arabic Thought in Liberal Age*.

10. Mustafa Kemal Atatürk (1881–1938) is considered the founder of modern Turkey. He led the Turkish national movement that ended the Ottoman rule of Turkey, which had prevailed for more than four centuries, and replaced it with a national republic. For more on this point see Ghanim, *Al-fikr assiyasi lil'imam Hasan Al-Banna*, 103–110.

11. Gershoni and Jankowski describe the reaction to the removal of the Ottoman caliphate as a "shock at the abrupt termination of such a hallowed Muslim

institution. Egyptians of a traditionalist orientation, in particular, seem to have felt a personal sense of loss and dismay over the end of the Caliphate." Israel Gershoni and James P. Jankowski, *Egypt, Islam, and the Arabs: The Search for Egyptian Nationhood, 1900–1930* (New York: Oxford University Press, 1986), 56.

12. For more on this issue see Martin Kramer, *Islam Assembled: The Advent of the Muslim Congresses* (New York: Columbia University Press, 1986).

13. Ghanim, *Al-fikr assiyasi lil'imam Hasan Al-Banna*, 130.

14. Gershoni and Jankowski, *Egypt, Islam, and the Arabs*, 58.

15. Hasan al-Banna, *Majmuat ar-rasail* (The Epistles of Hasan Al-Banna) (Cairo: Shorouk Press, 2002), 23.

16. Zakariyya Bayumi points out that Egypt had a significant number of Islamic associations and societies after World War I. He estimates this number to be approximately 135 moral, social, and religious societies. However, these groups were mainly preoccupied by religious and social activities without any political role. This might explain why al-Banna chose to establish the Brotherhood instead of joining an existing Islamic society. For more see Zakariyya Bayumi, *Al-Ikhwan al-Muslimon wa'l-jama'at al-Isalmiyya fil-hayah al-Siyasiyya al-Masriyya 1928–1948* (The Muslim Brotherhood and the Islamic Associations in the Egyptian Political Life, 1928–1948) (Cairo: Maktabt Wahba, 1991), 85–87.

17. Al-Banna, *Majmuat ar-rasail*, 25.

18. Al-Banna identified in detail the social and moral problems that overwhelmed Egyptian society during the 1930s. He repeatedly stressed that the only way to recover from these problems and "diseases" was to restore Islamic principles and values in everyday life ("Our Internal Problems in Light of the Islamic Order," in *Majmuat ar-rasail*, 255).

19. Al-Banna, *Majmuat ar-rasail*, 25.

20. Brynjar Lia, *The Society of the Muslim Brothers in Egypt: The Rise of an Islamic Mass Movement 1928–1942* (London: Ithaca Press, 1998), 58, 59.

21. Ghanim, *Al-fikr assiyasi lil'imam Hasan Al-Banna*, 112, 113.

22. Wilfred Cantwell Smith, *Islam in Modern History* (Princeton, NJ: Princeton University Press, 1977), 126.

23. Mohamed Abdullah al-Simman, *Hasan al-Banna: al-rajul wa-l-fikra* (The Man and the Idea) (Cairo: Dar al-Nasr, 1977), 23.

24. This concept is central in the Brotherhood's ideology, and al-Banna was the first Islamic scholar to coin and use this term. To internalize it within the Brotherhood, he determined seven principles of *al-fikra al-islamiyya* that were published on the cover of the Brotherhood's weekly magazine during the 1930s.

25. According to Ghanim, al-Banna was always preoccupied by Egypt's identity crisis. Ghanim highlights al-Banna's tendency to stress and delineate the meaning of identity as a part of everyday life art. Ibrahim El-Bayoumi Ghanim, interview with the author, Cairo, December 24, 2010.

26. Al-Banna, *Majmuat ar-rasail*, 171.

27. Commins, "Hasan al-Banna," 134.
28. Abdullah Essam, interview with author, March 25, 2012.
29. Many scholars hold that al-Banna created a distinctive discourse that enabled the Brotherhood to reach out to different audiences. For more see Lia, *The Society of the Muslim Brothers in Egypt*, 42; Commins, "Hasan al-Banna," 135.
30. Al-Banna, *Majmuat ar-rasail*, 13.
31. Ibid., 171.
32. Ibid., 173, 174.
33. Commins, "Hasan al-Banna," 136.
34. Al-Banna, *Majmuat ar-rasail*, 25.
35. Lia, *The Society of the Muslim Brothers in Egypt*, 140.
36. Al-Banna, *Majmuat ar-rasail*, 42.
37. Al-Banna's epistles encompass a clear and sophisticated platform for comprehensive reform. In a well-known tract called "Our Internal Problems in Light of the Islamic Order," he extensively analyzes the problems that Egypt faced and proposed solutions in a petition sent to King Farouk and Egypt's prime minister Mustafa al-Nahas (in *Majmuat ar-rasail*, 209).
38. To create this paradigm I read tracts and statements by al-Banna. That is, the seven components or elements of the *jama'a* paradigm are drawn from al-Banna's thoughts and ideas about *al-fikra al-islamiyya*. Some of them were explicitly mentioned in the tracts; others I deduced from al-Banna's speeches and essays published in the Brotherhood's publications.
39. Al-Banna, *Majmuat ar-rasail*, 168.
40. Robert Bemford and David Snow, "Framing Processes and Social Movements: An Overview and Assessment," *Annual Review of Sociology* 26: 614.
41. Al-Banna, *Majmuat ar-rasail*, 145–160.
42. Melucci, *Challenging Codes: Collective Action in The Information Age* (Cambridge: Cambridge University Press, 1996), 320.
43. Al-Banna, *Majmuat ar-rasail*, 114, 115, 116.
44. Ibid., 45.
45. Ibid., 48, 65.
46. Ibid., 161, 336, 188, 187.
47. Ibid., 178.
48. Munson points out the Brotherhood had over 2,000 branches throughout Egypt, with an active membership of 300,000 to 600,000 by 1949. For more details about the spread of the Brotherhood during the 1930s and 1940s see Ziad Munson, "Islamic Mobilization: Social Movement Theory and the Egyptian Muslim Brotherhood," *Sociological Quarterly* 42, no. 4 (2001): 487–510.
49. Al-Banna, *Majmuat ar-rasail*, 101.
50. Ibid., 174.
51. Mohamed Badie, "Oh, Brothers: Let's Work," *Weekly Statement*, March 31, 2011, http://www.ikhwanismailia.com/ismailia/12345.html, 174.

52. Zakaria Bayumi, *Al-Ikhwan al-Muslimon wa'l-jama'at al-Isalmiyya fil-hayah al-Siyasiyya al-Masriyya 1928–1948* (Cairo: Maktabt Wahba, 1991), 75–82.

53. Salah Ghorab, interview with author, Cairo, December 28, 2011.

54. The Fifth Annual Conference of the Brotherhood was a hallmark in the movement's history. It was the first conference after the remarkable growth of the Brotherhood, when the number of local branches jumped from five in 1930 to fifteen in 1931, then to 300 in 1938. The conference also marks a shift in the Brotherhood's strategy from being politically inactive to being a political force. It is after this conference that al-Banna decided to enter parliamentary elections and reveal the Brotherhood's political agenda and aspirations. For more see Hasan al-Banna, *Majmuat ar-rasail*, 165.

CHAPTER 5

1. Salah Abdul Halim, interview with author, December 26, 2011.

2. Samer S. Shehata, "Political *Da'wa*: Understanding the Muslim Brotherhood's Participation in Semi-Authoritarian Elections," in Samer S. Shehata, ed., *Islamist Politics in the Middle East: Movements and Change* (London: Routledge), 120.

3. Salah Abdul Halim, interview with author, December 28, 2010.

4. Wickham, *Mobilizing Islam: Religion, Activism, and Political Change in Egypt* (New York: Columbia University Press, 2002) 160.

5. Ibid., 152.

6. Abdul Khaliq Al-Sherif, interview with author, April 5, 2012.

7. Most of these schools were closed by the government after the coup of July 3, 2013.

8. Traditionally *du'ah* should acquire a sophisticated religious knowledge and education. However, most *du'ah* in Islamist movements are professionals with non-religious educational backgrounds (e.g., teachers, lawyers, engineers). For them preaching, or making *da'wa*, is not about religion per se but rather about creating an active member who can change society.

9. Al-Sherif interview.

10. Al-Banna, *Majmou't Rass'il Al-Imam Al-Shahid Hasan Al-Banna* (A Collection of Hasan Al-Banna Messages) (Cairo: Dar Al-Da'wa Publications, 2002), 178.

11. In the Fifth Conference epistle, al-Banna stressed the necessity of spreading the Brotherhood's ideology throughout the country in villages and cities (ibid., 120).

12. Eslam Ahmed, interview with author, January 11, 2012.

13. Mustafa Mashhur, *Ad-da'wa al-Fardiyya* (The Individual Call) (Cairo: Dar Ammar, 1990), 22.

14. Al-Banna, *Majmuat ar-rasail*, 179.

15. Bert Klandermans and Dirk Oegema, "Potentials, Networks, Motivations and Barriers: Steps towards Participation in Social Movements," *American Sociological Review* 52, no. 4 (1987): 519.

16. Sherif Ayman, interview with author, January 12, 2012.

17. Klandermans and Oegema, "Potentials, Networks, Motivations and Barriers," 520.
18. Ahmed interview.
19. Al-Banna, *Majmuat ar-rasail*, 179.
20. Abdul Halim al-Kinani, *Ad-da'wa al-Fardiyya bayin an-nazriyya wa-tatbiq* (The Individual Call between Theory and Practice) (Cairo: Dar Iqra', 2007), 15.
21. Alaa Muharram, "Essential Tools for the Individual Call," February 15, 2012, http://www.ikhwanonline.com/new/Article.aspx?ArtID=69083&SecID=0.
22. Al-Sherif interview.
23. Ayman interview.
24. Mashhur, *Ad-da'wa al-Fardiyya*, 24.
25. Ibid., 25.
26. Fathi Yakan is the former secretary general of the Lebanese Islamic Group (al-Jama'ah al-Islamiyya) and an influential leader who wrote many books and epistles that are widely read among Islamists.
27. Mashhur, *Ad-da'wa al-Fardiyya*, 27.
28. Ayman interview.
29. Florence Passy, "Socialization, Connection, and the Structure/Agency Gap: A Specification of the Impact of Networks on Participation in Social Movements," *Mobilization* 6, no. 2 (2001): 173–192.
30. Abdurrahman Ayyash, interview with author, January 14, 2012.
31. Ayman interview.
32. Abdelmoniem Aboul Fottouh is a key leader who rebuilt the Brotherhood in the 1970s after the imprisonment of senior leaders during the 1950s and 1960s. He was expelled from the movement in 2011 when he decided to run for the Egyptian presidency after the January 25 uprising. For more on his role see Hossam Tammam, *Abuel Fottouh: Shahid ala al-haraka al-islamiyya min 1970 ila 1984* (Abuel Fottouh: A Witness on the Islamist Movement from 1970 to 1984) (Cairo: Shorouk Press, 2010).
33. Ammar El-Beltagi, interview with author, March 28, 2012.
34. Marriage within the Brotherhood is a key feature of the movement's social base. Since its foundation in the early 1930s, the Sisters Section (Qism al-Akhawat) has played an important role in facilitating and maintaining marriage and kinship relationships within the movement. Fatima Abdelhady, the first secretary of the Sisters Section, points out her role in facilitating the marriage of many leaders. For more see, Fatima Abdelhady, *Rihlati ma' al-Akhawat al-Muslimat* (My Journey With the Muslim Sisters) (Cairo: Shorouk Press, 2011), 38.
35. Noha El-Hennawy, A split in the Muslim Brotherhood? Not so easy, *Egypt Independent*, April 17, 2011, http://www.egyptindependent.com//news/split-muslim-brotherhood-not-so-easy, *Al-Masry Al-Youm*, May 24, 2011.
36. Mohamed Ayoub, interview with author, April 3, 2012.
37. Mohamed Yussif, interview with author, March 29, 2012.
38. Wickham, *Mobilizing Islam*, 247.

CHAPTER 6

1. See, for example, William A. Gamson, "The Social Psychology of Collective Action," in Aldon Morris and Carol Mueller, eds., *Frontiers in Social Movement Theory* (New Haven, CT: Yale University Press,1992); Jeff Goodwin, James M. Jasper, and Francesca Polletta, *Passionate Politics: Emotions and Social Movements* (Chicago: University of Chicago Press, 2001); Jeff Goodwin and James M. Jasper, *Rethinking Social Movements: Structure, Meaning, and Emotion* (Oxford: Rowman & Littlefield, 2003).

2. Al-Banna, *Majmou't Rass'il Al-Imam Al-Shahid Hasan Al-Banna* (A Collection of Hasan Al-Banna Messages) (Cairo: Dar Al-Da'wa Publications, 2002), 44.

3. Abdelhamid El-Ghazali, *The Way to the Revival of the Muslim Ummah: A Study of the Thinking of Imam al-Banna* (Cairo: Al-Falah Foundation), 128, 130.

4. Ali Abdul Halim Mahmoud, *Wasa'il al-Taribiyya 'ind al-Ikhwan al- muslmiyyn* (*Tarbiyya* tools in the Muslim Brotherhood) (Cairo, Dar al-Tawzi' wal' Nashr al-Islamiyya, 1997), 11.

5. Interview with Mohamed Badie by Abdelgalil Al-Sharnoubi, March 7, 2010, http://www.dakahliaikhwan.com/viewarticle.php?id=4041.

6. Sherif Ayman, interview with author, March 26, 2012.

7. Amer Shemakh, "Al-tarbiyya al-islamiyya dakhil al-ikhwan al-muslmiyyn" (The Islamic *Tarbiyya* in the Muslim Brotherhood), March 27, 2011, http://www.ikhwanonline.com/new/Article.aspx?ArtID=90818&SecID=0.

8. Al-Banna, *Majmuat ar-rasail*, 92, 94.

9. Mohamed Hamza, interview with author, February 12, 2012.

10. Mohamed Yussif, interview with author, March 29, 2012.

11. Abdurrahman Mansour, interview with author, March 26, 2012.

12. Mohamed Mustafa, interview with author, March 28, 2012.

13. Ibid.

14. Interview with Mohamed al-Qassas by Noha El-Hennawy, *Egypt Independent*, April 17, 2011.

15. Mohamed Abdul Rahman, *Manhaj al-islah wataghiyyir fi al-ikhwan al- muslmiyyn* (The Approach of Reform and Change in the Muslim Brothers) (Cairo, Dar al-Tawzi' wal' Nashr al-Islamiyya, 2006), 25.

16. Abdurrahman Ayyash, interview with author, January 12, 2012.

17. Some accounts claim that al-Banna founded *kata'ib* units to prepare Brotherhood members for *jihad*, particularly against Israel in the 1940s. It is also believed that the *kata'ib* system was the cornerstone in establishing the Secret Apparatus, the military wing of the Brotherhood.

18. Mahmoud Abdul Halim, *Al-Ikhwan al-Muslimun: Ahdath sana'at al-tarikh* (The Muslim Brotherhood: Events That Made History) (Alexandria: Dar al-Da'wa, 1979), 150.

19. Ibid., 152.

20. Ibrahim Saleh, interview with author, March 30, 2012.

21. Mustafa interview.

22. According to Brynjar Lia, al-Banna established the Rover Scout units in the mid-1930s, and they were officially registered in the Egyptian National Scout Movement in 1938–1939. The functions of the Rover Scouts were to recruit new members through sporting activities, to maintain order and security in large meetings and conferences, and to prepare Brotherhood members to resist British imperialism and Zionism. For more see Brynjar Lia, *The Society of the Muslim Brothers in Egypt: The Rise of an Islamic Mass Movement 1928–1942* (London: Ithaca Press, 1999), 170–172. However, Lia points out that the Rover Scouts were rarely involved in militant activities: "The Rover Scout served as a reservoir of trained youth who could easily be rallied to social welfare services and public health projects which became a preoccupation of the Society during the war [World War II]" (172). The Brotherhood's 1944 bylaws outline the organization, membership, and structure of Rovers Scouts. According to Abdul Halim, the Brotherhood had many scout teams by the end of the 1930s. This is when it became mandatory for all members to join Rover Scout branches, including al-Banna himself, who led Rover Scouts in national ceremonies and celebrations (Mahmoud, *Wasa'il al-Taribiyya 'ind al-Ikhwan al- muslmiyyn*, 280).

23. Mahmoud, *Wasa'il al-Taribiyya 'ind al-Ikhwan al- muslmiyyn*, 282.

24. Ibid., 282–284.

25. Mohamed Soliman, interview with author, March 29, 2012.

26. Salah Abdul Halim, interview with author, December 28, 2010.

27. Mahmoud, *Wasa'il al-Taribiyya 'ind al-Ikhwan al- muslmiyyn*, 283.

28. Sherif Ayman, interview with author, January 12, 2012.

29. Mahmoud, *Wasa'il al-Taribiyya 'ind al-Ikhwan al- muslmiyyn*, 306–310.

30. *Bay'a* is an Islamic term that derives from the Qur'an. It refers to an oath given by a subordinate to his leader as a token of allegiance and was practiced by the Prophet Muhammad.

31. This degree was added to the bylaws in 1935 and sowed the seeds of the Special Apparatus (Al-tanzim al-hhas), the military arm of the Brotherhood, which became operationally active in the beginning of the 1940s.

32. Article 7 of the 1951 Bylaws specifies that the candidate should be eighteen years of age, honorable and upright, able to comprehend the ideas of the Brotherhood, willing to pay membership dues, and willing to swear an oath to the Brotherhood, Richard Mitchell, *The Society of Muslim Brothers* (London: Oxford University Press, 1969) 183.

33. Ibid., 183–184.

34. Mitchell, *The Society of Muslim Brothers*; Lia, *The Society of the Muslim Brothers in Egypt*.

35. Eslam Ahmed, interview with author, January 11, 2012.

36. Abdurrahman Ayyash, interview with author, January 11, 2012.

37. Ahmed interview.
38. Abdurrahman Ayyash, interview with author, January 12, 2012.
39. Mansur interview.
40. Ahmed interview.
41. Ayyash interview, January 12, 2012.
42. Ayman interview, March 26, 2012.
43. Ayyash interview, January 12, 2012.
44. Interview with author, Ammar El-Beltagi, March 28, 2012.
45. Mansur interview.
46. Ahmed interview.
47. Al-Banna, *Majmuat ar-rasail*, 211.
48. Ibid., 212.

CHAPTER 7

1. Mitchell, *The Society of Muslim Brothers*; Lia, *The Society of the Muslim Brothers in Egypt*.
2. See, for example, Mona El-Ghobashi, "The Metamorphosis of the Egyptian Muslim Brothers" *International Journal of Middle East Studies* 37, no. 1 (2005): 373–395; Nathan Brown, *When Victory Is Not an Option: Islamist Movements in Arab Politics* (Ithaca, NY: Cornell University Press, 2012); Carrie Rosefsky Wickham, *The Muslim Brotherhood: Evolution of an Islamist Movement* (Princeton, NJ: Princeton University Press, 2013).
3. See, for example, Doug McAdam, John D. McCarthy, and Mayer N. Zald, *Comparative Perspectives on Social Movements: Political Opportunities, Mobilizing Structures, and Cultural Framings* (Cambridge, UK: Cambridge University Press, 1996); Donatella Della Porta and Mario Diani, *Social Movements: An Introduction* (Massachusetts: Blackwell Publishing, 2006).
4. Della Porta and Diani, *Social Movements*, 137, 138.
5. See, for example, David S. Meyer, Nancy Whittier, and Belinda Robnett, *Social Movements: Identity, Culture and the State* (Oxford: Oxford University Press, 2002); Jo Reger, "Organizational Dynamics and Construction of Multiple Feminist Identities in the National Organization for Women," *Gender and Society* 16, no. 5 (2002): 710–726.
6. Mayer N. Zald and John David McCarthy, *Social Movements in an Organizational Society: Collected Essays* (Piscataway: Transaction Books, 1987), 134.
7. Melucci, *Challenging Codes: Collective Action in the Informative Age* (Cambridge, UK: Cambridge University Press, 1996), 314.
8. Ibid., 317.
9. Zald and McCarthy, *Social Movements in an Organizational Society*, 20.
10. Della Porta and Diani, *Social Movements*, 145–149.
11. Melucci, *Challenging Codes*, 326–327.

12. Al-Banna, *Majmou't Rass'il Al-Imam Al-Shahid Hasan Al-Banna* (A Collection of Hasan Al-Banna Messages) (Cairo: Dar Al-Da'wa Publications, 2002), 168, 169.

13. Brown, *When Victory Is Not an Option*, 66, 67.

14. Mitchell calls this axis the "technical" or operational level, which is mainly responsible for executing and implementing the Brotherhood's plans and programs. He divides this level into the administrative machinery of the movement, consisting of different committees (*lijan*; e.g., financial, policy, legal, statistics, and services), and the sections (*aqsam*), which are concerned with ideology and indoctrination (e.g., propagation section [*nashr al-da'wa*], students; Mitchell, *The Society of Muslim Brothers*, 170).

15. Mohamed Mustafa, interview with author, April 1, 2012.

16. The Brotherhood's bylaws were amended many times over the past three decades. This section is based on the amendments that were made in May 2009 and were significant particularly in identifying the structure and tasks of each organizational level. See the Brotherhood's internal bylaws, March 11, 2012, http://www.egyptwindow.net/news_Details.aspx?News_ID=17766.

17. Usually *shu'ba* includes members who live in a specific geographical area and receives names based on this area.

18. Historically the general guide selected the head of the *shu'ba*. But since 2005 internal elections have taken place within the Brotherhood on all levels. Mohamed Hamza, interview with author, January 11, 2012.

19. Each governorate has a Shura Council (Majlis al-Shura muhafza) that consists of a number of active members determined by the Guidance Bureau and based on the number of members in that governorate. Members of the governorate's Shura Council should be at least thirty years old and have been active members for at least five years. The term of each council is four years. The Guidance Bureau has the authority to appoint a number of members in the governorate's Shura Council, not to exceed one-fifth of the total and after consulting with the Administrative Office.

20. During the Mubarak era the Brotherhood could not hold the Shura Council's election. The last election was held in 1995, when the security forces raided the Council's first meeting and arrested many of its members. After the January 25 uprising the Brotherhood was able not only to hold the Shura Council elections but also to make its meetings public. After the coup of July 3, 2013, and the arrest of many of its senior members, the movement again could not hold Shura Council meetings.

21. The actual number of members in the Guidance Bureau used to be more than nineteen. This was mainly because of the arrest of members and the inability to conduct elections to choose their successors. For example, between 1995 and 2008 the number reached twenty-one, but many of them were arrested and kept their membership.

22. One of the key criticisms of the Brotherhood is the old age of the Guidance Bureau members, who used to be in their fifties and sixties. The only exception to this was Mohi El-Din Hamed, who joined the Guidance Bureau after being elected in 2008, when he was thirty-eight.

23. The bylaws allow the Guidance Bureau to make exceptions on the second and third conditions (membership in the Shura Council and membership in the Brotherhood for ten years) when they appoint the three additional members. However, this is contingent upon the approval of at least eleven elected members.

24. Hamza interview.

25. This rule remains theoretical as many members in the Guidance Bureau were imprisoned for years without losing their membership. In fact the opposite has happened: members who are arrested remain in the Guidance Bureau as a sign of appreciation for their sacrifice and solidarity with them.

26. Some media reports and analysts erroneously call *al-Murshid al-'Am* the supreme guide, confusing him with Iran's supreme guide (*al-Murshid al-A'la*). Linguistically *general guide* is more accurate and reflects the English translation of the Arabic phrase *al-Murshid al-'Am*.

27. Although it is not stipulated in the bylaws, the general guide receives a monthly salary from the Brotherhood so that he can focus on serving the movement.

28. According to the old bylaws, the general guide remained in his position until death. Therefore the movement has had only eight general guides during its eighty-seven years of existence.

29. Mohamed Mustafa, interview with author, April 3, 2012.

30. Khalil al-Anani, "Who Is Running the Brotherhood?," *Al-Hayat*, April 17, 2014.

31. To avoid the conceptualization polemic of ideology, this study treats ideology as an operational concept, or a "cover term for [a] relatively stable and coherent set of values, beliefs, and goals associated with a movement or a broader, encompassing social entity, and is assumed to provide the rationale for defending or challenging various social arrangements and conditions." David Snow, "Framing Processes, Ideology, and Discursive Fieds," in D. Snow, S. Soule, and H. Kriesi (eds.), *The Blackwell Companion to Social Movements* (Oxford: Blackwell, 380–412, 409).

32. See, for example, Stathis N. Kalyvas, *The Rise of Christian Democracy in Europe* (Ithaca, NY: Cornell University Press, 1996).

33. Brown, *When Victory Is Not an Option*, 73.

34. Said Hawwa, *Jundu' Allah Tanzimann* (Organized Soldiers of God) (Cairo: Maktabbat Wahba, 2004), 15, 51–52, 54. Hawwa (1935–1989) joined the Brotherhood while he was in high school and became one of its eminent leaders during the 1970s and 1980s. Islamists regard him as one of the most influential ideologues and theorists in the Brotherhood. He published about fifteen books, which are widely used by branches around the world. His most important books are a series on *Jund Allah* (Soldiers of God), which are studied in the Brotherhood's circles and are part of its *tarbiyya* curriculum.

35. Fathi Yakan, *Abjadiat at-tassur al-haraki lil' amal al'-Islami* (The Fundamentals of Islamic Activism) (Beirut: Muassasat Ar-Risala, 1981), 14. Yakan (1933–2009) was one of the most influential ideologues of Islamist movements modeled on the Brotherhood. He was born in Tripoli and was one of the founders of the Islamic Action Front in Lebanon in the 1950s and the leader of the Islamic Group (al-Jama'a al-Islamiyya) movement. According to Sebastian Elsässer, "Yakan is regarded as one of the most important contemporary protagonists of Muslim. Furthermore, many Islamists regard Yakan as the mastermind of Islamic activism and pragmatism. His books focus primarily on Islamic activism, organization, and socialization in Islamist movements." Sebastian Elsässer, "Between Ideology and Pragmatism: Fathi Yakan's Theory of Islamic Activism," *Die Welt des Islams* 47, no. 3 (2007): 376–402.

36. Ziad Munson, "Islamic Mobilization: Social Movement Theory and the Egyptian Muslim Brotherhood." *The Sociological Quarterly* 42, no. 4 (2001): 487–510, 498.

37. Esaam al-Erian Interview with author, December 24, 2010.

38. Brown, *When Victory Is Not an Option*, 72.

39. Ibid., 67.

40. An interview with Sayyid El-Melegi, *Al-Masry Al-Youm*, July 24, 2008.

41. I explain this point further in chapter 9.

42. Haitham Abu Khalil, *Ikhwan Islahiyun* (Reformist Brothers) (Cairo: Dawwin House, 2012), 38.

43. Husam Tammam, *Tahwlat al-Ikhwan al-Muslimin* (The Transformations of the Muslim Brotherhood) (Cairo: Maktabat Madbouli, 2010).

44. Ibid., 34.

45. Strikingly the Muslim Sister Section is not mentioned in the Brotherhood's current bylaws. While some interviewees justified this absence by the fear of regime repression against Sisters, others believe it reflects the marginalization of women inside the Brotherhood.

46. Omayma Abdel-Latif, "In the Shadow of the Brothers: The Women of the Egyptian Muslim Brotherhood," *Carnegie Papers*, no. 13 (Washington, DC: Carnegie Endowment for International Peace, 2008), 10.

47. Mahmoud Ezzat, the deputy general guide, asserts that the best place for a woman is in her house as a wife and a mother. He believes women should not undertake administrative tasks, which are beyond their physiological capacity. An interview with Mahmoud Ezzat, Ikhwan Online, December 16, 2004, http://www.ikhwanwiki.com/index.php?title=%D8%A5%D8%B4%D9%83% D8%A7%D9%84%D9%8A%D8%A7%D8%AA_%D8%B9%D9%85%D9%84_ %D8%A7%D9%84%D8%A3%D8%AE%D9%88%D8%A7%D8%AA_ %D8%B9%D9%84%D9%89_%D9%85%D9%83%D8%AA%D8%A8_%D8% A7%D9%84%D8%A5%D8%B1%D8%B4%D8%A7%D8%AF#.D8.A7.D9.84. D9.85.D8.B5.D8.AF.D8.B1.

48. Abdel-Latif, "In the Shadow of the Brothers," 10.

49. Some historians and scholars argue that al-Banna was influenced by fascism and similar movements that emerged in Europe during the 1930s. They claim he admired the nationalist and totalitarian structure of these movements. See, for example, Ana Belen Soage, "Hasan al-Banna or the Politicization of Islam," *Totalitarian Movements and Political Religions* 9, no. 1 (2008): 21–42. On Islamism and totalitarianism see, for example, Michael Whine, "Islamism and Totalitarianism: Similarities and Differences," *Totalitarian Movements and Political Religions* 2, no. 2 (2001): 54–72; Hendrik Hansen and Peter Kainz, "Radical Islamism and Totalitarian Ideology: A Comparison of Sayyid Qutb's Islamism with Marxism and National Socialism," *Totalitarian Movements and Political Religions* 8, no. 1 (2007): 55–76.

50. Several interviewees agreed on the lack of internal accountability in the Brotherhood. Some blamed this on the repressive environment wherein the Brotherhood operates; others relate it to the movement's internal norms and regulations.

51. Abu Khalil, *Ikhwan Islahiyun*, 36.

52. Tammam, *Tahwlat al-Ikhwan al-Muslimin*, 34.

CHAPTER 8

1. Melucci, *Challenging Codes: Collective Action in the Informative Age* (Cambridge, UK: Cambridge University Press, 1996), 317, 318.

2. This section draws upon the study of leadership and *bay'a* in the Brotherhood by Ella Landau-Tasseron, "Leadership and Allegiance in the Society of the Muslim Brothers," *Research Monographs on the Muslim World*, no. 2 (December 2010). Landau-Tasseron provides a sophisticated historical account of the role of *bay'a* in the Brotherhood, particularly during al-Banna's era (the 1930s and 1940s).

3. The term *bay'a* appears repeatedly in the Qur'an in different contexts. Historically *bay'a* was an Islamic tradition, "a pledge exchanged with a leader, entailing obligations of leaders and the led, towards one another" (ibid., 2). Muslim caliphs and sultans used to be given *bay'a* by the *'ulama* (*ahl al-hal wa'l-aqd*), and then by the entire society, or *umma*.

4. Ibid., 1.

5. It is stated in the Qur'an that the Prophet Muhammad took *bay'a* from those who converted to Islam: "Those who exchange pledges with you [Muhammad], it is with Allah that they exchange them" (48:10). Landau-Tasseron highlights that al-Banna was smart enough to deliberately invoke and emulate the Prophet when he established the Brotherhood: "Like the Prophet in his time al-Bannā created an enclave, that is, a new society that consolidated around an ideology and a way of life and separated itself as far as it could from the society in which it lived" ("Leadership and Allegiance in the Society of the Muslim Brothers," 5).

6. Cited in Landau-Tasseron, "Leadership and Allegiance in the Society of the Muslim Brothers," 1.

7. Landau-Tasseron highlights the link between the emergence of the concept of *bay'a* and the Sufi character of al-Banna. She points out that the relationship between al-Banna and his followers resembles the spiritual relationship between the Sufi sheikh and his followers. Hence al-Banna chose for his title general guide (*al-murshid al-'am*), similar to a Sufi sheikh being called *murshid* ("Leadership and Allegiance in the Society of the Muslim Brothers," 3–4).

8. Al-Banna, *Majmou't Rass'il Al-Imam Al-Shahid Hasan Al-Banna* (A Collection of Hasan Al-Banna Messages) (Cairo: Dar Al-Da'wa Publications, 2002), 185.

9. Many Brotherhood ideologues consider *bay'a* the most important norm. For instance, Hawwa treats *bay'a* as the core value and norm of the Brotherhood in order to achieve its goals. Although Hawwa views *bay'a* as nonbinding, he believes that it is the only way to solidify and strengthen the Brotherhood's organization, Said Hawwa, *Jundu' Allah Tanzimann* (Cairo, Maktabbat Wahba, 1988), 101.

10. Quoted in Richard Mitchell, *The Society of Muslim Brothers* (London: Oxford University Press, 1969), 165.

11. The main distinctions between these bylaws are the oath of *bay'a* and membership criteria. For instance, the first bylaw in 1930 did not mention the *bay'a*, which was added in 1944. In the 1990s *bay'a* was removed from the bylaws, along with the degrees of membership. Landau-Tasseron posits that this removal was the result of members' familiarity with the movement's regulations and norms, but I contend that it was due to the Brotherhood's security obsession. Revealing the levels of membership could imperil members and allow security forces to monitor and arrest them.

12. Ammar El-Beltagi, interview with author, March 26, 2012.

13. Abdurrahman Ayyash, interview with author, March 26, 2012.

14. Mohamed Mustafa, interview with author, April 1, 2012.

15. Landau-Tasseron, "Leadership and Allegiance in the Society of the Muslim Brothers," 12.

16. Mohamed Ayoub, interview with author, March 27, 2012.

17. The internal bylaws of the Muslim Brotherhood can be found at http://www.egyptwindow.net/news_Details.aspx?News_ID=17766.

18. An Interview with Karim Radwan, *Al-Masry Al-Youm*, July 15, 2012.

19. Abdul Rahman al-Barr, "Bay'at al-murshid wa bay'at ar-raiys" (The Allegiance of the General Guide and Allegiance of the President), April 3, 2013, http://dakahliaikhwan.com/viewarticle.php?id=13503.

20. Al-Barr was defending President Mohamed Morsi, whose *bay'a* to the Brotherhood's general guide, Mohamed Badie, created controversy over his relationship with the movement. After the elections he had to break his *bay'a*, and Badie publicly released him from his pledges and commitment to the Brotherhood. See the video of Badie at http://www.youtube.com/watch?v=TfoyRRmKKus.

21. According to Mustafa (interview), rejection of the leadership's commands is not considered a violation of *bay'a* and does not necessarily result in the termination of an individual's membership. However, it reflects his lack of commitment and can complicate his future prospects for promotion in the movement.

22. Landau-Tasseron, "Leadership and Allegiance in the Society of the Muslim Brothers," 17.

23. Ayoub interview.

24. Landau-Tasseron, "Leadership and Allegiance in the Society of the Muslim Brothers," 24.

25. Many Quranic verses and prophetic traditions urge Muslims to obey their leaders. Historically some Muslim caliphs and sultans abused the principle of *ta'a* to prolong their rule and suppress opposition.

26. Al-Banna, *Majmuat ar-rasail*, 185.

27. Landau-Tasseron, "Leadership and Allegiance in the Society of the Muslim Brothers," 7.

28. Amer Shemakh, "Obedience in the Muslim Brotherhood," July 12, 2012, http://www.ikhwanonline.com/new/Article.aspx?ArtID=90818&SecID=0.

29. Mustafa interview.

30. Four members resign from the Brotherhood, *El-Badil*, July 12, 2012, http://elbadil.com/2012/04/01/35353/.

31. Mustafa al-Naggar, "The Muslim Brotherhood between the Public and the Private," http://2mwag.blogspot.co.uk/2009/06/blog-post_15.html.

32. Mohamed Hamza, interview with author, January 11, 2012.

33. Ayyash interview.

34. The internal rifts are discussed in greater detail in chapter 7.

35. Ayyash interview.

36. Ayman Ashraf, interview with author, March 28, 2012.

37. Mohamed Hamza, interview with author, January 12, 2012.

38. Anwar Hamed, "Awaraq min waq' ashtuh" (Papers from the Reality I Lived), July 10, 2012, http://2mwag.blogspot.co.uk/search/label/%D9%86%D9%82%D8%AF%20%D8%B0%D8%A7%D8%AA%D9%8A.

39. Al-Banna, *Majmuat ar-rasail*, 190.

40. Mohamed Hamed Eliwa, "*Thiqa* as a Pillar of our *Da'wa*," July 12, 2012, http://www.ikhwanonline.com/new/Article.aspx?ArtID=86931&SecID=373.

41. Emad Ghanim, "Trust as a Pillar of Allegiance in the Muslim Brotherhood," July 12, 2012, http://www.ikhwan.net/forum/showthread.php?16788.

42. Mustafa interview.

43. Hamza interview, January 11, 2012.

44. Abdurrahman Mansour, interview with author, March 26, 2012.

45. Amr Soliman, interview with author, March 25, 2012.

46. Peter J. Burke and Jan E. Stets, "Trust and Commitment through Self-Verification," *Social Psychology Quarterly* 62, no. 4 (1999): 348.

47. Melucci, *Challenging Codes*, 318.

48. Francesca Polletta and James M. Jasper, "Collective Identity and Social Movements," *Annual Review of Sociology* 27 (August 2001): 292.
49. Salah Ghorab, interview with author, December 24, 2012.
50. Mohamed al-Naggar, interview with author, April 3, 2012.
51. Sherif Ayman, interview with author, March 26, 2012.
52. Sayyid Shoa'iyb, "What Does My Commitment to the Brotherhood Mean?," July 12, 2012, http://www.daawa-info.net/article.php?id=686.
53. Mohamed Sarhan, interview with author, April 2, 2012.
54. Al-Banna, *Majmuat ar-rasail*, 35.
55. Fathi Yakan, *What Does My Belonging to Islam Mean?* (Beirut: Mu'assasat ar-Risala, 1983), 137–140.
56. Shoa'iyb, "What Does My Commitment to the Brotherhood Mean?"
57. Sarhan interview.
58. Ayyash interview.
59. Mohamed al-Naggar interview.
60. Sherif Ayman, interview with author, January 12, 2012.
61. Melucci, *Challenging Codes*, 312.
62. Salah Ghorab, interview with author, December 24, 2010.
63. Husam Tammam, *The Muslim Brotherhood: The Years before the Revolution* (Cairo: Shorouk Press, 2012), 48.
64. Mustafa interview.
65. Hamza interview, January 11, 2012.

CHAPTER 9

1. Since the end of the 1970s many authoritarian regimes have become semi-authoritarian, hybrid, or competitive-authoritarian systems that attempt to maintain power by ostensibly democratic means but with no genuine changes. See, for example, Andreas Schedler, "Elections without Democracy: The Menu of Manipulation," *Journal of Democracy* 13, no. 2 (2002): 36–50; Jason Brownlee, *Authoritarianism in the Age of Democratization* (New York: Cambridge University Press, 2007); Steven Levitsky and Lucan A. Way, *Competitive Authoritarianism: Hybrid Regimes after the Cold War* (New York: Cambridge University Press, 2010); Lisa Blaydes, *Elections and Distributive Politics in Mubarak's Egypt* (New York: Cambridge University Press, 2013).
2. Schedler, "Elections without Democracy," 36.
3. Blaydes, *Elections and Distributive Politics in Mubarak's Egypt*, 1.
4. Melucci, *Challenging Codes: Collective Action in the Informative Age* (Cambridge, UK: Cambridge University Press, 1996) 323.
5. Hanspeter Kriesi, "Political Context and Opportunity," in David A. Snow, Sarah A. Soule, and Hanspeter Kriesi, eds., *The Blackwell Companion to Social Movements* (Oxford: Blackwell, 2004), 74.

6. See, for example, Sidney Tarrow, *Power in Movement: Social Movements and Contentious Politics* (Cambridge, UK: Cambridge University Press, 1998); Doug McAdam, John D. McCarthy, and Mayer N. Zald, eds., *Comparative Perspectives on Social Movements* (Cambridge, UK: Cambridge University Press, 1996).

7. Manuel Castells, *The Power of Identity: The Information Age, Economy, Society, and Culture* (Oxford: Wiley-Blackwell, 2010), 2: 9.

8. Several liberal and leftists parties witnessed schism and splits under Mubarak, including the Al-Ahrar Party and the Al-Ghad Party.

9. See, for example, Mai Kassem, *Egyptian Politics: The Dynamics of Authoritarian Rule* (Boulder, CO: Lynne Rienner, 2004); Brownlee, *Authoritarianism in the Age of Democratization*; Blaydes, *Elections and Distributive Politics in Mubarak's Egypt.*

10. Hesham Al-Awadi, *In Pursuit of Legitimacy: The Muslim Brothers and Mubarak, 1982–2000* (London: I.B.Tauris, 2004).

11. For more on this, see Carrie Rosefesky Wickham, *Moblizing Islam: Religion, Activism, and Political Change in Egypt* (New York: Columbia University Press, 2002); Mona El-Ghobashy, "The Metamorphosis of the Egyptian Muslim Brothers," *International Journal of Middle East Studies* 37(1) (2005): 373–395.

12. El-Ghobashy, "The Metamorphosis of the Egyptian Muslim Brothers," 380.

13. Ibid., 384.

14. Wickham, *Mobilizing Islam*, 3.

15. Al-Awadi, *In Pursuit of Legitimacy*, 189.

16. Esam al-'Aryan, interview with author, December 25, 2010.

17. Nathan Brown, *When Victory Is Not An Option: Islamist Movements In Arab Politics* (New York: Cornell University Press, 2012), 85.

18. Essam El-Din Gamal, "Brotherhood Steps into the Fray," *Al-Ahram Weekly*, March 11–17, 2004.

19. The initiative can be found at this link (in Arabic): http://www.aljazeera.net/specialfiles/pages/a7d9e130-0f09-4b77-bbb0-ee07dd61afd3.

20. The Kefaya movement was established in 2004 by various political activists and forces, including the Brotherhood. Its main objective was to end Mubarak's reign and prevent the succession of his son, Gamal. For more see Nadia Oweidat, Cheryl Benard, Dale Stahl, Walid Kildani, Edward O'Connell, and Audra K. Grant, "The Kefaya Movement: A Case Study Of A Grassroots Reform Initiative," (Washington, DC: Rand Corporation, 2008).

21. For more on the inclusion-moderation hypothesis, see Carrie Rosefsky Wickham, "The Path to Moderation: Strategy and Learning in the Formation of Egypt's Wasat Party," *Comparative Politics* 36, no. 2 (2004): 205–228; Jillian Schwedler, *Faith in Moderation: Islamist Parties in Jordan* (Cambridge, UK: Cambridge University Press, 2006); Janine A. Clark, "The Conditions of Islamist Moderation: Unpacking Cross-Ideological Cooperation in Jordan," *International Journal of Middle East Studies* 38, no. 4 (2006): 539–560.

22. On criticism of the inclusion-moderation thesis, see Gunes Murat Tezcur, "The Moderation Theory Revisited: The Case of Islamic Political Actors," *Party Politics* 16, no. 1 (2010): 69–88; Jillian Schwedler, "Can Islamists Become Moderates? Rethinking the Inclusion-Moderation Hypothesis," *World Politics* 63, no. 2 (2011): 347–376.

23. Mohamed Mustafa, interview with author, April 1, 2012.

24. Interview with Mahmoud Ezzat by Zahraa Bassam, Ikhwanonline, March 24, 2008, http://www.ikhwanonline.com/new/v3/Article.aspx?ArtID=35751&SecID=211.

25. Ibid.

26. Islam Lofti, "The Brotherhood and Rabbit Culture," April 16, 2008, http://kawakby.blogspot.com/2008/04/blog-post.html.

27. Melucci, *Challenging Codes*, 319.

28. Mohamed Mustafa, interview with author, April 3, 2012.

29. It was not until the Egyptian uprising in 2011 that the Brotherhood revealed its bylaws on its official website, www.ikhwanonline.com. While there is no significant difference between the old and new bylaws, the section pertinent to membership levels and procedures was omitted.

30. Mohamed Hamza, interview with author, January 11, 2012.

31. Abdurrahman Ayyash, interview with author, March 26, 2012.

32. Hamza interview.

33. Brown, *When Victory Is Not An Option*, 130.

34. The Brotherhood provides a different narrative for expelling al-Sokkary. It claims he was spying on al-Banna and involved in corruption transactions under the name of the Brotherhood. For more on this see Brynjad Lia, *The Society of the Muslim Brothers in Egypt: The Rise of An Islamic Mass Movement 1928–1942* (London: Ithaca Press, 1998).

35. According to Tammam, this group embraced an extreme ideology that was derived from Sayyid Qutb's thoughts. Hosam Tammam, *The Muslim Brotherhood: The Years Before the Revolution* (Cairo: Shorouk Press, 2012), 46.

36. El-Ghobashy, "The Metamorphosis of the Egyptian Muslim Brothers," 382–383.

37. Wickham, *Mobilizing Islam*, 218.

38. The establishment of Al-Wasat Party was a contested issue between the Brotherhood and Madi. While many of the senior leaders insisted that the Guidance Bureau supported the idea of establishing the party, Madi emphasized it was his original idea. An Interview with Abu Ela Madi, *Al-Masry Al-Youm*, March 27, 2009.

39. Wickham, *Mobilizing Islam*, 218.

40. Husam Tammam, *Abdul Moniem Abulfotouh: Shahid 'ala tarkikh al-haraka al-islamiyya* (Abdul Moniem Abulfotouh: A Witness of the Islamist Movement's History) (Cairo: Shorouk Press, 2010), 41.

41. Ibid., p. 42.

42. An Interview with Abu Ela Madi, *Al-Sharq Al-Awsat*, October 5, 2003.

43. Esam Sultan, "The Story of Al-Wasat Between The Brotherhood and National Democratic Party," *Al-Youm Al-Sabi'*, September 3, 2009.

44. In September 1981 Sadat unleashed a harsh campaign against his opponents covering the entire range of the political spectrum. Many of the Brotherhood's leaders fled the country and did not return until the second half of the 1980s.

45. Mashhur left the country in 1981 and was living in Kuwait and Germany. He returned in 1986 and became deputy general guide. After a fierce debate about his competency he then became the Brotherhood's fifth general guide and governed from 1996 to 2002. Ma'mun al-Hudaybi left Egypt in 1981 for Saudi Arabia, where he worked at the Ministry of Interior before returning to Egypt in 1986. He ran in the 1987 elections and became the spokesperson for the Brotherhood's parliamentary bloc. He became the sixth general guide and governed from 2002 to 2004. Mahdi Akef fled Egypt in 1981 for Germany, where he established the Islamic Centre in Munich. He returned in 1986 and joined the Guidance Bureau. He became the seventh general guide and governed from 2004 to 2010.

46. Habib points out that the selection of Abu al-Nasr was a surprise to the Brotherhood's members because he was ill and old. He claims Mashhur and Ma'mun al-Hudaybi orchestrated Abu al-Nasr's selection process. Esam Sultan agrees with Habib's account and emphasizes that the selection of Abu al-Nasr occurred because he was unaware of the internal dynamics of the Brotherhood, which according to Sultan, were controlled and directed by the conservatives. See the memoirs of Mohamed Habib in the *al-Shorouk* newspaper between February 9 and 25, 2015, and Sultan's article "The Story of Al-Wasat," in *Al-Youm al-Sabi*, September 3, 2009.

47. This incident has become widely known in the Egyptian media as the "Salsabil case." The roots of this case dates back to the end of 1986 when Khairat al-Shater and Hasan Malek established the company to sell electronics and computer devices. Within a few years the company expanded and brought on a new partner, Taher Abdelmoniem. In February 1992 the security forces raided Salsabil and confiscated its computers and many secret documents. Al-Shater, Malek, and Abdelmoniem were arrested, along with other prominent leaders in the Brotherhood, among them Ezzat and Gomma Amin, a member of the Guidance Bureau. For more see Al-Awadi, *In Pursuit of Legitimacy*, 162.

48. El-Ghobashy, "The Metamorphosis of the Egyptian Muslim Brothers," 384.

49. Esam Sultan says that Mashhur was pushed by al-Hudaybi to become the general guide. He refers to a meeting he had with Mashhur after the of Al-Wasat crisis where he asked Mashhur about the illegal manner in which he took the allegiance oath (*ba'ya*). Mashhur replied, "I was really surprised by what al-Hudaybi did," referring to al-Hudaybi's profound role in *bay'at al-maqabir*. Sultan, "The Story of Al-Wasat," *Al-Youm Al-Sabi'*, September 3, 2009, http://www.youm7.com/NewsPrint.asp?NewsID=132880.

50. El-Ghobashy, "The Metamorphosis of the Egyptian Muslim Brothers," 386.

51. An Interview with Mustafa Mashhour, *Al-Ahram Weekly*, April, 17–23, 1997.

52. Other members of the generation of the 1960s include the incumbent general guide, Mohamed Badie, Mahmoud Ezzat, Sayyid Nezzili, Rashad El-Bayoumi, Mahmoud Hussein, and Gomma Amin. For more see Haitham Abu Khalil, *Ikhwan Islahiyun* (Reformist Brothers), (Cairo: Dawwin House, 2012).

53. Ibid., 223.

54. There are different estimates of al-Shater's fortune. While he admits that his wealth is no more than five million dollars, others value it at more than fifteen million. Regardless of the accuracy of these numbers, it is widely known that al-Shater is the most important business tycoon in the Brotherhood. His fortune came mainly from a range of businesses that include furniture, textiles, supermarkets, car manufacturing, banking, and software. Many claim that his business empire flourished even when he was in prison. For more on this see Matthew Kaminski, "Khairat Al Shater: The Brother Who Would Run Egypt," *Wall Street Journal*, June 22, 2012, http://www.wsj.com/articles/SB1000142405 27023047653045774826903790620 50.

55. Despite the blurred relationship between al-Shater and the Brotherhood's financial resources, it is clear that he is the Brotherhood's economic and business strategist.

56. Several interviewees highlight Ezzat's role in shaping election results through his connections and influence over Shura Council members.

57. A Profile of Mahmoud Ezzat, *Elwatan*, June 2, 2015.

58. Salah El-Din Hussein, "Mahmoud Ezzat: The Castle's Guardian," *al-Islamiyun*, January 2, 2010, http://www.islamyun.net/index.php?option=com_ k2&view=item&id=74:%D9%85%D8%AD%D9%85%D9%88%D8%AF- %D8%B9%D8%B2%D8%AA-%D8%AD%D8%A7%D8%B1%D8%B3-%D8%A 7%D9%84%D9%82%D9%84%D8%B9%D8%A9&Itemid=156.

59. Abu Khalil, *Ikhwan Islahiyun*, 223.

60. Some media reports claim al-Shater and Mohamed Morsi, who by then was the head of the Brotherhood's Political Bureau, coordinated and negotiated with the Mubarak regime over the Brotherhood's share in the parliamentary elections of 2005. Mohamed Habib claims that he too held a meeting with officials of the State Security Apparatus (Jihaz amn al-dawla) to negotiate the Brotherhood's participation in the elections. See An Interview with Mohamed Habib, *al-Shorouk*, February 16, 2015. Mahdi Akef, the former general guide, admitted that the Mubarak regime offered to let the Brotherhood participate in the elections in exchange for not pressing or embarrassing the regime, particularly in light of mounting external pressure. An Interview with Mahdi Akef, *Al-Masry Al-Youm*, October 24, 2009.

61. Abu Khalil, *Ikhwan Islahiyun*, 225.

62. An Interview with Haitham Abu Khalil, *Al-Dostor*, October 26, 2009.

63. The Guidance Bureau's last election before 2008 was in 1995, when the regime cracked down on the Brotherhood and arrested many of the Shura Council's members, trying them in a military court. The selection of the new members was to fill the vacuum in the Guidance Bureau. By that time seven of the sixteen members were unable to exercise their role: three of them were in prison (al-Shater, Badie, and Mohamed Ali Beshr) and four of them were old and ill (Mohamed Hilal, Sabry Arafa, Abdullah al-Khatib, and Lashin Abu Shanab).

64. Brotherhood's Elections, *Al-Youm Al-Sabi'*, June 9, 2008.

65. The Meeting of Guidance Bureau Ends with Withdrawal of Akef, *Al-Masry Al-Youm*, October 19, 2009; "A Crisis Within the Brotherhood," *Elaph*, October 19, 2009, http://elaph.com/Web/Politics/2009/10/494812.htm.

66. An Interview with Mahdi Akef, *Al-Masry Al-Youm*, October 24, 2009.

67. Akef Announced He Will Step Down as A General Guide by End of 2009, *Al-Arabiya*, March 26, 2009, http://www.alarabiya.net/articles/2009/03/26/69275. html; Muslim Brotherhood Leader to Step Down, Ikhwanweb, March 29, 2009, http://www.ikhwanweb.com/article.php?id=19723.

68. Akef explained his decision to step down as setting a precedent that any member who reaches seventy should step down. An Interview with Mahdi Akef, *Al-Masry Al-Youm*, October 24, 2009.

69. Mohamed Habib's Memoirs, *Al-Shorouk*, February 23, 2015.

70. Mohamed Habib Threatens to Leave the Brotherhood, *Al-Masry Al-Youm*, December 30, 2009.

71. Al-Za'farani Rejects the Results of Brotherhood's Elections, *Al-Dostor*, December 21, 2009.

72. The Brotherhood Elects A New General Guide, *Al-Masry Al-Youm*, January 17, 2010.

73. Egypt's Brotherhood Gets New Leader, Ikhwanweb, January 16, 2010, http://www.ikhwanweb.com/article.php?id=22666.

Index

Abdel Halim, Mahmoud, 88
Abdel-Latif, Omayma, 116
Abdel Rahman, Mohamed, 153
Abdel Raziq, Aly, 53
Abdu, Mohamed, 51, 54
Abdul Halim, Salah, 69, 88,
    90, 177n22
Abu Khalil, Haitham, 116, 150, 151, 152
Abu Ra'ia, Mahmud, 96
Al-Adawy, Mohamed, 149
adversity/affliction narrative (mihna).
    See Mubarak regime repression,
    response to
Ahmed, Akbar, 25
Ahmed, Eslam, 72, 73–4, 93–4, 95, 96
Akef, Mohamed Mahdi, 1, 80, 147–8,
    151–2, 153–4
Al-Adl wal-Ihsan movement
    (Morocco), 46
Al-Azhar University, 52, 53, 71, 145
allegiance (bay'a). See ikhwanism
    (code of identity)
Anan, Sami, 157
Al-Anani, Khalil, 1
Anderson, Lisa, 20
Arab nationalism, 20
Arafa, Sabri, 149
"Are We Practical People?" (al-Banna), 58

Al-Arian, Abdullah, 30
al-'Aryan, Esam, 147, 149, 152, 153, 154
Ashraf, Ayman, 124
Atatürk, Mustafa Kemal, 53, 171n10
athletic training. See socialization
    process (tarbiyya)
authoritarianism and social
    movements, 136–7
Al-Awadi, Hesham, 31, 139
Ayman, Sherif, 73, 75, 77, 79–80, 82,
    85, 90, 130, 131
Ayoub, Mohamed, 81, 124
Ayubi, Nazih, 18, 20–1
Ayyash, Abdurrahman, 67, 79, 88, 93,
    95, 122, 126, 131

Badie, Mohamed, 7, 65, 84, 124, 148,
    154, 158
al-Banna, Ahmed Abdelrahman, 51
al-Banna, Hasan: assassination of
    (1949), 92; on Brotherhood
    objectives, 45–6; elections of 1942/
    1944, 6, 162n7; emulation of
    religious figures, 121, 182n5, 183n7;
    as founder of Muslim Brotherhood,
    5, 12, 29; as general guide, 115; grad-
    ualist approach of, 63; introduces
    jama'a paradigm (1938), 66;

self-description, 56–7; writings of, 50, 58, 62, 66, 76, 77, 85, 96, 97, 120, 121, 127, 130. *See also jama'a* paradigm and al-Banna; Muslim Brotherhood, introduction

al-Barr, Abdurrahman, 124

Bauman, Zygmunt, 35

Bayat, Asef, 18–9

El-Beltagi, Ammar, 80, 95, 122

El-Beltagi, Mohamed, 80

Benford, Robert, 40, 45, 59

Berger, Peter, 8–9, 24, 42

Al-Bishri, Tariq, 20

Blaydes, Lisa, 136

blind vs. sighted obedience, 125, 128

Brewer, Marilynn, 35

Brothers under the Banner of the Qur'an (al-Banna), 77

Brown, Nathan, 31, 32, 103, 112, 113, 114, 139, 144

Brubaker, Rogers, 37–8

bureaus of Muslim Brotherhood. *See* organizational structure and ideology

Burgat, François, 20

Burke, Peter J., 36, 37, 128

Burr, Vivien, 9

Bush, George W., 139

bylaws. *See* organizational structure and ideology

Calhoun, Craig, 2, 40–1

Callero, Peter, 36

camps (*mu'skar*). *See* socialization process (*tarbiyya*)

Casanova, Jose, 24

Castells, Manuel, 137

Cerulo, Karen, 42

Challenging Codes (Melucci), 42

chasing the prey. *See* recruitment and mobilization strategy

code of identity. See *ikhwanism* (code of identity)

Cohen, Jean, 41

collective action (Tarrow), 27–8

collective identity: construction of Islamic, 43–9; defined, 38–9; scholarship on, 40–1; and social constructivism, 42–3

comparative politics approach, 10, 29

Comprehensiveness of Islam, The (al-Qaradawi), 75–6

conservatives vs. reformists, 10–1, 46, 114, 136, 144–54

constructivism, defined, 8–9

Cooper, Frederick, 37–8

Corbin, Juliet, 11

crisis approach, 19–22

cultural approach. *See* essentialist approach

cultural framing process, 28–9

Daoud, Khaled, 80

Della Porta, Donatella, 41, 47, 100–1, 102

departments of Muslim Brotherhood. *See* organizational structure and ideology

Dessouki, Ali E., 20

Diani, Mario, 41, 47, 100–1, 102

Drury, John, 9

dues. *See* Muslim Brotherhood, introduction

Durkheim, Emile, 16

Eder, Klaus, 28–9

Egypt: Constitutional amendment (2004), 139; elections favorable to the Brotherhood, 7, 138, 140, 156; identity crisis (modernists vs. reformists), 52–3, 171*n*11; income inequality in, 21; January 25 Revolution (2011), 91, 93, 155, 179*n*20;

July 2013 coup, 111, 157–61, 179n20; relations with G.W. Bush administration, 139; urbanization and alienation in, 21

Eickelman, Dale, 24, 28

elasticity and adaptability. See *jama'a* paradigm and al-Banna

Eliwa, Mohamed Hamed, 127

"The Empowerment" ("Al-tamkin"), 148

enforced coherence. *See* Mubarak regime repression, response to

Ennahda movement (Tunisia), 20, 24, 141

al-'Aryan, Esam, 80, 113

Esposito, John, 17

Essam, Abdullah, 56

essentialist approach, 18, 22–5, 165n39

exclusive internal systems, 47

expressive objectives, defined, 46, 102–3

Ezzat, Mahmoud, 80, 142–3, 148, 149–54, 158

family (*usra*), 87–8, 105–6

Farouk regime, 57–8, 173n37

Fifth Annual Conference of the Brotherhood (1938), 66, 174n54

Fifth Conference Tract, The (al-Banna), 77

Fottouh, Abdelmoniem Aboul, 80, 124, 147, 149, 152, 154, 175n32

Foucault, Michel, 19

Freedom and Justice Party (FJP) (Egypt), 7, 11

Gamson, William, 39

al-Gazzar, Helmi, 80, 147

general guide (*al-murshid al-'am*), 107–8, 109–10, 115, 116, 123, 180nn26–27. *See also specific individuals*

the generalized other (Mead), 35

Ghanim, Emad, 127–8

Ghanim, Ibrahim El-Bayoumi, 54–5

el-Ghanouchi, Rachid, 20, 45

El-Ghazali, Abdelhamid, 84

El-Ghobashy, Mona, 31–2, 149

Ghorab, Salah, 66, 129, 133

Ghozlan, Mahmoud, 80

Giddens, Anthony, 19

Goffman, Erving, 45

Goodwin, Jeff, 26–7

Guidance Bureau (Maktab al-irshad). *See* organizational structure and ideology

Habermas, Jürgen, 28–9

Habib, Mohamed, 80, 124, 149, 152, 153, 154

Haddad, Yvonne, 20

Hafez, Mohammed, 26

Halliday, Fred, 24–5

Hamas (Palestine), 15, 140

Hamed, Anwar, 127

Hamed, Mohei, 153

Hamed, Yehia, 158

Hamza, Mohamed, 85, 126, 128, 134

Hassanin, Ahmed, 151

Hawwa, Said, 112, 180n34, 183n9

Heshmat, Gamal, 149

Hogg, Michael, 36

Horizons of the Teachings, The (al-Banna), 77

al-Hudaybi, Hasan, 30, 115, 144

al-Hudaybi, Ma'mun, 145, 147–9, 151

Hudson, Michael, 19–20

human agency, 9

Human Rights Watch, 158

Hunt, Scott, 40

Huntington, Samuel, 17–8

Hussein, Mahmoud, 158

al-Husseini, Sa'ad, 153

Ibrahim, Saad Eddin, 21

identification, 37, 67

identity, defined, 2, 34

identity, uses of (Brubaker and Cooper), 37–8

identity consolidation and *tarbiyya*, 12–3, 82–98; history of membership system, 91–3; incubation model, 82, 83–4; membership levels, 177n32; pillars of *tarbiyya*, 85. *See also ikhwanism* (code of identity); membership levels; socialization process (*tarbiyya*)

identity construction process, 12, 34–49; collective identity and social movements, 39–41; components of, 48f; concept of identity, 35–9; construction of Islamic collective identity, 43–9; from self-identity to group social identity, 36–8; social constructivism and identity, 42–3; from social identity to collective identity, 38–9

identity of resistance (Castells), 137

identity salience, defined, 38

identity theory, 35–8

ideology, defined, 180n31. *See also* organizational structure and ideology

ikhwanism (code of identity), 4–5, 13, 32, 101, 118–34, 167n82; allegiance (*bay'a*), 121–4, 182n3, 182n5, 183n9, 183n11; commitment (*iltizam*), 128–30; as frame of identity, 120–32; institutionalization of, 132–4; loyalty (*intima*), 130–2; norms and values of, 5, 119–21, 132; obedience (*ta'ah*), 124–7; punishment for violations of, 85, 92, 114, 117, 119, 123; trust (*thiqa*), 127–8. *See also* identity consolidation and *tarbiyya*; *jama'a* paradigm and al-Banna

inclusion-moderation thesis, 140–1

income inequality, 21

incubation model. *See* identity consolidation and *tarbiyya*

individual call (*ad-da'wa al-fardiyya*), 74–9, 78t. *See also* recruitment and mobilization strategy

instrumental objectives, defined, 46, 102–3

internal elections. *See* Muslim Brotherhood, introduction

internalization of norms. See *ikhwanism* (code of identity)

Iranian Revolution (1979), impact on scholarship, 19

Islam and the Foundations of Governance (Abdel Raziq), 53

Islamic business (Ibrahim), 21

Islamic constitutionalism (Rutherford), 32

Islamic organizational theory (Hawwa), 112

Islamic Salvation Front, 21

Islamic State of Iraq and al-Sham (ISIS), 14, 17

Islamism, defined, 163n2

Islamism and Islamist movements, study of, 11–2, 14–33; comparative politics approach to, 10, 29; crisis approach to, 19–22; cultural framing process, 28–9; essentialist approach to, 18, 22–5, 165n39; Orientalist approach, 15, 18, 24, 25, 31, 32; political opportunity structures approach to, 27–8; and political process theory, 26–7; and political scholarship, 16–8; and religious scholarship, 16; social movement theory, 26–9; studies on Muslim Brotherhood, 15–6, 29–33, 167n82

Islam is the solution (motto), 112, 113

Ismail, Salwa, 21–2, 28

al-Jama'a al-Islamiyya, 138

jama'a paradigm and al-Banna, 5–6, 12, 50–66; activating identity in everyday life, 64–6; aims and objectives, 59–60; applicability and practicality, 58; Brotherhood as identity-created movement, 54–5; creation of *jama'a* paradigm, 58–64, 59*f*; duties (*al-wajibat*), 61–2; early influences on al-Banna, 51–2; and Egypt's identity crisis, 52–3; elasticity and adaptability, 57–8, 99; inclusiveness and comprehensiveness, 56–7; and Islamic identity (*al-fikra al-islamiyya*), 55–8, 56*f*, 172*n*24, 173*n*37; means (*al-wasa'il*), 62; methodology (*al-manhaj*), 62; mission (*al-muhema*), 60–1; phases (*al-marahil*), 63–4. See also *ikhwanism* (code of identity)

January 25 Revolution (2011) (Egypt), 91, 93, 155, 179*n*20

Jasper, James, 26–7, 40, 41

Jihad Movement, 138

Johnston, Hank, 9, 41

July 2013 coup (Egypt), 111, 157–61, 179*n*20

Justice and Development Party (Morocco), 15

Justice and Development Party (Turkey), 15, 24

Kamal, Mohamed, 158

al-Katatni, Mohamed Sa'ad, 153

Kefaya (Enough) movement, 139, 140

Kepel, Gilles, 30–1

al-Kinani, Abdul Halim, 74

Klandermans, Bert, 9, 41, 73

al-Koumi, Ahmed Samir, 125

Krämer, Gudrun, 20

Kriesi, Hanspeter, 136

Laban, Ali, 94

Landau-Tasseron, Ella, 121, 123, 124, 125, 182*n*5, 183*n*7

Leary, Mark, 37

Lebanese Islamic Action Front, 112

Lewis, Bernard, 17–8

Lia, Brynjar, 29–30, 100, 177*n*22

Lights of Islam, The (*Anwar al-Islam*) (Abu Ra'ia), 96

Listen and obey (motto), 125–7

Lotfi, Islam, 143

Luckmann, Thomas, 8–9, 42

Madi, Abu El-Ela, 80, 145, 147

Mahmoud, Ali Abdul Halim, 89, 91

Malek, Hasan, 140, 148, 151

Mansour, Abdurrahman, 86, 94, 96, 128

Martin, Richard, 17

Mashhur, Mustafa, 72–3, 75–7, 78*t*, 145, 147–9, 151

Masoud, Tarek, 31

Maudidi, Abul A'la, 45

McCarthy, John, 101, 102

Mead, George Herbert, 35–6

meaning construction, and cultural framing process, 28–9

meetings and seminars. *See* socialization process (*tarbiyya*)

El-Melegi, Sayyid, 114

Melucci, Alberto: on collective action, 2–3, 42, 43, 44, 47, 48, 101; on collective identity, 39, 40, 60; on commitment, 129; on norms, 5, 119, 132; on response to repression, 143; on social movements, 101, 102, 136

membership levels, 91–8, 93*f*, 103, 177*n*32; active ('*amil*), 92, 96–7, 106; assistant member (*musa'id*), 91–2; associate (*muntasib*), 92, 95, 106; history of, 91–3; military arm (*mujahid*), 92, 177*n*31; regular (*muntazim*), 95–6; supporter (*mu'ayyid*), 94, 106; sympathizer/ lover (*muhib*), 93

mental training. *See* socialization process (*tarbiyya*)

Metamorphosis of the Egyptian Muslim Brothers, The (El-Ghobashy), 31–2

methodology of research, 11

mihna (adversity/affliction) narrative. *See* Mubarak regime repression, response to

militant Islamists, rise of during 1980s–90s, 19

Mind, Self, and Society (Mead), 35

Mitchell, Richard P., 29, 100, 179n14

mobilization. *See* recruitment and mobilization strategy

modernity paradigm and religion, 15, 40–1. *See also* essentialist approach

Montasser, Mohamed, 158

Morsi, Mohamed, 7, 111, 154, 156, 157, 161, 162nn8–9

Mubarak, Hosni, ouster of (2011), 7

Mubarak regime repression, response to, 8, 13, 135–54; from accommodation to confrontation, 137–40; and al-Shater, 140, 148, 149–54; arrest/imprisonment of Brotherhood leaders, 30–1, 140, 143; authoritarianism and social movements, 136–7; balance of power within, 146–54; conservatives vs. reformists, 136, 144–54; construction of adversity narrative (*mihna*), 10, 137, 141–6; development of solidarity, 140–6; division management, 144–6; and Ezzat, 142–3, 148, 149–54; fraudulent 2010 elections, 7; self-preservation, 46, 135, 137, 143. *See also ikhwanism* (code of identity); organizational structure and ideology

Muhammad's Youth, 144, 159

Muharram, Alaa, 74

Munson, Ziad, 28, 30, 113

Muslim anomie (Pipes), 23–4

Muslim Brotherhood, introduction, 1–13; branches of, 173n48, 174n54; conservatives vs. reformists, 10–1; defense against state infiltration, 3–4, 67, 98, 117, 132; encouragement of economic liberalization, 21; founding of, 22; identity and activism, 2–4; identity as social construct, 8–9; internal elections, 96, 106, 108, 116–7, 179nn20–21; *jama'a* paradigm, 5–6; literature review, 29–33; membership dues, 92, 94, 95, 96–7, 150; multidisciplinary approach, 9–11; number of members, 173n48; organization of book, 11–3; preaching schools, 71; research methodology, 11; resilience and durability of, 6–8; rise of during 1930s–40s, 28, 30, 54, 65, 80, 113; rise of during 1970s, 6–7, 20, 30, 32, 80, 145; rise of during 1980s–90s, 7, 30–1, 80, 138–9, 145, 147. *See also* identity consolidation and *tarbiyya; ikhwanism* (code of identity); *jama'a* paradigm and al-Banna; organizational structure and ideology; recruitment and mobilization strategy

Muslim Brotherhood in Egypt: Gerontocracy Fighting against Time, The (Al-Anani), 1

Muslim Sisters (Qism al-akhwat al-muslimat), 116, 181n45

Mustafa, Mohamed, 86, 89, 99, 104, 111, 123, 128, 133, 142

Nadawi, Abul Hasan Ali, 76

al-Naggar, Mohamed, 129, 131

al-Naggar, Mustafa, 126

al-Nasr, Mohamed Hamed Abu, 115, 148

Nasr, Osama, 153
Nasser regime, 30; relations with
    al-Hudaybi, 144; repression under,
    6, 80, 142, 147, 150–1
National Democratic Party (NDP)
    (Egypt), 137, 138, 140, 155
National Salvation Front (Egypt), 156
new social movement theory
    (NSM), 40–1
9/11 attacks, impact on
    scholarship, 18, 19

oaths of allegiance, 92, 96, 121–6, 129
obedience (*ta'ah*). See *ikhwanism*
    (code of identity)
Oegema, Dirk, 9, 73
organizational structure and ideology,
    13, 99–117, 133; Administrative
    Office (Maktab Idari), 106–7, 116,
    148, 151, 153; Battalions Unit (Nizam
    al-kata'ib), 88; conservatives vs.
    reformists, 114; decision making
    mechanism, 110–1; districts
    (*mantiqa*), 106, 111; divisions
    (*shu'ba*), 106; family (*usra*), 105–6;
    function of ideology, 111–3; General
    Bylaws (Al-la'iha al-'ama), 104,
    105–6, 107, 110, 114, 115, 117, 122, 123,
    143, 153, 183n11; general guide
    (*al-murshid al-'am*), 107–8,
    109–10, 115, 116, 123, 180nn26–27;
    Governorate Administrative Office,
    94, 95, 106; Guidance Bureau
    (Maktab al-irshad), 92, 96, 104,
    105f, 107, 108–9, 110, 114, 116, 148–9,
    150, 151, 152–3, 154, 158, 179n19;
    hierarchal structure, 103–6;
    horizontal axis of structure, 104–5,
    105f, 179n14; and identity, 100–3,
    104–5f; institutionalization
    and critiques of, 113–7, 182n49;
    internal protests/boycotts, 124,

125, 128, 143–6; Muslim Sisters
    (Qism al-akhwat al-muslimat),
    116, 181n45; Shura Council (Majlis
    al-Shura), 104, 107–8, 109, 110, 114,
    116, 123, 148–9, 151, 152, 153, 154,
    158, 179nn19–20; Socialization
    Department (Qism al-tarbiyya),
    84, 151; Special Apparatus
    (Al-tanzim al-hhas), 6, 144, 147,
    177n31; Students Section (Qism
    al-talabah), 79–80, 151, 152; vertical
    axis of structure, 103–4, 104f
Organized Soldiers of God (*Jund Allah
    Tanzimann*) (Hawwa), 180n34
Orientalist approach, 15, 18, 24,
    25, 31, 32
Ottoman Empire, demise of, 53, 171n11
Our Call (*Da'watuna*) (al-Banna), 130

Passy, Florence, 79
Pipes, Daniel, 17–8, 23
Piscatori, James, 17, 24, 28
political opportunity structures
    approach, 27–8
political process theory, 26–7
Polletta, Francesca, 40, 41
postculturalism. *See* essentialist
    approach
preaching (*da'wa*), 10, 71, 75, 174n8
privatization and income equality, 21
public seminars, 91

Al-Qaeda, 17, 24
al-Qaradawi, Yusuf, 75–6
al-Qassas, Mohamed, 86
Qur'an: allegiance (*bay'a*) in, 182n5;
    differing interpretations of, 24;
    historicizing of, 23; and *jama'a*
    paradigm, 51, 54, 56; in
    socialization process, 86, 89,
    94, 96, 97
Qutb, Sayyid, 30, 45, 96, 149–51

Radawan, Karim, 123

recruitment and mobilization strategy, 12, 67–81; Brotherhood's recruitment strategy and stages, 70–81, 72f; disseminating the call (*nashr al-da'wa*), 72–3; general connectivity (*ar-rabt al-'am*), 73–4; individual call (*ad-da'wa al-fardiyya*), 74–9, 78t; and Islamist movements generally, 68–70; marriage among members, 80, 175n34; preachers as recruiters, 71, 75, 174n8; recruitment of students, 79–80, 86; social networks, 69–70, 79–81

reformist movements, 10–1, 46, 52–3, 114, 136, 144–54, 171n11

regime repression. *See* Mubarak regime repression, response to; *specific regimes*

Reicher, Steve, 9

repression: and radicalization, 48; social movements under, 136–7. *See also specific leaders/regimes*

research methodology, 11

revolutionary movements, 46

Rida, Rashid, 54

role identity theory, 36

Rover Scouts. *See* scouts (*jawwala*) system

Roy, Olivier, 25, 44

Rushdi, Mohamed, 145

Rutherford, Bruce, 32

Sadat regime, 6, 144, 147, 150

Said, Edward, 17–8

Salafis, 155, 156

Saleh, Ibrahim, 88

Saleh, Sobhi, 80

Salsabil, 148, 150, 151

Sarahn, Mohamed, 130, 131

Sayyid, Bobby, 25

Schedler, Andreas, 136

scouts (*jawwala*) system, 89, 177n22

secularization theory, 19, 25, 164n5

self-categorization, 37

self-education. *See* socialization process (*tarbiyya*)

self-identity, defined, 37

Sets, Jan, 37

shari'a (sacred law): and politicization of Islam, 18; westernization views on, 23–4

al-Shater, Khairat, 80, 140, 148, 149–54

Shehata, Samer, 68–9

Shemakh, Amer, 85, 125

Al-Sherif, Abdul Khaliq, 71, 75, 118, 133

Shoa'iyb, Sayyid, 130, 131

"Shura and Party Pluralism in Muslim Society" statement, 145, 156

Shura Council (Majlis al-Shura). *See* organizational structure and ideology

al-Sisi regime, 157, 158–61

Smith, Wilfred, 55

SMT. *See* social movement theory (SMT)

Snow, David, 28, 40, 45, 59

social constructivism, 8–9

social entrepreneurs (*du'ah*), 36

social identity, defined, 37–9

social movement, defined (Melucci), 101

social movement theory (SMT): commitment, 128; cultural framing process, 28–9; effects of authoritarianism, 136–7; limitations of, 9–11; and new social movements (NSMs), 40; political opportunity structures, 27–8; political process theory, 26–7; and social constructivism, 12, 83

social networks. *See* recruitment and mobilization strategy

social psychology, 9, 29, 83

socialization process (*tarbiyya*), 67, 84–91, 87f; battalion meetings (*katiba*), 88–9; camps (*mu'skar*), 89–90;

congress/annual national meetings (*mu'tamar*), 91; family (*usra*), 87–8; pillars of *tarbiyya*, 85; trips/monthly retreats (*rihla*), 89; weekly seminars (*nadwa*), 91; workshops/study groups (*dawra*), 90–1. *See also* identity consolidation and *tarbiyya*

society-oriented movements, 46

sociology of religion, 9–10, 16, 24, 29

al-Sokkary, Ahmed, 144

Soliman, Amr, 128

Soliman, Mohamed, 90

Spaces of Islam (*Fi rihab al-Islam*) (Laban), 94

spiritual readiness. *See* socialization process (*tarbiyya*)

state-oriented movements, 46

Stets, Jan E., 128

Strauss, Anselm, 11

structural adjustment policies, and income equality, 21

Stryker, Sheldon, 36, 37

Sufism, 171n6

Sultan, Essam, 80, 145, 147

Sunna: differing interpretations of, 24; and *jama'a* paradigm, 51, 54

Syria: urbanization and alienation in, 21

tactical violence, 160

Talimah, Essam, 158

Tammam, Husam, 80–1, 116, 117, 133

Tangney, June, 37

Tantawy, Mohamed Hussein, 157

tarbiyya. *See* identity consolidation and *tarbiyya*; socialization process (*tarbiyya*)

Tarrow, Sidney, 27

Taylor, Charles, 37, 38

Taylor, Verta, 39

The Teachings (*Risalat at-Ta'alim*) (al-Banna), 85, 97, 120, 121, 127

Terry, Deborah, 36

Tessler, Mark, 21

Tibi, Bassam, 17–8, 22–3

al-Tilmisani, Omar, 115, 147, 148

Touraine, Alain, 28–9, 40

Turkey: removal of Ottoman caliphate (1924), 53, 171n11

ulama (Muslim scholars), politicization of Islam, 18

urbanization, 20–1

Vandewalle, Dirk, 21

virtuous society (Roy), 44

War of 1967, and rise of Islamist movements, 19, 20

Al-Wasat Party (Egypt), 144, 145–6, 147, 149, 159

Weber, Max, 16

What Does It Mean My Belonging to Islam? (Yakan), 76–7, 131

What Has the World Lost with the Degradation of Muslims? (Nadawi), 76

White, Katherine, 36

Whittier, Nancy, 39

Wickham, Carrie, 30, 31, 69, 81, 138, 145

Wiktorowicz, Quintan, 27–8

women, marginalization of, 116, 181n45

Yakan, Fathi, 76–7, 112, 131, 175n26, 181n35

Yavuz, Hakan, 9, 22, 27, 28, 43, 46

Yussif, Mohamed, 81, 86

al-Za'farani, Ibrahim, 124, 147, 149, 152, 154

Zahran, Mohammed, 52

Zald, Mayer, 101, 102

Zollner, Barbara, 30

Inside the Muslim Brotherhood :
religion, identity, and politics

BP 10 .J383 A635 2016 cop.1